Catarina Belo

Spirit in Philosophy

A Metaphysical Inquiry

Catarina Belo

Spirit in Philosophy

A Metaphysical Inquiry

WiSa

Bibliografische Information der Deutschen Nationalbibliothek
Die Deutsche Nationalbibliothek verzeichnet diese Publikation in der Deutschen Nationalbibliografie; detaillierte bibliografische Daten sind im Internet über http://dnb.d-nb.de abrufbar.

Bibliographic information published by the Deutsche Nationalbibliothek
Die Deutsche Nationalbibliothek lists this publication in the Deutsche Nationalbibliografie; detailed bibliographic data are available in the Internet at http://dnb.d-nb.de.

Abbildungen: © leafart - Fotolia.com
Coverfoto: © Duarte Belo. Abdruck mit freundlicher Genehmigung

ISBN: 978-3-95538-032-8

Stuttgart 2019

something spiritual underlies all sensible existence and . . .
what is actually excellent lies in the spiritual

Schelling, *Clara*

Contents

Acknowledgments

The research for this book was carried out primarily during a sabbatical leave in 2014–2015 granted by my home institution, the American University in Cairo.

I received much useful advice on the manuscript from William Melaney, Professor of English and Comparative Literature at the American University in Cairo.

Class discussions with my students at the American University in Cairo provided inspiration for many aspects of this book.

I am also grateful to Johanna Baboukis for the careful proofreading of the manuscript.

My mother, Maria Teresa Belo, always encouraged my philosophical pursuits, from the early stages of my interest in philosophy. This book is dedicated to her memory.

Foreword

The concept of "spirit" appears in the history of philosophy in various forms, some-times explicitly, sometimes implicitly. It is a broad concept and therefore it features under different names and aspects. The precise meaning of spirit is a complex question and it will become clearer as we proceed with the analysis of the philosophical tradition on the topic. It relates primarily to questions of metaphysics and theory of knowledge, although it can be seen to be present in all the philosophical disciplines.

The present text, in the form of a dialogue between a student and a teacher (fol-lowing a literary tradition in philosophy which goes back to Plato and has such dis-tinguished champions as Cicero, Augustine, Anselm, and Berkeley, to name a few), proposes to look into the question of spirit and its varied meanings from a historical and a conceptual perspective within philosophy. We will not limit ourselves to ex-plicit references to spirit, which would confine us to specific philosophers—such as Hegel, in whose work the term "spirit" is most explicit, Aquinas, and other medieval philosophers, who take spirit primarily in its theological sense, differently from what Hegel was to do later. In other words, if we were to speak of spirit in philosophy in a literal way, we would have to limit ourselves to Hegel and perhaps a few other phi-losophers, mostly from the medieval period.

In the medieval tradition spirit has primarily a theological meaning. More spe-cifically, this meaning is tied to Christian dogma, and in particular the dogma of the Trinity and the Holy Spirit as the third person of the Trinity. The theological and the scriptural or biblical sense of spirit makes an important contribution to the discussion, not least because philosophers in the European tradition from the Middle Ages on-wards were heavily influenced by the scriptural meaning of spirit. Therefore, it is appropriate to include the theological aspect in addition to the philosophical aspects of spirit, which are the focus of our analysis of the concept.

Therefore, while focusing on the philosophical meaning of "spirit," the theo-logical aspect should not be overlooked, since it informs the philosophical meaning.

Moreover, if we search for this concept in the history of philosophy, we find that spirit is a central topic for a modern philosopher such as Berkeley, who contrasts it to matter, rendering it not only actual but the only reality. However, it is in the philosophy of Hegel that spirit becomes explicitly and repeatedly the central theme. It is such an important aspect of Hegel's philosophy that it appears as a central concept in all the main philosophical disciplines treated by him, and is more explicitly and extensively treated in his works than in previous philosophers. In Hegel, this term has primarily a philosophical or general meaning but the theological meaning is not far to seek, and sometimes Hegel refers explicitly to the theological meaning, as grounding the philosophical meaning and justifying it.

In Hegel's works, spirit has various complex meanings and various associations with other concepts. Based on these associated concepts, related to knowledge, being, and existence, to mention but a few, we can trace it back to the Presocratic philosophers and find other exponents in the history of philosophy, who may have written on interrelated issues without calling them explicitly "spirit." Hence spirit is here taken in a general and far-reaching sense. Spirit would thus comprise the notions of "idea," "mind," "soul," "intellect," "form"—as they appear in ancient, medieval, and modern philosophy—to mention some of the most central concepts associated with spirit.

Consequently, this work draws inspiration primarily from Hegel, but also from other philosophers, such as Saint Thomas Aquinas and Berkeley. In the medieval period, particularly in medieval Christian philosophy, as we have seen, the term was studied primarily within a theological context, but for Hegel the philosophical connotations are as, if not more, important. While the concept "spirit" plays an important role in other fields of human experience, particularly in religion, Hegel treats it as a philosophical concept, without, however, disregarding the religious aspects, especially within Christian theology. One could say that in Hegel, the philosophical aspect of spirit is more general than the theological aspect and would include the latter, although Hegel himself claimed that they are at bottom the same. For the content of philosophy is for him the same as the content of religion or even theology, although the two disciplines, philosophy and religion, express themselves in different ways. From a medieval perspective, however, the theological element should dominate, and it could be argued that in the medieval sense of the term, all spirit comes ultimately from the ultimate or infinite spirit, God himself.

Hegel wrote profusely on "spirit," and his *Phenomenology of Spirit* is especially devoted to this topic, including and starting from finite subjective human spirit, to infinite divine spirit. Hegel traces the development of spirit and the process through which subjective and finite spirit attains to absolute knowing in a gradual development towards infinite or absolute spirit. However, even the *Phenomenology of Spirit* does not exhaust all meanings of spirit for Hegel, who wrote on the subject in other works, including his lectures given in Berlin. The present work proposes to take Hegel's works into account, but also the great medieval works on spirit and intellect, and to look at the meaning of spirit in a more general way.

Spirit may seem too general a topic since it straddles several disciplines, but in actual fact it has various but interrelated meanings which can be articulated in a coherent and focused way.

The first part of the present work deals with spirit in the history of philosophy: in the form of intellect, and the various kinds of intellect, and also as the object of the intellect, which are ideas, forms, or knowledge itself. Different periods in the history of philosophy have focused either on the objective aspect or on the subjective aspect. The former, or objective, aspect dominated the history of philosophy up to the modern period, more specifically the early 17th century, and the latter, or subjective, aspect has predominated since the modern period.

Intellect broadly construed can be understood as subjective spirit, and the object of subjective intellect or spirit can be termed objective. This work also looks at the combination of or meeting point between these two kinds of spirit, subjective and objective. The distinction between the different kinds of spirit features in Hegel (who develops a specific conception of subjective and objective spirit) but also, more recently, in Edith Stein.

Moreover, in this work the emphasis of the research on spirit is primarily the history of philosophy up to and including Hegel, given that the presence and meaning of spirit is a topic that belongs primarily in metaphysics, interest in which declined after Hegel, in spite of a recent revival of interest in metaphysics and especially ontology.

The second part of the work looks at the various philosophical disciplines, such as metaphysics, theory of knowledge, and ethics, and the meaning and role of spirit in them, in an attempt to bring together the various historical accounts of the term as presented in the philosophical tradition. The entire work is a dialogue with the philosophical tradition since the question of spirit is prominent in it in an explicit or implicit way. However, and while continuing the dialogue with the history of philosophy, the second part looks at the question of spirit in a more systematic way as it features in the various philosophical disciplines. This second part does not aim primarily to interpret the meaning of spirit in specific philosophers but looks at its meaning within the various philosophical disciplines in order to find a unitary position.

The main inspiration for this work is Hegel, given his explicit mention of spirit in his works, without disregarding the medieval Christian tradition, including the theological aspects. These two aspects, philosophical and theological, as we have seen, are related, and Hegel considered that we cannot neglect the theological or religious aspect of the problem; but our emphasis lies on a philosophical approach, since the theological treatment of spirit deserves and has been the subject of an entire specialized literature.

One might ask: why tackle the question of spirit and seek a unitary approach to this topic within the history of philosophy and the philosophical disciplines? Why would the question of spirit warrant this attention? One might argue that even in Hegel this term is too vague to be pinpointed and too broad to deserve a detailed study. However, we believe that in Hegel and in philosophy in general (its history and its disciplines) there is clearly a unitary approach that can be taken, and the point of this study is precisely to look at the tradition from a Hegelian perspective and from a unitary perspective. This does not mean to follow exclusively Hegel's categories and understanding of spirit, or to use his methods, and in particular his dialectical logic, but it does imply an approach that is close to Hegel (although it does not follow him in every respect), given that he arguably devoted more time and effort to this question than any other philosopher.

At the same time, Hegel's philosophy does not exhaust the meaning of spirit, and any study of spirit, including the present one, is a work in progress since the topic is inexhaustible. The theological tradition of Christianity, in which spirit plays such an important role, does contribute to the enrichment of the philosophical concept, as we have seen.

In seeking to understand the meaning of spirit, the question of its relation to matter cannot be ignored, since this dichotomy appears clearly in the history of philosophy. Already in ancient philosophy this opposition features in Plato, in association with the distinction between soul and body, with its philosophical and religious connotations. In the Christian tradition, ancient and medieval, the difference between spirit and matter is also apparent. We find it again clearly spelled out in the modern period, for instance in Berkeley, who denies altogether the existence of matter. In Hegel the same opposition is mentioned, more frequently in the form of the dichotomy between spirit and nature. The two poles of reality, spirit and matter, must be part of the discussion. In other words, matter must be included in the discussion of spirit.

The mention of spirit raises many questions within the various philosophical disciplines. Speaking of spirit evokes the metaphysical question concerning the nature of reality, and whether it is spiritual or material, or both. It also raises the associated question of whether, for instance, knowledge is spiritual and mental, or real and material. Therefore, one of the major questions involved is an epistemological one, pertaining to the debate between realism and idealism, and whether knowledge originates outside the mind or issues from it. The problem can be formulated in various ways, depending on one's definition of realism or idealism. Philosophers in whose works spirit plays a prominent role, such as Hegel and Berkeley, have traditionally been considered idealists of some sort. Even if they, alongside Plato, hold that reality, and the corresponding knowledge and ideas, exist in God or some absolute spirit as in an independent reality—and so independently of the human subjective mind or spirit—the question of idealism is always present. There are various kinds of idealism (for instance, subjective or objective), and these philosophers could be considered objective idealists, but the meaning of idealism would nevertheless have to be taken into account.

The discussion of spirit raises questions in metaphysics and theory of knowledge, and therefore the very term "idealism" in this sense could refer to knowledge or to reality. Within the theory of knowledge idealism could be defined as the view according to which knowledge is in the mind or some mind instead of originating in an external reality. Within metaphysics, idealism would mean that reality itself is purely ideal or spiritual and not material. These two understandings of idealism usually go hand in hand.

Generally speaking, philosophers who emphasize the role of spirit over matter or spirit over nature, and defend the primacy of ideas or ideals versus material things, tend to be considered idealist philosophers, independently of whether they favor a metaphysical or an epistemological version of idealism, or both. They emphasize spiritual aspects (ideas or intellects) in opposition to matter, or they even deny matter, as we have seen in the case of Berkeley. In a nutshell, idealism can be seen as the view that what matters are ideas or the knowing subject as it sees the world. These are all issues related to the question of spirit, perennial issues that have to be addressed as part of this discussion.

Obviously, it is not possible to exhaust the treatment of spirit in one work or solve all the associated issues, but this study aims at contributing to the debate on a theme which is so central in the history of philosophy, and therefore deserves our current attention, regardless of one's position on these issues and regardless of the contemporary philosophical school one identifies oneself with.

PART I: SPIRIT AND THE HISTORY OF PHILOSOPHY

Student: Spirit is a topic which is mentioned by various philosophers, for instance Berkeley and Hegel. How can we understand "spirit" from a philosophical perspective?

Teacher: Spirit is said in many ways. It is a multifaceted concept with various but interrelated meanings, to be found in different disciplines of knowledge. We can find it in philosophy, most explicitly in Hegel, but also in theology, especially Christian theology, and in the various religious traditions. We have to remain focused on the philosophical level and treat the religious and theological aspects only in so far as they are related to philosophy. Although spirit may be an obvious concept, its exact meaning may not be immediately apparent. We can say, generally speaking, that spirit may be negatively defined as the opposite of matter, and also as something infinite, unextended, invisible, or incorruptible—all of which may be considered as negative ways of defining spirit.

Student: In order to define spirit, would it help to relate spirit to mind or soul?

Teacher: Traditionally, mind and soul are more specific than spirit. Mind usually refers to the human mind with its intellectual or mental abilities, or faculties, and the soul is usually related to the body, which is the natural counterpart of the soul. Soul is perhaps primarily a theological concept, although it can be considered from a philosophical perspective (that is, independently of a particular religious tradition), and many philosophers have discussed the theme of the soul. In relation to mind or intellect, it can be said that, in the history of philosophy, the mind or intellect was considered a part of the soul, so it is a more specific concept than soul. Therefore spirit is more general than soul, and soul is more general than mind.

We will take these concepts into account as part of our investigation. Spirit is a rather broad concept, and thus not easy to define in one sentence. Our discussion will be about the different aspects of spirit within philosophy. Spirit is not necessarily something human or subjective, as we shall see. It thus transcends the purely human domain, although it is also associated with the human mind. There are various kinds of spirit, which are the subject of the various philosophical disciplines.

Student: You defend the idea that spirit is an obvious concept, but would not some philosophers deny that there is spirit or rationality outside or beyond the human mind?

Teacher: Even if we were inclined to take that position, some sciences show signs that contradict it. Looking at mathematics and the structure of languages, it is clear that reality and language display a structure and rationality, and even spirituality, which is independent of the human mind. That spiritual or rational reality is discovered by the human mind, rather than invented by it.

Student: I understand that spirituality is not confined to the human mind. If we invoke a different kind of mind or spirit, such as an infinite mind, does it involve including religion and theology as a central subject of our discussion?

Teacher: Different religions talk about spirit, so it is not possible to do justice to all the different traditions. For instance, in eastern religions such as Hinduism or Buddhism spirit and spirituality are a very important element, to mention just a couple of them, but spirituality as a general concept or even as a religious concept is not really within the remit of our discussion.

In addition, spirit features in the scriptures of three main Western religions, Judaism, Christianity, and Islam, but we will not deal in detail with the meaning of spirit in scripture. We can mention in passing the question of spirit in the Bible, in which spirit is associated with God's activity, word, wisdom, and generally with life (especially in Hebrew). There it often means breath, and also air, wind, and the breath of life. Spirit is linked to wisdom, revelation (and thus divine inspiration), God's creative activity and knowledge, as it appears clearly in the Old Testament. In the New Testament it is contrasted with matter and with the body. In the Old Testament it features prominently, and in the New Testament it is identified with God and with the third person of the Trinity, the Holy Spirit, Trinitarian theology having developed in the course of the first few centuries of Christianity.

Student: Spirit is an obvious religious topic, but I wonder if its philosophical meaning is as obvious as the religious one.

Teacher: It is important to stress the intersection between religion and philosophy from its beginnings in ancient Greece, when the religious question was never far from the concerns of the philosophers, and also in the medieval period when religion takes center stage. Often the same questions are addressed by religion and philosophy.

Philosophy has close relations with the sciences also, but in comparison with religion, it is actually the younger sister, as we know (although some philosophers, for instance the medieval Islamic philosopher Alfarabi, claim that philosophy is older than religion).

We will see that the interrelation between philosophical and religious meanings becomes especially significant during the Middle Ages, and later in Hegel (without disregarding modern philosophers such as Leibniz and Berkeley). In religion itself, spirit has a theoretical and a practical dimension which relates to the practice of religion and its influence on one's lifestyle as a result. Our discussion is more concerned with the theoretical dimension, since this is more closely related to the philosophical meaning of spirit. We will consider other aspects in so far as they are related to the theoretical aspect.

Student: It is clear that spirit straddles both religion and philosophy. Should we not first define spirit precisely, in order to ascertain how it features in the history of philosophy?

Teacher: We can start with a general understanding of spirit and then ascertain the meaning of spirit from the history of philosophy, especially from Hegel, who was explicit in writing about spirit, which is at the center of his philosophical system. The meaning of spirit will become clear from the history of philosophy itself.

We can subsequently speculate on the implications of the historical-philosophical meaning of spirit.

Student: What does the history of philosophy have to say about spirit? If spirit is mainly dealt with by Christian philosophers and by Hegel, can we find this concept in Greek philosophy?

Teacher: We should first look at the philosophical tradition, comprised in the history of philosophy, including Greek philosophy, before analyzing further the concept in itself. Looking at the history of philosophy will ensure a solid basis for further investigations. While it is not possible to take into account every philosopher, it is important to take the history of philosophy into account because of the meaningfulness of the debates which will serve as an inspiration for our discussion. Hegel, who writes profusely on spirit, also believes that the history of philosophy is not a mere description, following a chronological order, of the various systems and ideas proposed by philosophers in the course of time. Each philosophy contains a grain of truth—often more than that—such that the history of philosophy cannot be ignored.

Spirit has many dimensions, and has strong religious and theological connotations, but we will focus on philosophy.

Student: Before we start on the history of philosophy, what are the most important philosophical disciplines that treat of spirit?

Teacher: All disciplines within philosophy are involved in and influenced by one or more philosophical meanings of spirit, as we shall see, but spirit is particularly important within metaphysics or ontology. The latter, according to Aristotle, is one of the two branches of metaphysics, alongside theology, and it is also important for theory of knowledge or epistemology. The concept of spirit is associated primarily with being and existence, and also with knowledge and the concept of soul, mind and intellect, as we shall see. In this sense, we must inquire into the nature of reality and whether it is spiritual or material, or both, and into the nature of knowledge and whether it also is material or spiritual or both. Within theory of knowledge it is important to take into account the distinction between subject and object.

Spirit also has implications for ethics, aesthetics and philosophy of nature.

We will see that, within philosophy, we must take a metaphysical approach.

Student: I understand the need to focus on metaphysics and theory of knowledge, but are we going to privilege one over the other? And is this a metaphysical inquiry? In what sense?

Teacher: Metaphysics has been the central discipline within philosophy since its birth in Ancient Greece, because it deals with the nature of reality itself and so constitutes the most fundamental part of philosophy. *Metaphysics* is the title of one of Aristotle's main works, although this title was probably not Aristotle's own designation, but a later addition by Andronicus, who edited Aristotle's works and arranged them according to a specific order. He also grouped various works composed by Aristotle pertaining to logic under the title *Organon*, thus forming a collection of logical works.

For Aristotle, metaphysics was "first philosophy," and the Aristotelian tradition, in Antiquity and in the Middle Ages, continued to employ the expression "first philosophy" to designate metaphysics. This philosophical discipline, according to Aristotle, treats of being as being, and of the supreme being, that is, God. In other words, it comprises ontology and theology. In addition, metaphysics may be considered the science of first principles, and, as the Greek term indicates, that which comes after physics, which is the science of nature. This indicates that metaphysics does not deal with physical reality itself, but with another kind of reality, which is spiritual, rather than natural or material.

Student: Does this mean that one has to accept the existence of a spiritual reality if one accepts the existence of metaphysics and engages in its study?

Teacher: I am afraid so; in accepting metaphysics one must accept also the existence of some kind of spiritual or theoretical reality. In addition, because metaphysics is such a broad and abstract branch of philosophy—while it considers and takes into account knowledge obtained from experience (following as it does in the wake of physics and natural philosophy)—it is in charge of examining the presuppositions established or discovered prior to empirical knowledge, and so presupposes a knowledge which is independent of sensible experience. Metaphysics therefore precedes and goes beyond empirical knowledge and experience. In connection with this question, it is important to bear in mind that, according to Aristotle, these first principles that are known in first philosophy cannot be proved. For some philosophers, including some medieval Islamic philosophers (for instance, Alfarabi) these first principles can be obtained from experience, but it is not clear that this is the case for Aristotle. As a general and fundamental discipline of philosophy, metaphysics treats of general principles, the first causes of being. It deals with the origin or the causes of things. In this sense, it is sometimes identified with philosophy itself, that is, a branch of knowledge which is general and theoretical. It is associated with a general outlook on life, on reality and the world. Aquinas holds that the metaphysicians, and not the natural philosophers, are the ones who consider the origin of things, universal being, and things that are devoid of movement. He further claims that all the speculative sciences depend on metaphysics.

Student: So should we assume that there is a close connection between metaphysics and theory of knowledge?

Teacher: That is right. In the same way that we can say that reality is material or spiritual or both, knowledge can be said to have the same characteristics; and since knowledge is supposed to mirror reality, what is assumed in metaphysics will influence one's theory of knowledge. There are different ways of distinguishing knowledge and reality, for reality concerns the things themselves while knowledge describes our conception or understanding of things or objects. Aquinas, for instance, considers that "truth" goes hand in hand with knowledge (or language, since "truth" applies to propositions), while being goes hand in hand with reality and is studied by metaphysics.

Naturally, there should be a correspondence between the things and the knowledge we have of them, which is something we will discuss later.

Returning to the meaning of metaphysics, according to Hegel, philosophy is the study and knowledge of the causes of things, which overlaps with the meaning of metaphysics.

Student: Has there not been a rejection of metaphysics in the recent history of philosophy?

Teacher: In recent times, this philosophical discipline has been discredited, in connection with a growing lack of confidence in the power of human reason to grasp reality. A lack of confidence in reason, or a belief in the limits of reason, need not necessarily lead to the downfall of metaphysics or to a skeptical or a relativist position. In the Middle Ages, for instance, there was another guide to truth other than reason, namely scripture. In modern and in contemporary philosophy, following an attack on authority, an attack on human reason ensued.

However, the major metaphysical questions are still with us. As a fundamental part of metaphysics, ontology as the reflection on being (and more generally reality) never really went away, and there is currently a great deal of research within this field, for instance in analytic ontology, which is part of analytic philosophy.

Student: Since metaphysics or at least ontology never completely disappeared as a philosophical discipline, was there a particular part or aspect of metaphysics which was discredited?

Teacher: One main aspect of mainstream metaphysics which was discredited in the modern period was a certain metaphysics of the substance (or of individual things), based on particular aspects and interpretations of Aristotle's philosophy. Substance for Aristotle and Aristotelian philosophers was the building block of reality, at a physical and a metaphysical level—in fact, the concept of substance (or "thing") straddles these two disciplines of philosophy.

In natural science, this emphasis on individual substances or things went hand in hand with the notion of substantial forms—namely, essential qualities in substances which were used in ancient and medieval philosophical discourse to explain natural phenomena. They were later set aside in favor of a quantitative approach to scientific phenomena. There was also criticism of certain aspects of substance which did not fit with the empiricist model of modern scientific practice, in particular spiritual aspects like the soul, which was considered to be a spiritual substance.

In connection with Aristotelian metaphysics, it is important to note that this traditional metaphysics is still alive in Christian theology today, especially in Catholic theology, which draws its principles primarily from the theology of Saint Thomas Aquinas.

Student: Metaphysics has a long history within philosophy and it has several branches. Which sense of metaphysics should we take as the basis of our discussion?

Teacher: Metaphysics has a strong theoretical side, and also a strong rationalist side. In this sense our discussion is a metaphysical inquiry. Spirit is here analyzed in its metaphysical dimensions since its various meanings are not primarily or directly related to sense experience, and so spirit is squarely placed in the metaphysical domain, which is essentially speculative and theoretical.

Student: Given that metaphysics has come under sharp criticism in recent times, how can we justify a metaphysical study, and a study of spirit?

Teacher: We saw that ontology was never truly discarded, even if some philosophers rejected the theological branch of metaphysics, which some consider separately from ontology. Therefore, a part of metaphysics has always remained the subject of study by philosophers.

In addition, we must stress, in our defense of metaphysics, that philosophy, in its theoretical and even metaphysical aspect, treats not only of essential aspects of reality and reality itself as a whole, but it also studies, analyzes, and even judges the other disciplines and branches of knowledge. One could say that it studies or judges their principles and most abstract aspects. This is still the case today and is a legacy from Aristotle's conception of metaphysics, which towered over all the other branches of knowledge. Therefore one might say that a philosophy of the other sciences or branches of knowledge, such as philosophy of physics, contains metaphysical aspects because it considers the abstract principles of the other sciences. Therefore, one aspect of philosophy as it relates to other disciplines (which were once part of philosophy but attained their independence in the post-Aristotelian period of modern science) may rightfully be considered a domain of metaphysics in its theoretical aspects.

Student: Hence for Aristotle all the disciplines were united under metaphysics or philosophy?

Teacher: Yes; the Aristotelian tradition takes the unity of the sciences very seriously. The higher sciences judge and guide the lower sciences, and these in turn serve the higher sciences. One science proves the subject matter of another—and a science cannot prove the existence of its own subject matter, to avoid circularity—in a hierarchy which is clearly established. This close articulation among the different sciences has been lost and sometimes the links within the same science are lost, given the growing specialization which affects the various disciplines. For our purposes we should stress the need for metaphysics to continue paying attention to other philosophical and scientific disciplines and all aspects of human experience.

Moreover, the question of spirit is central to the history of philosophy, as will become clearer later. Naturally, one could deny the existence of spirit, but that itself is a metaphysical position, and therefore arguably a self-defeating theory.

Furthermore, since religion and religious studies, for instance, address essential issues from a spiritual and a metaphysical perspective, we must not ignore them. As in religious studies, we are justified in studying spirit from a metaphysical—that is to say, not naturalistic or empiricist—perspective. Spirit is an essential aspect of religion and religious studies, and therefore it should not be ignored by philosophy or metaphysics.

Chapter 1
Ancient Philosophy

The Presocratics

Student: Is it possible to find the term or the concept of spirit in ancient philosophy?
Teacher: The first philosophers in ancient Greece were primarily interested in giving a naturalistic account of reality. According to Aristotle, they provided a different kind of explanation of reality from the one which had recourse to myth, and in this way they were considered to have founded a new discipline, namely philosophy. They studied nature from a material and physical perspective. In particular, they wanted to explain natural phenomena, such as eclipses and rainfall. Some of them looked for one material principle that would explain all reality, as its grounding principle, in the sense that everything would require it in order to come into being. Thales asserted that this was water, Anaximenes held that it was air. Heraclitus highlighted fire as the eternal element, and he also held that there is one divine law that grounds the laws of the cosmos and human laws. This means that for Heraclitus the cosmos is in itself intelligible, a claim that other Presocratic philosophers would also endorse. Heraclitus clearly holds that we must use the testimony of the senses as well as reason in order to understand the nature of reality.
Student: Is the Presocratic account of nature purely natural and materialistic?
Teacher: In spite of the fact that these philosophies clearly rest on an observation of nature, the spiritual element is not altogether absent. Cicero, for instance, gives an account of how the philosophers who preceded Socrates mention the work of the gods. For instance, he mentions Thales as claiming that God was the mind shaping everything out of water. In addition, Heraclitus defends the idea that everything is in motion, which is a general philosophical or metaphysical position regarding reality, and Parmenides also makes general claims about reality. However, Cicero himself states that it is only with Anaxagoras, a pupil of Anaximander, that the world is seen to be conceived and ruled by the power of an infinite mind.

The theory that all natural bodies are made up of four elements, earth, water, air and fire, is attributed to Empedocles. The Presocratics had various explanations for how the combination of different elements made up the natural bodies which we see, Empedocles stating that they are generated through love and dissolved through strife. However, some Presocratic philosophers also gave an intellectual or spiritual account of the world and reality, as we see already with Heraclitus. Xenophanes, for instance, thought of a deity greater than all, an all-knowing divinity whose thinking controls the universe.

Student: So not all the Presocratics were bent on a naturalistic explanation of reality?

Teacher: No. Among the precursors who favored the significance of a spiritual account of reality, or the role of spirit in reality, other than Heraclitus and Xenophanes, before Socrates, is Parmenides, who mentions reason as a sure guide to understanding reality, instead of the senses. He has a focus on logos, reason or intellect. Other philosophers see in Parmenides an important aspect in that he distinguishes being from non-being, a position which has metaphysical and logical consequences. In logic, it would entail a form of the principle of non-contradiction, in that the same thing cannot have two opposite predicates at the same time and in the same sense. What other philosophers, such as Hegel, admire in Parmenides is his identification between thought and being. Being is what is thought. Hegel would later claim that the real is rational and the rational is real, which is another way of explaining the same principle. There is thus an identity between thinking and being. It is clear that for Hegel thinking is spiritual rather than material.

Other philosophers in the Eleatic school, of which Parmenides was the founder and the most important exponent, were preoccupied with physical questions that were related to metaphysics, for instance, the question of the one, and infinity, developed in particular by Melissus.

Student: This means that fundamental metaphysical questions surrounding being and thought were already posed by the Presocratics. And are these not perennial questions?

Teacher: Yes, since the question of being (and also existence) is the fundamental question of philosophy, and more specifically metaphysics.

These questions have continuously been debated through to the modern and contemporary period, and had an impact on scientific questions, although there was not a strict separation between science and metaphysics in Presocratic philosophy. Some philosophers, such as Parmenides, were more interested in metaphysical questions, but there were metaphysical elements also in other Presocratic philosophies.

Pythagoras viewed the universe along mathematical lines, and sought to explain the cosmos through numbers. He considered the nature of soul in itself, defending the idea of the reincarnation of the soul in human beings and even animals, a view that appears to influence Plato later, as it becomes clear in various Platonic dialogues.

Student: Therefore, the Presocratics take an interest in the question of the soul, which is clearly an important aspect of spirit?

Teacher: Yes, the soul is related to spirit and evokes the related issues of thinking and personal identity. Naturally, the questions surrounding the soul in the ancient world go hand in hand with religion—and this could also be said of the modern period. One might even say that the question of the soul, its nature and existence, is primarily a religious and not a philosophical question. However, in the history of philosophy it is treated from a philosophical perspective, as it is very clear at least from Aristotle's works—which give momentum to a philosophical treatment of soul.

Student: If "soul" has such strong religious connotations, what is distinctive about a philosophical approach?

Teacher: The philosophical approach to soul is apparent with regard to both form and content. With regard to form, philosophical arguments and logic are used to prove the existence, the nature, and/or the immortality of the soul—instead of the arguments from authority which are more commonly found in religion or theology. In addition, the close connection between soul and knowledge is explored by Plato and Aristotle. It becomes clear that not just the intellect but also memory have their seat in the soul, and sense perception is also "processed" in the soul. Knowledge is considered to be the result of the activity of the various faculties of the soul and therefore the question of soul becomes definitely a philosophical issue.

In Plato, the religious and the philosophical treatment of the soul are still very closely connected, as a result of the religious questions pertaining to the soul which arise in the ancient world. The relation of the soul to the body is one of the central aspects discussed in Plato's dialogues. Does a soul pre-exist its union with the body? Does it continue to exist after it is separated from the body? (Socrates defines death in the *Phaedo* as the separation of the soul from the body.) Is the soul immortal or does it disappear and dissolve like the body after death? Does each body have its own individual soul, or does the same soul inhabit various bodies in succession? Having been influenced by Pythagoras and the question of reincarnation, Plato addresses these issues in his dialogues.

Generally speaking, the ancients associated soul with life, which meant that they believed, for instance, that plants also have souls. Therefore, there is such thing as a vegetative soul, which is responsible for growth, and which is common to plants, animals, and human beings. There is also an animal soul which is responsible for movement, and finally the human soul has all these qualities, and thinking or intellect in addition.

Plato's views on the soul, as we have seen, are influenced by Pythagoras. As a philosopher, Pythagoras also helped to define philosophy as a discipline. He is credited with coining the term "philosophy"—love of wisdom—and explaining that a philosopher discusses every subject and is not specialized in any particular subject, as reported by Cicero.

Student: Were there discussions among the Presocratics based primarily on a conception of matter, or of nature as matter?

Teacher: Yes, in addition to the discussion of metaphysical reality, logic, and the soul, there were also theories of matter that prefigured later conceptions and discussions about matter. The atomists, like Leucippus and Democritus, thought of matter as consisting of atoms, indivisible units of matter, which traveled in the void. Epicurus, who founded his own school, accepted atomism, and it was later taken up by Latin-speaking philosophers, such as Lucretius. This position, stating that matter constituted the basic reality, influenced later thought, for instance Marx and his materialism. There were different views on how the atoms came together. Epicurus held that this happened by chance. In addition, he did not believe in divine providence. Consequently, he defends indeterminism in nature, and claims that if the gods exist, they do not become involved in human affairs. Atomism also influenced modern science, although the atoms are not currently considered to be indivisible, but rather are composed of various elements. Ancient atomists defended the existence of the void, later denied by Aristotle. Everything, on their account, is composed of atoms and void. Shapes of atoms explained the qualities of material objects.

Student: Were there Presocratics who defended the dominance of spirit over matter?

Teacher: We have seen that some Presocratic philosophers do not trust the senses and believe that reality should be investigated by reason. Some even hold that reason or intellect guides everything. Generally speaking, we must take into account the fact that the senses are particularly related to matter because they are in direct contact with material objects. Reason can also study the objects of the senses, but first through the intermediary of the senses, and reason can moreover think independently about abstract realities.

With regard to the Presocratics who defend the preeminence of the spiritual, we have, for instance, Diogenes of Apollonia, who holds that everything is ordered by an intelligence. This is air or God, and in human beings and animals it is intelligence and mind or soul, respectively. Things are ordered according to the good.

The main philosopher defending intellect as the cause of reality and individual things is Anaxagoras, who states that *nous*, or intellect, rules the world and accounts for the creation and existence of all natural bodies and phenomena. This intellect is eternal, it animates living beings, and it creates movement and the world. Some ancient philosophers, like Socrates, for instance, were not entirely convinced by the account of the agency of the intellect as described by Anaxagoras and held that he ultimately only indicated material causes to account for existing beings, such as the natural elements. Socrates' approach to Anaxagoras is described in Plato's dialogue *Phaedo*, in which Socrates recounts how he was initially impressed by the philosophy of Anaxagoras, because of his description of a *nous* that guided everything towards the good, including in nature; but he then became disillusioned when he realized that Anaxagoras did not take the concept of intellect far enough. Although Anaxagoras mentioned intellect, he then used material causes to explain natural and celestial phenomena.

Student: If Socrates considers Anaxagoras' account of intellect ambiguous, what does spirit mean for Anaxagoras?

Teacher: In Anaxagoras, *nous* or intellect is a spiritual, nonmaterial cause, but Socrates takes it much further. According to Socrates, spirit is related to knowledge and also to ethical questions, since both knowledge and morality come from the rational soul. Spirit here can mean the human spirit which is able to learn and know. It also includes the concept of will, and hence the related ethical questions, which for Socrates ground and explain human morality. These are the theoretical and the practical aspects of the intellect, respectively.

In Socrates, according to the Platonic dialogues, we already see some of the major concepts pertaining to spirit: it is related to the human intellect, knowledge, and ethical questions. And, most importantly, it appears to be opposed to matter, a theme which is developed in Plato's dialogues. According to Socrates, if the world were directed by intellect (*nous*), as held by Anaxagoras, it would mean that it had a final cause or purpose and was not constituted at random. Goodness would prevail and render reality and life meaningful. The world would be directed towards the good in a purposive way by a superior intelligence. This approach, in contrast to the naturalistic accounts of many Presocratics, highlights the purpose or final cause of events instead of the efficient cause, which immediately precedes its effect. However, Socrates complains that Anaxagoras, although mentioning a universal intelligence, does not put it to work, and instead falls back on the material causes already invoked by the naturalist philosophers. With Anaxagoras we are still unsure if the world and the events which happen in it are truly directed towards the good by an intellect.

Socrates and Plato

Student: Socrates, then, takes spirit more seriously than his predecessors.
Teacher: It is with Socrates, on Plato's account and in Plato's works, that we find a major turn to spiritual aspects of philosophy, and so a turn towards metaphysical and ethical questions. In fact, we could say that Plato is the first to establish clearly the philosophical meaning of spirit, with his conception of the human soul and the forms whose nature the soul imitates.
Student: It is clear that Socrates introduces new themes into his philosophical discussions, and in this way he distinguishes himself from the previous philosophers. It is not for nothing that his predecessors are known as the Presocratics. Does Plato follow in the same vein as Socrates when it comes to spirit?
Teacher: From the various accounts about Socrates and his philosophical interests, it appears that Plato follows in the footsteps of Socrates and expands on his understanding of spirit.

In Plato, spirit can be identified with the human intellect or with reason. But spirit in this sense is not confined to the human intellect or mind. Plato introduces in his dialogues the description of certain eternal essences, the forms or ideas, such as the good, the beautiful, the just, the equal. This spiritual reality, in the shape of ideas, is to be found outside the human mind, in a different, timeless reality, although these two spiritual aspects, the intellect and the forms, are related. Some of these forms are described in the dialogue *Phaedo*, where Plato has Socrates defend a theory of ideas, which are the paradigms of the things that exist here in the earthly realm. As we have seen, some of those ideas or forms are the just, the good, the pious, the equal, or justice, goodness, and piety. No entity, human or non-human, although it may display some of these qualities, exhausts any of them, and these are just some examples of the eternal forms. This means that if a human being is just, he or she shares in the form of justice. If something is beautiful it shares in the eternal form of the beautiful, but it does not exhaust it, otherwise nothing else would be beautiful. Therefore, that quality exists by itself as an eternal essence in a different reality from ours. And the same applies to the other qualities. Consequently, there is a realm of forms in a different world, where all the forms exist in their pure state. It is very important to stress that these qualities are eternal, indivisible, simple, and unchanging, unlike the corruptible things we see on earth. It was precisely the search for an eternal reality which seems to have prompted Plato to devise his theory of forms, because it is not possible, according to the ancient Greeks, to know that which keeps changing. The forms explain that which is stable in an otherwise unstable terrestrial world.

Student: I understand that the theory of forms is a central aspect of Plato's philosophy and how the forms are purely spiritual. But what exactly do these forms mean, and are there forms of all qualities?

Teacher: These forms could refer to general concepts, qualities, or mathematical or quantitative properties—like equality and magnitude. So the forms are not just qualities, although they are treated as qualities and not as quantities as such, since a quantity is divisible and the forms are indivisible. In addition, the soul is of a similar nature to that of the forms, as being invisible, unchangeable, immortal, intelligible, eternal, incorruptible. The forms and the rational soul are both spiritual. Reality is spiritual, and so these forms account for the intelligibility of things but also for their existence. If things cease to participate in the forms, they also cease to exist. For Plato, as for Hegel later, reality is at bottom spiritual or rational rather than material.

Plato believes that this rational aspect is that which does not change, come to be or pass away. For Plato the ideas are the eternal forms which exist in a reality which our soul has seen. Therefore these forms or ideas are to be found in three ways: they are in our souls, and exist in them implicitly, and explicitly when we remember those forms, such as the good and the pious. They exist in sensible objects, which can be called good or equal if they participate, or share, in those forms. Those forms also exist separately in a superior realm. The terms Plato uses for these spiritual realities refer to reality, logic, and the intellect or reason, but we can call them spiritual in a broad way.

In Plato an important aspect of spirit or the soul is that it is opposed to matter, and this becomes a constant feature in later philosophy through to the modern period. In a certain sense, matter and spirit are understood in relation to each other, as opposites which, however, can be found together in individual things or persons in this world.

Student: The opposition between spirit and matter in Plato is clear, but how is spirit precisely to be distinguished from matter? What characterizes spirit specifically?

Teacher: Generally speaking, that which is spirit is apprehended by the mind or the intellect alone, while matter is apprehended by the senses. If something cannot be seen, heard, smelled, touched, or tasted it is not material. Naturally, it is possible to talk about matter in an abstract way. Some philosophers have attributed specific properties to matter in itself, such as extension and divisibility. Aristotle believed that prime matter, or pure matter, is a pure abstraction as something which has no form or shape and can never be known by the mind or apprehended by the senses precisely because it has no shape or form. There are many ways to describe matter, and current scientific discussions about matter are quite abstract.

Spirit, on the other hand, is perceived by the intellect, and it is not extended or divisible. Plato's distinction between the forms and matter set the tone for philosophical discussions on these topics up to the modern period. For Plato, forms are changeless, and they not only allow us to know things but they also constitute the being of things, as we have seen. Without forms everything would fall apart because they lend some stability even to finite beings, which come to be and pass away.

Student: We saw what the nature of the forms is and how they are present in this world and in the other world, and we saw that the soul understands the forms, but in what sense is the soul something spiritual?

Teacher: The soul really belongs in the realm of the forms, and is akin to them. Therefore it is truly spiritual. Generally speaking, Plato appears to have been influenced by the religious tradition and in particular by Pythagoras and his followers. So he equates soul with life and he believes that animals also have souls. In fact a human soul can reincarnate in an animal. It is clear that he believes that the soul is immortal, as held by Socrates. And this is because it shares many characteristics with the forms. The soul is invisible, indivisible, incorruptible, immaterial, and not extended, and so it also endures forever. However, it can admit of the good and the bad, that is, it can be virtuous and it can be evil. It can let itself be dominated by the body and the passions of the body. In this way it becomes distracted and can forsake its main activity, which is to contemplate the good. Plato, as expounded by Socrates, holds that the soul exists eternally, that is to say, before it enters the body and after it leaves it. It is the principle of life. Therefore, a body without a soul is an inanimate, lifeless body. In the same way that we see forms present in material beings in this world, the soul is also found in this world as present in and managing a living body. The soul stands to the body as the other forms stand to individual things which participate in the forms.

Student: The forms are said to be incorruptible. Does Plato prove that the soul is immortal?

Teacher: Plato proves the immortality of the soul precisely through the association of the soul with the forms, particularly with the form of life. Since the soul is inextricably linked with life, it cannot die. Moreover, there is a clear link between ethics and metaphysics in connection with Plato's views on the soul. The soul ought to know the most perfect form, the form of the good, which could claim priority among the forms. By knowing the good, it will be virtuous, and the person who possesses such a soul will be a good person who will practice good deeds. This good conduct will ensure a good afterlife, for Plato defends in the *Phaedo* the notion of a judgment of a person's deeds after death. There is recompense for the virtuous and punishment for the evildoers through the kind of reincarnation which they will experience in the afterlife. The good will be in the company of the gods or reincarnate as virtuous people, while the bad will reincarnate as violent animals.

Student: The link between metaphysics and ethics is clear in Plato. It is also clear that those who know the good are bound to practice it. The spiritual element in ethics also informs our conception of the virtues. What does it mean to be virtuous in this life, that is to say, how can the virtues be practiced?

Teacher: Plato's philosophy opposes the two kinds of reality, the eternal reality of the world of forms and the material reality of this earthly world. While the soul is akin to the eternal world, the body resembles more the physical world, in a kind of duality. In order to observe the proper order of things, the soul should control the body and not let the body's desires and needs dominate it. Therefore the soul has to be strong and focus on seeking knowledge, which is the hallmark of wise men and philosophers. The idea of virtue is premised on the principle that reason prevails over the senses. In principle, everyone is expected to follow these precepts. In the dialogues, we see that Socrates is willing to converse with anyone and use his dialectical method regardless of his interlocutor's social standing, and so appears to assume that any person, citizen or stranger, can potentially become a philosopher. Reason or the spiritual must prevail in us; the virtues are based on that principle and they must be based on knowledge or wisdom.

Student: What kinds of things should the philosopher avoid, according to Socrates?

Teacher: In the same way that the philosopher should seek wisdom and goodness, respectively a metaphysical and an ethical pursuit, he (or she) should not be too worried about the needs of the body (eating and drinking, for instance) and external goods that are related to the body, such as honors, glory, and material possessions. Consequently, Socrates holds that one is only evil through ignorance of the good, given that the true and the good and inextricably connected. One can only be good by knowing goodness. There is no ethics without epistemology, according to what we find in the Platonic dialogues.

Student: It seems that knowledge or wisdom is the defining feature of human beings, and Socrates does state in the *Apology* that "the unexamined life is not worth living" for human beings. But how does one attain knowledge?

Teacher: The similarity between the soul and the forms—the soul being the subject of knowledge and the forms the object of knowledge, although this terminology (the terms "subject" and "object") is not explicitly used by Plato—comes from the fact that the soul before inhabiting a body was together with the forms in the other world, as described in the dialogue *Phaedrus*. In fact, the soul belongs in that other world. If the soul, who is forever contemplating the forms in that realm, becomes distracted and unfocused it loses its bearings and becomes heavy. It finally comes down to this world and incarnates in a body, as a punishment, for the soul is not material and wants nothing to do with material reality. This sudden attachment to a body is such a violent event that the soul forgets all about the forms it has seen, and is born in an infant body ignorant of everything. Slowly, by seeing the reflections of the forms in this world, or by being asked the right questions which Socrates asks as part of his dialectical method, it comes to remember the forms which it saw in the other world, and it always longs to return to that world. Socrates proposed a theory of knowledge as recollection or remembering in the *Meno*. The main point of this position, and the stories that illustrate it, is the similarity between the mind and the forms.

Plato gives us a complete notion about the soul in these dialogues. For him, knowledge and learning are recollection. All the forms are in the rational soul to start with; we simply need to remember them. Learning is a process of remembering, bringing out, and recalling long-lost knowledge to the soul. The soul is not just rational: other parts of the soul manage the body and its needs.

Student: Is knowledge something simple or does it have different parts or aspects in Plato?

Teacher: In the *Republic*, Socrates mentions the different parts of knowledge. He distinguishes knowledge from opinion, and then distinguishes within the rational part of the soul the discursive part (*dianoia*) and the intelligible part (*nous*), which directly attains knowledge. The distinction between discursive and non-discursive thought becomes very important, not least in the Middle Ages, a period when direct or non-discursive knowledge is clearly preferred as being the prerogative of God and the angels. Some philosophers defend the idea that it can also be present in human beings, albeit rarely. This kind of knowledge is immediate and intuitive, and it does not need to go through steps but is attained instantly. The distinction between knowledge and opinion is often discussed by Socrates in the dialogues. Naturally, knowledge for Plato is knowledge of the forms and of the unchangeable, and knowledge itself is considered unchangeable. As we have seen, truth should be sought with the mind or the rational soul. In some cases, the senses will help us recall some forms we have seen in a previous life, but on the whole the senses mislead us and so we must follow reason instead. Plato, following the lead of Parmenides, holds that reality as well as knowledge is primarily spiritual. The forms, which are the building blocks of reality, are purely spiritual, and not material. Many philosophers after him would claim that reality is spiritual. We could argue that this view dominates the history of philosophy, as opposed to other views. Aristotle, who studied under Plato, differs in many ways from Plato in his philosophical views, but one could argue that he does not challenge the idea of a spiritual knowledge or even of a spiritual reality.

Aristotle

Student: Plato was a very influential philosopher and his most famous pupil, as we know, was Aristotle. At first blush, Aristotle seems keener on studying individual or particular existing things or substances than ideas. These things are material or have a material substratum, so can we talk about spirit in Aristotle? For instance, does Aristotle, who studied in Plato's Academy, accept the existence of these separate realities, the eternal forms?

Teacher: Aristotle does not accept the existence of separate forms in a superior realm, although he does not deny the existence of forms (or rather, universals or essences) in this world and in our minds. He also expands on the characteristics of form and matter, and on their differences.

Student: How does he understand matter and form?

Teacher: Form has various expressions in Aristotle's philosophy, and he also has a complex theory of matter, arguably more complete than that of his predecessors. For Aristotle, form is something intangible and pertaining to the domain of knowledge and the intellect, while matter is generally related to the senses since material objects are apprehended by the senses.

Moreover, form and matter are two of the four causes he distinguishes in nature, alongside the end, or purpose, and the efficient cause. These are more familiar to us, because we think of cause primarily as that which produces something. Sometimes we refer to a goal as a cause—for instance when we say that someone defends a certain cause. These four causes explain the basic nature of an individual thing. Matter is the material a thing is made of (for instance, the wood of the table), the end is the purpose of that substance (for instance, writing), and the efficient cause designates that which or the person who produced it (for instance, a carpenter). The formal cause consists in the definition of a thing (for instance, "this wooden object with four legs"). Therefore, matter and form are essential in Aristotle's philosophy, primarily in his physics and metaphysics, two disciplines in which the question of form and matter features prominently.

Student: Clearly, for Aristotle, as for Plato, form is a cause of being and existence, and also of intelligibility. If the form defines something, it allows us to understand that thing. Consequently form is a central aspect of Aristotle's philosophy and it shares certain common aspects with Plato's conception of form, although Aristotle denies that forms exist independently of the intellect or of existing things. In addition to the formal cause, are there other meanings of "form" in Aristotle?

Teacher: The other meanings are relative to form as cause of being and of understanding. Form is what defines or shapes something, it is an active principle, and it is related to the universal concepts with which we analyze existents. Primary substances are individuals which actually exist, such as this table, or this pen. In order to describe primary substances we use the ten categories, substance being the first category, and accidents—such as, for instance, time, place, and relation—constituting the remaining nine categories. We have substance and nine categories, or the concepts we use to describe the substance. Substance is sometimes considered the essence of something, sometimes the substrate of its qualities or accidents.

Secondary substances are universal concepts such as "man," "animal," rather than "this man" or "this animal," so they can be genera or species, general notions or concepts. The categories also have a formal aspect, in so far as they are accidents. A secondary substance is also a universal, and has therefore a formal aspect.

Student: If, for Aristotle, the formal cause is a counterpart of the material cause in individual substances, is there a stark difference between matter and form?

Teacher: The difference between matter and form remains, as for Plato. Form relates to the universality of the concept, while matter ensures that we have an individual existent. Matter is therefore the principle of individuation, while the form is something universal. Form is an active principle, and matter a passive principle, which means that it is only effective through form.

Student: If form is related to knowledge and being universally conceived, can it be considered something spiritual?

Teacher: This conception of form can be related to spirit because the form is related to the intellect. Forms or universal concepts are that which the intellect can know, and they assume different aspects in Aristotle. They are not primarily apprehended by the senses. Rather, these general qualities are abstracted from sense perception, which means to extract the abstract or universal elements from the individuals which are apprehended by the senses. Abstraction means to concentrate on the form by disregarding the material element in the individual thing. According to this model, we abstract form from matter if we, for example, think of "horseness" as a result of seeing one or several horses, and concentrate on what makes a horse a horse, and what is specific to horses and not shared with other species. The forms are thus not material but concepts in the mind. In addition, they are related to other general concepts which Aristotle devised, such as genus (for instance, animal) and species (for instance, human). These terms are still used in biology, as well as family, order, class, division, and kingdom.

A more general way of classifying particular objects (more general than the ten categories) was developed and systematized by Porphyry in the 3rd/4th century AD. He devises a system of five predicables, which are genus, species, differentia (the quality that singles out a species within a genus), property (a quality of a certain species, which however does not define it—Aquinas states that it is a medium between the essence and the accident), and accident (a quality which may or may not belong to a thing). In the Middle Ages, even more general categories were defined, namely the transcendentals, on which more later.

Student: In that case, spirit in Aristotle's philosophy is interchangeable with the form or the formal cause?

Teacher: Yes, in the case of Aristotle, the spiritual is tied up with form and its several meanings. In addition, for him (as with Parmenides previously) there is a logical dimension to the question of form and substance. In fact, the categories and the predicables apply to real existing things and they consist in what we can say about them. These general concepts or forms are predicated of individual substances. The metaphysical and logical aspects, pertaining to reality and language respectively, are intertwined. As a result, Aristotle's logic deals with formal aspects of thinking, which are not separate from his metaphysics. Parmenides is considered to have first formulated the principle of non-contradiction. Aristotle defines the general rules of logic (the principles of identity, non-contradiction, and excluded middle) in the *Metaphysics* and he also developed the first system of formal logic, syllogistic logic. Naturally the metaphysical, which considers reality, and the logical, which represents our language about reality, go together.

Student: I understand that Aristotelian metaphysics emphasizes form and the spiritual element to the detriment of matter. Form is considered to be active and to render actual those individual substances in which it exists, while matter is the passive element, in which the form and the accidents inhere.

Teacher: The difference between form and matter as active and passive respectively is an important issue, as we have mentioned. Form is active and not in potentiality, or latent, by itself. In contrast, matter by itself accomplishes nothing, it only acts in combination with a form or several forms. So matter is not truly the cause of existence or being, while form, which is the spiritual, unextended aspect, is truly causative or efficient; it exists in actuality and it is efficient by itself. It is efficient in connection with matter, in material beings and individuals. This is a way of stressing that the material aspect is passive and accounts for the potentiality in something (the fact that something is latent and not fully developed in its characteristics) while the form is active and in actuality.

Student: Are there other spiritual aspects in Aristotle's works?

Teacher: Yes, this is obviously the intellectual element, which we must not neglect. The form is something objective, which is known or seen by the human intellect or subject, and the form is akin to the human intellect—in the same way that in Plato the forms are akin to the rational soul. Aristotle states that when the subject actually intelligizes a spiritual object, an object devoid of matter, the subject and the object become one. The human intellect shares in the nature of the spiritual. This theme is later developed by medieval philosophers, who establish a common origin for all that is spiritual, and naturally this is God, or the One.

Student: How does Aristotle describe the process of knowledge?

Teacher: According to Aristotle, knowledge starts from sense perception and from first perceiving individual material things. Subsequently, a process of abstraction follows, leading up to the knowledge of universals or forms. Knowledge itself is never of matter but of universal forms, secondary substances, genera or species, or knowledge of first principles. A definition is also something general or universal. That is to say, definitions are of the universal rather than of particular beings. There could be particular elements in knowledge, but knowledge (theoretical reason) itself is of the universal. In this way, the intellectual and the formal and spiritual are inextricably related.

Student: How does Aristotle describe the intellect?

Teacher: The intellect for Aristotle is the rational and the thinking part of the soul, and it pertains to human beings rather than animals or plants; the gods also have a contemplative activity, so thinking is clearly considered a superior activity. The intellect can be in actuality or potentiality. Initially it is in potentiality but when it intelligizes the universals in actuality, it becomes one with the intelligible object, as we have seen. The intellect then possesses these universals. Aristotle also mentions a separate intellect which is always in act, and this intellect was conceived in different ways by his interpreters, especially in the medieval period, as we shall see.

Student: What of his conception of the soul?

Teacher: Aristotle considers the soul to be also related to life, and he defines it as the first actuality of a natural body which potentially possesses life. He attributes a soul to plants, which is the vegetative soul and is responsible for growth, for instance. Then animals have an additional kind of soul, the sensitive soul, which is responsible for sensation, motion, and desire. Finally there is the rational soul or intellect, which only human beings possess, in addition to the vegetative and the animal soul.

As we have seen, there are various kinds of intellect in Aristotle, who is much more systematic in his analysis of human knowledge than Plato is, and this includes the study of the various human faculties of knowledge, from sense perception through to the active intellect which actually intelligizes, not excluding imagination and memory. He also mentions a divine intellect, whose activity consists in thinking itself constantly and eternally. He characterizes the deity as thought thinking itself, and this divine intellect is identified with God in the medieval philosophical tradition.

Student: The concept of spirit clearly has various meanings in Aristotle, including the notion of form, logical categories and intellect, which belongs to his study of human psychology.

Teacher: Yes, and the logical and the metaphysical aspects are not irrelevant to physics, because some topics, such as causality and the question of matter, are studied by both physics and metaphysics. We therefore find a metaphysical exposition of the four causes in Aristotle's *Metaphysics*, but they also feature in his *Physics*, where we see the application of the principle of the four causes in nature, physics being the study of nature. Matter naturally belongs to the natural, earthly world, where we see it combined with form. On the other hand, matter by itself, or prime matter, is a purely abstract or even speculative concept, and this is why it is analyzed in metaphysics rather than in physics, which studies nature and movement.

We can say that although Aristotle starts from the physical reality and from individual, material, actually existing substances, all the edifice of his philosophy and his conception of knowledge is purely spiritual because it focuses on universals and logical categories. He also values theoretical knowledge above practical knowledge. For all the interest in ethics and politics in ancient philosophy, it is clear that both Plato and Aristotle emphasize the theoretical and contemplative over the practical and political.

Student: What else does Aristotle have to say about matter?

Teacher: Matter is that which actually exists only in so far as it is perceived. All the matter we find in nature already bears a form or shape, or formal qualities, so we never perceive prime matter as such, or pure matter. In addition, we cannot define individuals. We can certainly perceive an individual material existing thing, but we cannot know it as such, any more than we can know an individual human being, although we may be able to define the characteristics of the human species (as a rational animal) and what it means to be human. Matter is a rather mysterious concept in Aristotle.

Therefore, the spiritual in Aristotle can be found in his metaphysical conception of reality, in his logic, which cannot be dissociated from his metaphysics, and also in his epistemology. Knowledge is purely spiritual for Aristotle, although he obviously does not deny the existence of matter. However much we try to come closer to the material, our knowledge is purely formal. He founded the disciplines of formal logic, and laid the foundations for physics and biology (with his differentiation between genus and species). With regard to metaphysics his views are not dissimilar to Plato's, since reality is really constituted by the forms, and pure matter is an abstraction that we should assume as underlying the forms. However, we can never know exactly what it is, and it remains an intellectual and abstract concept. In spite of his realism regarding individual material substances, the notion of knowledge as spiritual dominates his philosophy. An illustration of this point is that, according to

Aristotle, when we perceive a material object, we do not actually have the object in our minds but a picture of it.

Aristotle's views on the world, nature, and knowledge would shape the philosophical tradition for centuries to come, until the modern period in Europe. A new model of science was not found until the Renaissance.

Stoics and Epicureans

Student: Are there other schools in the ancient world defending a particular view of spirit?

Teacher: After Aristotle other schools emerged in Ancient Greece. One of them, Stoicism, defends the idea of a universal intellect that pervades and rules everything, a divine world soul (made of a special, intelligent kind of fire) which rules everything and disposes all matter. The Stoics held that spirit (*pneuma*), which for them was a body (only bodies truly exist for the Stoics), was a force pervading all things, including animated bodies and the universe, and keeping it together. In animate beings this spirit took the form of the soul. Although they defend the notion of an all-pervading spirit, they understand it in a materialistic way.

The Stoics developed important aspects of logic and physics. In ethics, they defended the principle of conformity to nature, which meant to follow one's nature and reason and to be tuned in to universal reason. Acting morally implies having the virtues, and knowledge is required for this. The wise man is virtuous and vice versa.

They also defended the notion of providence and the view that events do not happen randomly or haphazardly but follow a definite order—to such an extent that they were considered to be determinists.

In the Stoics spirit can be identified with this universal reason, in spite of its connection with matter.

Student: Do other schools of thought have a conception of spirit in this period?

Teacher: Alongside the Aristotelian school, which remained extremely influential, it is important to mention Plato's Academy, which had various versions throughout the Hellenistic period. Some of these versions had a strong skeptical element. This was a departure from Plato's philosophy, but it derived from some typical aspects of Plato's thought, in particular his distrust of sense perception to attain true knowledge. Cicero was a keen follower of the Academics, in his desire to avoid dogmatism. And although he admires certain aspects of Stoicism (which would be a dominant influence in later ancient Roman philosophy) he also mentions the other two major schools of philosophy, the Peripatetics, descended from Aristotle's school, and Epicureanism (stressing the principle that pleasure was the highest good), in addition to the Academy and Stoicism.

Student: Does this mean that other schools of philosophy became more influential than Plato's and Aristotle's schools, since they developed after Plato and Aristotle?

Teacher: The Stoic and the Epicurean schools were a novelty in comparison with the previous schools of philosophy, and they focused on ethics more than on the other branches of philosophy, but they also developed new metaphysical and logical theories. However, Aristotelian and Platonic philosophies came to dominate the following period, during the Middle Ages, and some of the questions posed by the Stoics and the Epicureans were incorporated into the later tendencies in philosophy rather than being treated as they had been by the Stoics and the Epicureans. Their influence as specific individual schools reemerges in the modern period in Europe.

Student: I understand the significance of Stoicism and Epicureanism in ancient philosophy, as well as the skeptical developments in Plato's Academy. I wonder how Plato's philosophy was transformed in the ancient period, in addition to the theories taught in the Academy?

Neoplatonism

Teacher: As formulated by Plotinus at the height of the Roman Empire, Neoplatonism became the most influential form of Platonism, through the medieval period and well into the Renaissance. Plotinus had a distinctive conception of the world and of an intellect ruling it. He conceives of the world as an emanation proceeding from three elements, starting from the One. From the One, the intellect proceeds, and from the intellect a soul proceeds. The concept of emanation was extremely important in subsequent philosophical traditions, but so were the concept of soul and intellect, which are initially conceived by Plotinus as universal. The soul then generates the sensible world, and the sensible world is a reflection of the intelligible world, which is generated by the intellect. Oneness is present with the One, which is the cause of being but above it, and multiplicity starts at the level of the intellect. The intellect is the cause of essence, which accounts for the multiplicity of thoughts or ideas. The ideas are thoughts in the divine mind. We find in Plotinus the same identity of being and thought as in Parmenides before him.

Again, we find the notion of a universal intellect and a universal soul ruling the world. The human soul straddles the two worlds, material and intelligible.

Student: Can we say that Plotinus systematizes Plato's philosophy? He also seems to include aspects of other ancient schools in his philosophical system.

Teacher: Plotinus added several new theories to, and chose particular aspects of, Plato's philosophy. In addition, he was influenced by Aristotle, since we also find in his philosophy the concepts of substance and accident, which are typically Aristotelian. We also find a reformulation of Platonism with its theory of forms which exist in a separate world.

Student: What are the spiritual or formal elements in Neoplatonism?

Teacher: We can say that the spiritual element explicitly dominates in Plotinus' philosophy as in Plato. As we have seen, there is a procession, a process of origination, from the One, which is above being, to the intellect, which possesses the forms, and to the soul. All these are spiritual realities. The earthly or material world follows subsequently. This kind of emanation is a causative process, and it means that the material world is an effect of the spiritual realm. In addition, the intelligible world is more truly existent than the material world. Plotinus equates matter with non-existence, and another expression of non-existence is evil. As the universe, in the emanation scheme, becomes more material, it is less real and possesses being to a lesser extent.

The Aristotelian and the Neoplatonic traditions would alternatively and sometimes simultaneously dominate the Western philosophical tradition, including Jewish and Islamic philosophy, until the Renaissance.

Student: Is Aristotle's philosophy transformed in the same way as Plato's during the Middle Ages?

Teacher: Aristotle's philosophy is by nature more systematic than Plato's, and Aristotle sought to cover all the knowledge of his time and even founded new disciplines, such as logic. In late Antiquity and throughout the medieval period, Aristotle's works, given their complexity, are the subject of many commentaries. Therefore his philosophy suffers primarily gradual transformations, rather than a fundamental transformation as in the case of Plato with Neoplatonism.

Chapter 2
Medieval Philosophy

Neoplatonism in the Middle Ages

Student: Given the predominance of Neoplatonism and Aristotelianism in the Middle Ages, do we find the same views on spirit in the medieval period, as intellect and
forms or ideas?

Teacher: In the medieval period, the links between philosophy and religion become
stronger, with the influence of Judaism first, in late Antiquity, and then Christianity
and Islam. The question of God becomes central during this period. The themes of
the divine and divinity were not absent from ancient philosophy, either in Plato or in
Aristotle. With Stoicism and Epicureanism the issue surrounding God's involvement
in human and earthly affairs becomes more pronounced. It is in the Middle Ages that
philosophy becomes heavily influenced by religion and theology, given the historical
developments in Europe as well as in Asia and North Africa. Therefore, the philosophical element has to be articulated in connection with religion, which dominates
all aspects of society in an organized and systematic way. Everything, including in
philosophy, is viewed in relation to God. The world and everything in it is seen as his
creation. God is the principle and the end of creation and of human beings. Naturally,
one's conception of God is an important aspect, and there are varying views in this
respect, theological and philosophical, in the medieval world, which is dominated by
a monotheistic religious outlook. Given that the philosophical tradition is continuous
and there is a strong influence of the philosophy of Plato and Aristotle, who agree on
a spiritual principle of the universe and individual substances, the predominant philosophical outlook during the Middle Ages is of God as an infinite intellect who is all-
powerful and all-knowing. There are debates regarding God's attributes, such as intellect and will. Some Islamic theologians, unlike the Islamic philosophers, stress his
will over his intellect, and add that God has the attributes of seeing and hearing. For
the philosophers, however, God does not have any attributes that can be associated
with a material body or the senses. God is a purely spiritual being, who does not have
a body, or a soul to manage a body; he is a pure infinite intellect and therefore knows
everything without needing the senses. In God, according to the philosophers, all

attributes are identical with his essence. Thus God is not corporeal, material, finite, extended, limited, but is incorporeal and infinite. Underpinning this philosophical conception of God are important elements from the philosophy of Plato and Aristotle, who associate matter with extension, corporeality, passivity, potentiality, and finitude. Therefore every material element is removed from God. This does not invalidate scriptural descriptions of God which ascribe to him bodily or soul-like qualities. God is pure intellect and does not have a soul with all its different faculties because he is not material or corporeal, and thus cannot have a body. The Godhead is spiritual and any anthropomorphic descriptions of God in scripture, or descriptions ascribing to God human or animal characteristics, are to be considered metaphorical according to many medieval philosophers. Consequently, we are enjoined to follow the spirit and not the letter of scripture. These metaphors are interpreted in different ways by philosophers from the various religious traditions.

Student: It appears that metaphorical interpretation is crucial in securing the agreement between scripture and philosophy. Do we find different positions among philosophers with regard to metaphors and allegories?

Teacher: Those who prefer to follow scripture more closely, such as Aquinas and other medieval Christian philosophers and theologians, value metaphors and allegories in scripture which describe the Godhead. They also tend to value scripture over philosophical works—because they consider the human intellect to be finite and limited, whereas the divine intellect, the source of scripture, is infinite and omniscient. Although God is purely spiritual, it is possible to represent his attributes by analogy with certain animals and other creatures.

Medieval Islamic philosophers, however, such as Avicenna and Averroes, reject any anthropomorphic passages as literal descriptions of God, while conceding their utility for non-philosophers. They hold that the philosophers know their true meaning and must interpret them metaphorically.

The question of metaphors is also important for the Jewish tradition, and it is related to the spiritual reading of scripture. In the Jewish religion God's transcendence is stressed in such a way that God's name cannot be pronounced and indeed cannot be known. God is moreover purely spiritual and not bound by matter and material circumstances like human beings and other living beings. Therefore, any anthropomorphic descriptions of God must be interpreted allegorically, that is to say, not literally, because God does not have human characteristics. Maimonides, the most famous medieval Jewish philosopher and thinker, is a strong proponent of this position. God does not have senses and does not manifest Himself in a sensible or material way.

Student: It is natural that the question of the interpretation of scripture should become so significant in the Middle Ages, especially in its articulation with the different contemporary philosophical tendencies. Do we find an influence of Aristotelianism and Neoplatonism also in medieval Jewish philosophy?

Teacher: Maimonides was an admirer of the medieval Islamic philosopher Alfarabi. Consequently, he was influenced by the Neoplatonic and the Aristotelian tradition, although Maimonides does not accept the emanation schema developed by Alfarabi. Alfarabi combined the ancient cosmology of Ptolemy with the basic principles of the emanation schema by Plotinus, which explains how everything comes to be from a first principle. The emanation schema ensures a gradation of being from the first principle to the lowest emanated being, until matter is reached, and finally, nonexistence. A distinction is maintained between the celestial world and the terrestrial world. Emanation is like an overflow from the first principle, and a flowing out from each being to the next, which is its emanation.

Student: How does Alfarabi combine the principle of emanation with Ptolemy's astronomy?

Teacher: The principle of emanation in Plotinus states that from the One an intellect proceeds, and subsequently a soul. Each principle produces from itself the next principle, in a total of three principles (the One, the intellect, and the soul), before the generation of the world takes place. Alfarabi accepts the principle that from one principle another proceeds, but he links those principles to the astronomy described by Ptolemy. More specifically, instead of three spiritual principles we find eleven, and they are all intellects. Only the first principle is purely one, and the following intellects contain a duality. They are not souls but intellects, and they have each a celestial sphere attached to them (for instance, the fifth, sixth, and eighth emanated intellects have Jupiter, Mars, and Venus respectively as their spheres, and these are the actual planets we see). This was perhaps Alfarabi's most ingenious philosophical innovation, the way in which he combined metaphysics and astronomy.

In this way, Alfarabi maintained the general principle of emanation and of the outpouring from the first being, but to each emanated intellect a sphere, following the Ptolemaic system, is attached, with the exception of the eleventh emanated intellect, which does not have its own sphere. Once the celestial world is formed in this way, we have the formation of the terrestrial world on the basis of the celestial world and the celestial spheres. This means that there is no creation as such but a seamless sequence of emanations. This schema was adopted by Avicenna with some modifications and additions (since he held that the spheres do not just have an intellect but also a soul). Maimonides does not accept this schema, although he follows the Islamic philosophers in saying that God's anthropomorphic descriptions are to be taken metaphorically.

Student: Is emanation a way of describing the creation of the world?

Teacher: Emanation is a way of explaining the origin of the world for Alfarabi and Avicenna, but some Muslim theologians oppose it because it does not presuppose a will on the part of the One who creates. According to them, emanation is an outpouring from the First, not a conscious decision and will to create the world. Therefore emanation is starkly different from the Qur'anic account of creation, which states that God created the world in six days.

Student: I see how this question pertains to the reading of scripture, although emanation clearly seems to depart from the notion of creation.

Teacher: These are complex issues related to creation and they were debated in the Middle Ages. Later, Hegel also tackles the issue and understands the principle of creation out of nothing as a metaphor whose purpose is to explain that God is spirit and cause. However, creation is a special kind of causation, as Hegel himself admits. It is also a unique kind of causation according to the medieval Christian philosophers, who for the most part defend the idea of creation as described in the Bible.

Returning to Maimonides, the Neoplatonic tradition is perhaps most obvious in the negative theology that he follows. This means that we can say nothing positive about God but can only say what God is not, because he is entirely transcendent. In referring to God, we can only use as attributes verbs of action which do not actually describe him. The use of metaphors in the Bible serves to illustrate this point, according to Maimonides. Therefore we cannot ascribe to God any material or anthropomorphic characteristics. And it is not possible to describe God by means of any attributes because this would mean to ascribe a plurality to him, and God is one. We saw how oneness is an important element in Plotinus. It is in fact the first element, and the start, of the emanation schema; from it proceeds the intellect and then the soul, both of which already entail some plurality. Also, according to Maimonides, we cannot truly apply the same attributes to God and to us, which means that our language is inadequate to speak about God. Consequently, we should understand any attributes ascribed to God in a negative way. If we say that God is powerful it means that he does not lack power. Our language is not capable of doing justice to God, and at any rate it is not possible to know God's essence. For instance, we cannot say that God possesses emotions, although scripture appears to ascribe them to God.

Student: And how does the question of God's attributes relate to spirit?

Teacher: For the medieval philosophers, God is purely spiritual. God is spirit in the most perfect way and sense. There are differences among the Western religious traditions, namely Judaism, Christianity, and Islam, but all consider God to be one. The notion of God as purely spiritual has deep philosophical roots. For the ancient philosophers, such as Plato and Aristotle, matter is naturally limited, divisible, and finite. It is clear for the medieval philosophers and theologians that these attributes are not compatible with God's omnipotence and omniscience. In Christianity the idea of God as spirit is emphasized. God is spirit and for Christian philosophers and theologians each person of the Trinity is also spirit, because God himself is spirit. The second person of the Trinity, the Son or the Logos, assumes a human shape in the person of Jesus Christ, and reveals himself to us.

Student: In what sense exactly should we think of God as spiritual?

Teacher: God is spiritual because he is not material, and also because he possesses the transcendentals, the most general attributes, such as being, one, truth, and goodness, to the utmost degree. He is infinite being; he is truly one and not composed of anything, conceptually or materially. He is true because he is the ultimate reality, and he is pure and infinite good. According to the medieval Christian philosophers these attributes are one with his essence, and so do not constitute a multiplicity in him. He does not have any material characteristics and therefore is not limited but is infinite, and possesses his attributes in an infinite way. They are identical with his essence, which is infinite being. In addition, God, in all these traditions, does not have anthropomorphic characteristics, because human beings are partly material and limited.

This means that God does not possess a body or any bodily parts. In addition, he does not have a soul, as we have seen. Some medieval philosophers debate whether God is a substance. For instance, Avicenna states that God is not a substance precisely because he is transcendent and substances are limited things. We saw how Aristotle thinks of substances primarily as individual particular things which surround us in the material terrestrial world.

Student: It seems strange to say that God does not have a soul. Why is this the case according to medieval philosophers? It makes it seem as though God were lacking something that human beings have.

Teacher: God does not have a soul because he does not have a body and the soul connects the body with the intellectual part of the soul. The soul is not pure intellect, as we have seen, but it is also in charge of managing the body, which God does not have. This is why medieval philosophers defend the idea that God is pure intellect, in the sense that he is purely spiritual. Matter is considered a limitation and something that impedes action. Some of these questions remain present in the modern period.

Because God does not have a soul he is pure intellect, and is not divisible or extended in any way, as we have seen. This means also that he does not have emotions, in the sense that he is not moved by anything outside himself. He cannot have emotions because again this would imply the existence of a soul and a body. For the emotions express themselves in a bodily way and through the body and they imply some kind of passivity. Will and intellect belong to God in an infinite way.

Student: Scripture appears to ascribe emotions to God. How do we interpret the emotions attributed to God in scripture?

Teacher: Medieval philosophers, for instance Anselm and Maimonides after him, state that God's actions produce effects that resemble human emotions or are interpreted by us as human emotions. To feel an emotion is to be moved and to be passive, and for that reason too God cannot possibly feel emotions, because God is active and is thus an infinite power. Anselm says that if God acts in a way that is merciful it is because his action is interpreted as a sign of mercy, but this does not mean that God feels mercy as such, or is moved by human beings, since it is always God who takes the initiative. Moreover, he is impassible. Equally, Maimonides does not believe that God can be perceived by the senses, given that he is not material and is to be perceived intellectually.

Student: Then God is the foremost exemplar of spirit.

Teacher: He is purely spiritual and infinite spirit. Therefore when we speak of spirit, God is spiritual in an absolute way. Consequently, Hegel later identifies God with absolute spirit. God can also be seen as the origin of spirit and of all that is spiritual. In this way the philosophical tradition is consistent in saying that God is spiritual. We find this position among most medieval philosophers and theologians, in spite of differences, primarily in the theological domain.

Student: Does it mean that not all medieval thinkers agree to read scripture metaphorically?

Teacher: Some Islamic theologians prefer not to read the Qur'an metaphorically and not to speculate about the ways in which it describes God. Obviously, the more conservative groups who read scripture literally opposed philosophy and the influence of Greek philosophy on theology and religion. Therefore the use of metaphors is extremely important in the Middle Ages when it comes to the interpretation of scripture. It goes hand in hand with the view that God is spiritual and the way in which this position can be defended in a rational way. In other words, it is more complicated to hold that God is spirit if anthropomorphic descriptions of God are not read metaphorically.

Student: I understand how the question of the metaphorical reading of scripture is related to the conception of God as spirit. As we have seen, another way of explaining this view held by the medieval philosophers is to say that God is a pure intellect?

Teacher: Yes, this is another way of saying that God is purely spiritual and it also shows the continuity with the ancient philosophical tradition.

Student: In this view of God as pure spirit, which aspect predominates, the philosophical or the theological? It seems that philosophy determines the outcome, since the idea that God is intellect goes back to Aristotle. Or does the theological element dominate philosophical analysis in the Middle Ages?

Teacher: There are various combinations of both elements, and sometimes the philosophical element dominates, sometimes the theological does. In the Christian world, it can be said, for instance in Scholasticism, but also in Patristics, that the theological element in philosophy predominates and philosophy becomes the handmaid of theology. In the Islamic world, on the contrary, for several centuries philosophers (such as Alfarabi, Avicenna, and Averroes) use Islamic themes in their thought and works, but the philosophical aspects predominate given their close adherence to Aristotle, a position which draws criticism from Islamic theologians.

Generally speaking, during the medieval period, theological debates became more influential and became intertwined with philosophical discussions. Theology and philosophy came to inform one another. The same topic could be discussed based on philosophy or on theology, and sometimes both theology and philosophy were involved in the discussion of the same question.

Student: With regard to philosophy, which philosophical movements predominate in this period?

Teacher: Neoplatonism dominated early Christian philosophy, especially for the Church Fathers, in what is called the Patristic period. This is because Aristotle's thought, particularly his system of the ten categories, was considered to apply to particular material beings rather than celestial and divine realities. Neoplatonism had a religious element that attracted the early Church Fathers. However, there was a growing interest in Aristotle's philosophy in the ancient world, from the first century BC onwards, with many commentaries being written on his works.

Student: Where do we find the major points of contact between religion and Neoplatonism?

Teacher: The conflation of both can be clearly observed in Augustine, who witnessed the transition from late Antiquity to the Middle Ages. He is thus an important exponent of Neoplatonism. His conversion to Christianity was linked to his reading of the Neoplatonic books, as he recounts in the *Confessions*. Among other things, Neoplatonic philosophy allowed him to solve the problem of evil which was tying him to the Manichean religion of which he had become a member. Manicheism represented a dualist thought which viewed good and evil as ever fighting each other. It admitted of a good god who, however, was not all-powerful because of the existence of evil, which was considered a real entity by Manicheans. So there was no one absolute principle of existence, but two principles that explained the existence of the world and all phenomena in it.

Student: How does Neoplatonism help to explain the problem of evil in a way which is compatible with a good and omnipotent God, as we find in Christianity?

Teacher: Like Plotinus, Augustine came to think of evil as relative to the good and as an absence of the good. This allowed him to think of an omnipotent God who is good and provident, and also omnipotent. We see that Augustine combines Neoplatonism and Christianity in a particular way. More specifically, the idea of one single principle and cause of the world was appealing to him and it was in harmony with the biblical account of creation by God. As we have seen, Plotinus appeared to have solved the problem of evil. In this way, the existence of evil did not detract from the biblical notion of a good God, or from the idea that the good was a principle of creation and prevailed in the world. Neoplatonism presents us with the notion of a gradation of being. God is the foremost being (although for Plotinus himself the One was above being and above any attributes, as an absolute principle). With the sequence of gradation of being, existents become gradually less spiritual and more material and also less truly existing, until we reach matter, which is in itself non-existence. With regard to the connection between the human soul and God, Augustine held that the human soul was illuminated by God, although knowledge could also be obtained by sense perception.

Student: How does Augustine conceive of God? One would expect him to accept that God is purely spiritual.

Teacher: He follows Christian dogma in saying that God is omniscient and omnipotent, as well as perfectly good. Augustine offers an early proof of God's existence by distinguishing three kinds of existing beings. There are three levels of existence: pure existence, life, and understanding. He starts by explaining the things which only exist, such as stones. Another kind of being is that which exists and lives, such as irrational animals. Finally there are existing, living, and rational beings, such as human beings, angels, and God. The second level necessarily includes the first, existence, and the third necessarily includes the first and the second, that is, existence and life. If God is an intellect he must therefore be also living and existing. This would lay the foundation for later proofs of God's existence, and would influence Anselm's proof as well as Descartes'. Augustine adopted many, but not all, aspects of Neoplatonic philosophy, since he espoused the biblical account of creation rather than explaining the origin of the world through a series of emanations from the One. He also had a tremendous impact on the development of Christian theology, for instance with respect to the role of the human will and human responsibility in sinning.

Student: It is clear that medieval Neoplatonism favored spirit over matter in its explanation of existence as well as the world and its origin. It is a position that emphasizes the fact that the spiritual is more real than the material. Were there other developments within the Neoplatonic tradition in the Middle Ages?

Teacher: From the Neoplatonic tradition, several aspects were adopted in medieval philosophy, such as for instance the idea of one single and absolute principle of the world. Medieval Neoplatonists hold that spirit or intellect is the origin of the universe. It is important to note here that most philosophers, under the influence of Aristotle, conflate the first two principles of existence in Plotinus, the One and the intellect, which become the one God who is intellect.

Student: Are there other elements adapted from Neoplatonism to fit a medieval worldview?

Teacher: We have seen that the notion of emanation was significant, as a gradual process whereby everything from the One or the intellect came to be, that is, from the divine intellect through to human beings and individual animate and inanimate substances. It was especially important for medieval Islamic philosophers. The emanation schema was adopted by Islamic philosophers such as Alfarabi and Avicenna, who did not explain how this might square with the account of God's creation of the world in six days in the Qur'an, as we have seen. Their views were based on the spurious *Theology of Aristotle*, a work attributed to Aristotle but in fact consisting of the three final books of the *Enneads* by Plotinus. In this way, they were unaware of the Neoplatonic influence they received and attributed it to Aristotle. It is worth noticing that some Neoplatonist Jewish philosophers also integrated the notion of emanation, with some modifications, into their philosophies, such as Isaac Israeli (with God creating a first matter and a first form), Solomon Ibn Gabirol, and Judah Halevi. Israeli holds that God creates first matter and first form, from which the first intellect proceeds. According to him, a second intellect emanates from the first intellect, and it is identified with the soul.

In addition, Neoplatonic views on matter and evil were highly influential, for Christian, Islamic, and Jewish philosophers. It is significant how the Neoplatonic tradition is combined with Aristotelianism in the Middle Ages.

We have seen that emanation was not adopted earlier by Augustine, who accepts the scriptural account of creation and wishes to maintain a clear distinction between God, on the one hand, and the world and creatures, on the other.

Generally speaking, as you mentioned, we have the primacy of intellect and soul over the material world and substances, and the primacy of good over evil, which is simply a privation, or lack of the good. This means that every evil is a lack of a certain good. One may indicate an as example the idea that war is the absence of peace, which is the good that is desired in this case. The idea of evil as privation of the good was immensely influential because it allowed for the existence of an omnipotent and omniscient and infinitely good God in spite of the existence of evil in the world.

We find several of these Neoplatonic elements in many of the medieval philosophers, who embraced them knowingly (like Augustine) or unknowingly (like some Islamic philosophers, who thought that they were reading Aristotle when in fact they were reading Plotinus).

Student: This dual influence by Plotinus and Aristotle appears to have been very fruitful.

Teacher: Yes, and this dual influence is adapted according to the religion professed by the philosophers in question. The spiritual element broadly construed dominates the philosophical (and naturally the theological) discourse. We find the hegemony of the spiritual in the guise of the One, or the intellect, and the souls which proceed from or are created by it. As in Plato, the material world is caused by spiritual agents, the first Intellect and, for Islamic philosophers, also by the celestial souls. As in Aristotle, there is a clear distinction between the celestial world and the earthly world, which contains material substances. This distinction shapes the medieval view of nature and the discipline of natural philosophy, which comprises physics and other disciplines, such as biology. Naturally, the philosophical and the religious aspects went hand in hand.

Student: How are Aristotelianism and Neoplatonism adapted with regard to the religious affiliation of the philosophers?

Teacher: Islamic philosophers refer to God as the First, which is tied up with their belief in the oneness of God, a core tenet of Islam. As in Aristotle, the One and the Intellect are identified with the one God. Both in Christian and in Islamic philosophy God becomes identified primarily with intellect and thinking, while other elements, such as will, sometimes become subordinated to the intellectual aspect. As we have seen, for many, though not all, philosophers, the Aristotelian and the Neoplatonic traditions become conflated.

Knowledge, as in ancient philosophy, is purely spiritual and the objects of true knowledge are also spiritual rather than material. Reality is ideal, constituted by the ideas, the images of which we find in this earthly world. Those who reject the Platonic theory of separate self-subsisting forms state that they exist not separately but within the divine intellect who creates the world on the basis of these ideas.

Student: This means that Plato's theory of ideas is still influential in the medieval period.

Teacher: Yes, a different version of the theory of ideas survives in the medieval period. These ideas no longer subsist separately, but they exist in God's mind and are generated by God, according to Aquinas. This means that they exist somewhere other than in our minds and things, and we can abstract them from these things in order to obtain knowledge. These ideas exist either in particular objects or in the human, the angelic or the divine mind. In this way, Plato's theories become influential again. Authors who, following Aristotle, reject the theory of self-subsisting ideas, such as Avicenna, still believe that they exist in a celestial intellect.

Student: Intellect is a form of spirit. How do medieval philosophers form their theories of the intellect? Are there different views on the intellect?

Teacher: There are different views on the human and the divine intellect, both based on Aristotle. Medieval philosophers elaborate on Aristotle's theories of the intellect, and on the relation of the intellect with the other faculties of the soul, which are inferior to the intellect. As we have seen, according to Aristotle, there are several types of intellect in accordance with its position with regard to the intelligible. We have different kinds of intellect, a kind that is in potentiality to intelligizing its object; another kind is actually intelligizing it. Finally, the intellect has retained the universals, the intelligible objects. Most controversial was Aristotle's mention of a separate intellect which was always thinking.

Student: How did the controversy arise?

Teacher: The controversy concerned the interpretation of this intellect and its relation to the other types of human intellect. Some philosophers, still in Antiquity, such as Themistius, held that this intellect was a part of the human intellect. But before him, Alexander of Aphrodisias defended the idea that this external intellect corresponded to the divine intellect, given Aristotle's indication to the effect that, unlike the human intellect, it was always thinking, and that it was separate.

Student: I understand how this "separate" intellect could be interpreted in different ways: as a separate part of the human soul or as entirely separate from the human soul. Which of these two views prevailed?

Teacher: The view that it was situated outside the human intellect prevailed among Islamic philosophers. It was identified with an active intellect which was a celestial intellect. For Alfarabi and Avicenna this active intellect was the tenth emanation from the One. For Averroes it was a separate intellect, although he did not accept the Neo-platonic emanation schema. In this intellect were contained all universals and ideas, which it transmitted to human beings. In addition, this separate intellect accounted for revelation and prophecy—which was naturally a central aspect within a religious context—and so it enabled philosophers to articulate the philosophical and the theo-logical accounts of revelation. Part of the rationale for upholding the separateness of this active intellect was the Aristotelian principle which stated that something poten-tial only becomes actual when it is actualized by something which is already in actu-ality. This meant that the human intellect was only rendered active in its intelligizing activity by this external active intellect which is never in potentiality. For these Is-lamic philosophers the universal ideas reside in this separate active intellect which thinks constantly, and does not cease in its intellectual and thinking activity.

On the other hand, medieval Christian philosophers like Aquinas believed that this active intellect was simply a part of the human intellect. Aquinas also condemned Averroes' view to the effect that the human intellect became totally fused with this external active intellect after death so as to lose its particularity and personal identity, as this would invalidate the notion of a final judgment of individual human beings. Generally speaking, universals and ideas are concentrated in the divine intellect, and for Islamic philosophers also in a celestial intellect. According to Aquinas, every form is a certain resemblance of God. And everything is modeled on these ideas, hence giving rise to a common spiritual principle which unites the intellect and the ideas, which are both active and effective as formal causes.

Student: We have seen in which sense God is spirit for medieval philosophers and theologians. In addition, the spiritual element in medieval philosophy clearly lies in the ideality of forms, and the fact that they exist in an intellect. We have again the preponderance of intellect and form or idea as the active and effective elements of reality.

Teacher: Yes, and the dominance of the spiritual aspect is tied, in the Middle Ages, to the fact that these ideas are inherent in a divine or celestial intellect. Naturally, ideas in human beings can also lead to the creation of particular substances, related to the arts, but in the case of the divine intellect we are talking about creation of the world and all reality coming from this divine intellect by way of its ideas. In Plato, these ideas existed autonomously and were active in a superior world, but in the medieval period the ideas inhere in an intellect, as we have seen. In this way God becomes the exemplar cause of everything in the universe.

Aristotelianism in the Middle Ages

Student: We know that besides Neoplatonism, Aristotle's philosophy also heavily influenced medieval philosophers. How did Aristotelianism become more influential later in the Middle Ages, after the initial impact of Neoplatonism in Patristic philosophy?

Teacher: Aristotelianism never died as a school of philosophy. It is described by Cicero as one of the main schools of philosophy in Antiquity, alongside the Stoics, the Epicureans, and the Academicians (Plato's school). Aristotelianism develops further in the Middle Ages. The tradition of commentaries on Aristotle's works goes back to the Hellenistic period and late Antiquity, and it continues in the medieval period, both in the Islamic and in the Christian world. The longest commentaries are written by the Islamic philosopher Averroes in the twelfth century, but we also find commentaries on Aristotle's works composed by Aquinas and by Jewish philosophers. This tradition of detailed study of Aristotle continued into the Renaissance and the early 17th century. The various theories found in Aristotle are developed and refined. As we have seen, there is, for instance, a plethora of theories on the different kinds of intellect, with important variations between Christian and Islamic philosophers.

Student: The tradition of commentaries on Aristotle spans a very long period. What transformations does Aristotelianism go through in this period?

Teacher: While Neoplatonism was influential primarily in Patristic philosophy and in the earlier period of Islamic philosophy, Aristotelianism becomes more influential later in the Middle Ages, and especially starting from Averroes, who made it his task to restore Aristotle's philosophy to its original form. There were reasons for this return to Aristotle, to the exclusion of other philosophical influences. Averroes' philosophical project consisted in a return to Aristotle as a response to his predecessors' espousal of Neoplatonism, which, as Averroes saw it, had drawn the criticism of the Islamic theologians and had given philosophy a bad name. For instance, the emanation schema did not truly indicate a will on the part of God to create the world. With emanation, creation is merely an overflow and not the result of deliberate action. Therefore, Averroes believed that with a return to Aristotle's true philosophy it would be possible to harmonize philosophy and religion, and particularly philosophy (which for him was convertible with Aristotle's thought) and Islam.

Owing to Averroes, and after him, Aristotle dominated philosophical thought in Scholasticism, the second major trend in medieval Christian philosophy after Patristics. The main concepts in Aristotle's philosophy, under the influence of the commentary tradition, were used to describe God and creation. There was an articulation of religion and philosophy in this period, as we have seen. Having been translated into Arabic first and then into Latin, Aristotle's works were studied, and commentaries were written and studied. A gradual process of adaptation was underway for several centuries, in the Islamic and in the Christian world.

Student: What did this adaptation of Aristotle's thought entail?

Teacher: This adaptation meant that Aristotle's concepts were understood in a certain sense, to serve a particular purpose which implied a comparison with scripture. His main logical categories and the notion of substance—central to Aristotle's philosophy and, as we have seen, sometimes meaning essence and sometimes a substrate of qualities—were still in use. However, Aristotle was primarily concerned with concrete individuals, existing beings, and therefore he did not truly consider in detail certain aspects of existence that would become so important during the Middle Ages given the religious and theological influence. For instance, Aristotle did not consider the ideas of creation and providence in the way that the medieval philosophers and theologians did. Although constituting a single principle of movement and therefore of existence in the world, his prime mover was not concerned about particulars in the earthly realm. In addition, Aristotle considered the possibility, on the part of human beings, to see future events in dreams, but the idea of prophecy was truly analyzed later by medieval philosophers in a detailed way, though not without having recourse to Aristotle's theories about the intellect. Aristotle's notions about causation, and the four causes, were still used to describe primary substances, and one finds a study of logic and physics in their own right during the Middle Ages. However, the question of God and his relation to creation, and particularly to human beings, becomes central in medieval philosophy. For instance, the four causes are attributed to God. God is considered (already by Themistius) to be the foremost efficient (as creator), formal, and final cause—God is considered to be the beginning and the end of things and creation, that from which everything comes and to which everything returns—in both the Christian and the Islamic traditions. Although God is not a material cause per se, since he is not material himself, he is the cause of matter, and for Aquinas he creates matter and the world out of nothing—creation out of nothing, connected with the efficient cause, being also a theme not truly considered by Aristotle. Aristotle's conception of causality and the four causes is therefore seen in a different light given the influence of religion and especially scripture. Some of these themes would continue to be debated in the modern period, notably the question of God's providence.

Student: Are there changes, in the medieval period, in the understanding of the relationship between human beings and God?

Teacher: Yes. There are specific issues concerning the relation between God and human beings and nature. The question of evil, as we have seen, becomes more central during this period, given the need to explain the notion of an absolutely good God—and here Neoplatonism is fundamental in solving some questions. Medieval ethics is also influenced by Aristotle's philosophy.

Student: How is medieval ethics influenced by Aristotle?

Teacher: Aristotle's theory of the virtues is generally adopted. According to this theory, acting in a right and moral way is to act virtuously, and the virtues consist in a mean between two extremes. There are various kinds of virtues, such as moral and intellectual, but they require the knowledge of the mean, the golden mean, and they are a guide to ethical action. In the medieval period the virtues continue to be a fundamental aspect of ethical theory, together with the notion of practicing the good as defined by scripture.

Student: Naturally, scripture must be taken into account in any medieval ethical theory.

Teacher: Yes, and in Christian theology, more virtues are discerned on the basis of scripture which surpass the moral and intellectual virtues. These are the theological virtues: faith, hope, and charity, which are infused by God and lead to happiness in the afterlife. Faith is a habit of the intellectual part of the soul, but it is also linked to the will. Therefore it can be described as an act of the intellect which is ordered by the will. Faith is the knowledge of things unseen, and it generates charity. Happiness is seen as a goal to be secured not just in this present life but also, and more importantly, for the next life, which is eternal. Already in the Platonic dialogues we find the stress on the need to lead a good life in order to secure a good afterlife. The question of the immortality of the soul is discussed and explained by medieval philosophers and theologians in the light of scripture.

Student: Do we also find changes in medieval metaphysics in relation to Aristotelian metaphysics, given the influence of scripture?

Teacher: Yes, with a creationist model (even if not all philosophers followed scripture literally) the questions concerning existence and its source become more complex. In particular, the difference between essence and existence is clearly established, as a result of the concept of creation. Aristotle simply assumes the existence of primary substances, but medieval philosophers explain their existence through God's creation, based on the ideas and the essences in his intellect. Avicenna, for instance, clearly distinguishes essence from existence, and considers existence to be an accident of the essence. This follows in the wake of early Islamic theological discussions on this issue, which stipulate that God contains the essences of all things and subsequently bestows existence on them according to his will. Later, in medieval Christian philosophy, existence becomes an attribute, and the question continued to be debated in the modern and even in the contemporary period.

Student: How do views on metaphysics and creation in the Middle Ages bear on the question of spirit?

Teacher: If we take the creationist model into account, as well as the issue of God and his attributes, it becomes clear that spirit dominates reality and provides an explanation for all existing things. Aquinas explicitly states that God is spirit, which means that the origin of the world is spiritual. God creates by his intellect and his will, and therefore it becomes clear that the source of the world is spiritual, with matter coming into existence later. Philosophers agree in saying that God himself exists from all eternity and will continue to exist into all eternity. He is purely spiritual, and the world is created by his intellect and will in accordance with his ideas and the essences he conceives. When it comes to the relation between spirit and matter—already present in Aristotle and in Plato before him—the latter is subordinated to the former, and is explained by the former.

Student: What is the medieval conception of matter? I suppose we can expect it to be heavily influenced by Neoplatonism and Aristotelianism.

Teacher: Medieval philosophers, for the most part, do not endorse materialism, which claims that matter is the main constituent of reality and grounds thought, while thought derives from matter. An extreme form of materialism states that everything is material, even our thoughts. Medieval philosophers believe that spirit comes first and grounds matter. Matter is not simply this abstract mass whose origin cannot be accounted for, but it is something that God creates out of nothing (as stated by Aquinas) although he himself is purely spiritual and has no physical dimension, extension, movement, or potentiality. He creates by his intellect, such that all creatures are in him in an exemplary manner. In the field of ethics, we find an intellectualist view, where the will is subordinated to the intellect. This follows in the wake of the tradition laid out by Plato and Aristotle, who stipulate that the intellect precedes the will, and that practical philosophy—of which ethics is a part, together with political philosophy, which treats of the organization of human communities—is subordinated to theoretical philosophy, which is the worthier of the two. It is only in modern philosophy that one finds the concept of will preceding the intellect, as for instance in Rousseau. In the ancient and the medieval periods of the history of philosophy the intellect is considered to precede the will and to direct it.

Student: There clearly is a distinction between Patristic philosophy and Scholasticism, the former being primarily influenced by Neoplatonism as a philosophical school. One the other hand, Scholasticism was primarily influenced by Aristotle—is there a particular reason for this?

Teacher: The term Scholasticism is related to school philosophy and the birth of universities in Europe. Instead of going to particular teachers to learn certain subjects, or attending a particular school of philosophy, as was the custom in Antiquity, in the later Middle Ages students attended universities. Medieval universities offered all subjects, and students came from different parts of Europe, which explains the origin of the term "university" to designate these new institutions. Naturally, in this context, where a need was felt to teach and study all the different subjects, namely logic, physics, and metaphysics (as well as theology, medicine, and law), Aristotle's thought, which covered all the philosophical subjects and all the different sciences, was considered to be the most appropriate and comprehensive to be taught in medieval European universities. However, Neoplatonism continued to be an important influence in philosophy and theology.

Student: I understand how philosophers and theologians were influenced by these two philosophical movements, but was there an opposition to the influence of these philosophical ideas in medieval theology?

Teacher: There are variations in the acceptance of Neoplatonic and Aristotelian philosophy, on account of different interpretations, for instance with respect to the intellect, as we have seen. The main opposition to philosophy comes from certain theologians. For instance, in the Islamic world there is opposition to a rather intellectualistic view of God. Al-Ghazali, who is very critical of the Islamic philosophers, stresses God's will and other attributes that are denied by the philosophers, such as hearing and seeing. In the Christian world, there is also opposition to what is thought to be an overly rationalistic conception of God and the corresponding approach to theology. As a consequence, Aristotle's positions are condemned regularly, until the synthesis produced by Aquinas is finally accepted.

Student: What kinds of variations do we find with regard to the interpretation of Aristotle by medieval philosophers?

Teacher: In the case of philosophy, we have variations on Neoplatonism and Aristotelianism, interpreted now in the light of scripture. An Aristotelian like Averroes holds that the prime mover, who according to Aristotle in the *Physics* is the generator of movement and therefore existence in the world, has knowledge, will, and intention, an expansion on Aristotle's views in the *Physics* on the mover who is never passive or potential. And there are many other such developments.

Student: Are there developments with regard to Aristotle's logic and metaphysics?

Teacher: Yes, and an important aspect which is developed is the theory of transcendentals, particularly in medieval Christian philosophy. They were called transcendentals because they transcended the ten categories (substance, quality, quantity, relation, place, time, position, state, action, and affection). The ten categories were deemed appropriate to designate earthly, particular material substances, but they could not be applied to spiritual beings, especially God. One cannot speak of time and place, or being affected, in relation to God; thus the categories were not appropriate to describe him, but only material, earthly beings, animate and inanimate. In this sense, the transcendentals are considered to be the most general concepts, and therefore appropriate to describe God. The main transcendentals are being, one, truth, and good; being is more general than one, which is more general than truth, which is more general than good. One is considered negatively, as undivided being. According to Aquinas, being, one, and good are said in many ways—and God's being is infinitely above ours. God does not share the same being, oneness, and goodness with us or with other creatures, and this goes to show God's absolute transcendence.

Both the Aristotelian and the Neoplatonic traditions in the Middle Ages strongly emphasize the spiritual and intellectual over matter, whether it refers to the intellectual nature of knowledge, or the primacy of spiritual substances and entities. Aquinas holds that no intellectual substance is a body. As we have seen, ethics is also very intellectualistic, with the intellect guiding the will.

Within theology, there are also developments as a result of philosophical influences. The inquiry into the nature of the soul, which had already been discussed by Plato, Aristotle, and other ancient philosophers, is expanded to accommodate a theological perspective informed by scripture, as we will see in greater detail.

Student: May we conclude that there are different and varied theological perspectives in the Middle Ages?

Teacher: Yes, and new disciplines are devised alongside the old ones. For instance, Aquinas clearly distinguishes two kinds of theology, a natural theology, which is part of metaphysics and is mentioned by Aristotle, and sacred doctrine, which is theology based on scripture and inspired by divine revelation.

Student: What exactly is the difference between the two kinds of theology?

Teacher: We have seen that metaphysics according to Aristotle is divided into ontology (the theory of being as being) and theology (the theory of God as the supreme being). This is a natural theology in the sense that it is accessible to the human intellect without the need to resort to other sources. According to Aquinas, there is another kind of theology, which belongs to a different genus of science given its different source, as it is grounded in scripture and not in the human mind. This is sacred doctrine and it is based on the Bible. For instance we can learn about God's existence through natural reason, but scripture gives us more detail about God's nature. In addition, according to Aquinas some Christian dogmas can only be known through scripture, such as the Incarnation and the Trinity. Not all theologians agree on the limits of human reason when it comes to theological matters. Anselm, for instance, believed that these two dogmas could be proved by reason alone, in contrast to Aquinas. Obviously, Aquinas believed that sacred doctrine was superior to natural theology, since the latter is based on the finite human intellect, while sacred doctrine is based on God's knowledge, which is complete and infinite, and is revealed to us. This is in harmony with Aquinas' view that the human mind is finite and prone to errors, which explains the need for scripture to reveal the central doctrines about God. Sacred theology is consequently considered to be more certain than the human sciences.

The Soul in Scholasticism

Student: We know that the views on the soul changed in the Middle Ages under the influence of scripture, in addition to the philosophical influences. What impact did Aristotle's view on the soul have on Scholasticism?
Teacher: In Scholasticism, as for Aristotle, the soul is identified with life, and any living being is considered to have a soul, including plants and animals as well as human beings, but the main focus is on the human soul. Part of the human soul is responsible for managing the body and the passions, but another part of the soul is purely spiritual, namely the intellect; naturally, this is the focus of medieval Aristotelian philosophers, since it is this part which distinguishes us from animals and plants and which allows us to acquire knowledge. The soul as a whole, and its immortality, is an important theme in ancient and medieval philosophy. The soul is a complete entity which belongs to each human being, but the intellectual part or faculty draws the attention of medieval philosophers, who expand on Aristotle's theories. The medieval philosophers see an important link between the human soul and the divine intellect, which is said to illuminate the human soul. The soul is also in contact with the angels (in the Christian tradition) or the separate active intellect (in the Islamic

tradition). Due to its intellectual nature, the human soul bridges the gap between the two worlds, celestial and earthly, which were considered as separate entities in the Aristotelian tradition, with different sets of laws. The laws governing the earthly world did not apply to the celestial world, and vice versa, a view that was only rejected in the Renaissance with the universal application of mathematics to physical and celestial phenomena.

Student: I understand that the soul is a unity and speaking of parts of the soul may not be the best way to describe the different faculties. How are we to understand the different faculties of the soul?

Teacher: The theory of the faculties of the soul becomes more complex in the medieval period. With regard to the soul and the intellect, different views were propounded by various philosophers. These faculties were classified according to their role in the acquisition of knowledge by the human soul. The starting point in the Aristotelian tradition is naturally sense perception, arising from the activity of the five senses. Then came a common sense which compared and united the sensations obtained through the five senses. Memory was closely related to sense perception. At the level of memory there was a retention of the forms perceived by the senses and their combination, in connection with a retentive imagination. Finally, and only to be found in human beings, who are rational animals, we have the intellect, whose main task is to deal with universals and with first principles, unlike the senses, which deal with particular, material objects.

Student: In Aristotle, we have seen that knowledge properly speaking is of universals and not of particular things, although these universal notions are abstracted from particular substances. For Plato too the objects of knowledge are the universal forms and not particular things. Does this tradition of knowledge as consisting in knowledge of the universal continue among medieval philosophers?

Teacher: Yes, the idea that knowledge is of the universal is for the most part accepted. This approach is very clear in Aquinas, and he generally endorses Aristotle's conception of knowledge, which starts from the senses. The sensible object is impressed on the external senses, and this form proceeds to the imagination and then to memory. He believes that forms are present both in material beings and in the mind or the intellect, but they are received in the intellect in an immaterial way. The act of the intellect is universal and immaterial. Immaterial things are intelligible in themselves, but in material things we must abstract the forms, and thus render those things intelligible. The forms in God's intellect are created by himself. Moreover, God creates the world as an intellectual and voluntary agent, and he causes knowledge in us. For Aquinas, the proper act of the human intellect is to know, but more specifically it is to know God, and this is what brings about everlasting happiness or beatitude. Aquinas understands idea as the form which a thing imitates intentionally; in this sense, where the idea entails an end, it is an end. The intellect can put things together or separate them, that is to say, it can synthesize or analyze them.

Student: I understand that knowledge for Aristotelian philosophers involves abstraction and the use of syllogistic logic and valid arguments. Are there other kinds of knowledge for Aquinas?

Teacher: For Aquinas, and for other medieval Christian philosophers, there was a distinction between discursive and non-discursive intuitive knowledge, as we have seen. An Islamic philosopher like Avicenna also makes this distinction. The main difference between these two kinds of knowledge lies in the process of knowing. In discursive knowledge, reason apprehends the universal object through a syllogism, in a mediated, progressive way, by means of premises and conclusions. On the other hand, non-discursive knowledge is an intellectual intuition which grasps the conclusion immediately, without having recourse to syllogistic logic. The rational soul tends to use a discursive method. Reasoning is characteristic of human beings, while angels understand intellectual objects immediately. God too does not require syllogisms but intelligizes everything instantly, in no time. And God is the cause of our knowledge, as well as the first principle of our counsels and wills. Human beings can be illuminated by angels, but Aquinas stresses that our will is subordinate to God, not to the angels.

Student: How does Aquinas understand the difference between reason and intellect (or understanding)?

Teacher: They are fundamentally the same (in terms of the object known), except for the process involved. The connection between them is the following: reasoning resembles movement, acquisition, and imperfection, while understanding or intellect resembles rest, possession, and perfection. Aquinas also distinguishes between a higher reason, which deals with eternal things, and a lower reason, which considers temporal things. Accordingly, two lower parts of the soul are the scientific (to deal with necessary beings) and the rationative (to deal with contingent beings). The intellect deals with the principles, while the conclusions belong to science. The higher reason is wisdom, and the lower reason corresponds to science. Aquinas states that the intellect reflects on itself by intelligizing.

In Aquinas and the medieval tradition reason is discursive; it understands step by step and has to go through the premises in order to reach the conclusion. On the other hand, the intellect, which is a habit of first principles (and to know habitually lies between actuality and potentiality), understands by intuition, immediately, unlike reason.

Student: I understand the difference between reason and intellect or understanding in Aquinas. Is this terminology still in use in the modern period?

Teacher: Later, for Hegel, reason is superior to the understanding: the understanding is discursive and goes through stages, while reason fathoms the deepest realities. The distinction between understanding and reason is also present in Kant, who holds that the understanding, unlike reason, is bound by empirical data. Therefore, in the modern period a different terminology is adopted, whereby reason deals with higher realities than does the understanding.

With regard to ideas, for Aquinas they are contained in divine wisdom, as we have seen. They do not exist separately, but they are contained in God's intellect which is interchangeable with his being, while in human beings the intellect is a power. The ideas are created by him, and therefore God is the exemplar of all beings and he acts by his intellect and will. Hegel later stresses the existence of things in their intellectual or spiritual dimension. God is the cause of all knowledge. For Aquinas, spiritual nature is higher than corporeal nature, and so the soul can know even without the body. However, certain operations, like imagination, memory, and even thought, require bodily forces. The forms available in the intellect are superior to the forms to be found in material bodies, for there they are purely immaterial.

For Aquinas, the mind is the intellect; they have the same meaning. And the forms constitute being. Human knowledge participates in divine knowledge. God is spirit, and the qualities of the intellect and the intelligible are the same, since the intellect in act and the intelligible in act are one. Among the characteristics of the intelligible are necessity and incorruptibility. As a result, knowledge of the intelligible is knowledge of the universal and the necessary. Regarding contingent things we have opinions, rather than knowledge. Aquinas opposed materiality to intelligibility.

Student: For Aquinas, then, knowledge is primarily universal and theoretical?

Teacher: There is also a distinction between theoretical and practical intellect in Aquinas, but they are closely related. The intellect is ordered towards theoretical knowledge and the will is directed towards practical reason. However, for Aquinas, the will is a rational potency. He holds that the will depends on the intellect, in the sense that we choose from among the things we know. Equally, the free will depends on the intellect, since we have a free will on account of being rational. Consequently ethical questions revert to the intellect and to knowledge as something spiritual. Even when it comes to practical matters, the source is the intellect, which is a spiritual principle. There is a distinction between the different virtues, and among the speculative virtues are knowledge, wisdom, and understanding.

Student: I understand that all the spiritual aspects of knowledge and being which are found in Aristotle are also present in Aquinas, and that for him all spirit has one infinite spiritual source, namely God. As a leading exponent of Scholasticism, Aquinas is strongly influenced by Aristotelianism. Is there also a Neoplatonic influence in Aquinas?

Teacher: Aquinas follows primarily Aristotle, who is dubbed "the philosopher," as did his teacher Albert the Great. On the other hand Aquinas is influenced by some Neoplatonic themes, for instance the idea that God is the exemplar of all beings, and that they participate in his existence in some way. He also defends the idea that God is in everything by his essence and power (as efficient cause), as cause of everything. He creates by his wisdom. All ideas are contained in God (including corporeal forms), which means that Aquinas places the Platonic ideas in the divine intellect. Therefore everything pre-exists in God before being created. The substantial forms constitute the species, and being comes from the forms.

Because God is purely actual and always thinking, he is his own act of understanding and will, and he is wholly identified with his intellect and with his will. In contradistinction, in human beings the intellect is a faculty or a power and not the essence. Only in God is the intellect his own essence. For Aquinas as for Aristotle, human knowledge starts with sense perception, and by a process of abstraction, forms are obtained and received in the intellect. In Aquinas human reason is the principle and the end of the intellect, and the act of the intellect is attributed to reason. Both conscience (as knowledge of good and evil) and reason are explicitly considered by Aquinas to be spirit.

In Aquinas we also find the view that the human intellect can be directly illuminated by God, and this is an important aspect of his epistemology. The mind knows all things in the divine truth or in the eternal ideas, and the ability of the intellect extends to all general species.

In a hierarchy of beings for Aquinas, the spiritual nature ranks higher than the corporeal. In accordance with the views of Dionysius (that is, Pseudo-Dionysius the Areopagite), spiritual substances have essence, power, and operation, to such an extent that corporeal things can be touched by an incorporeal thing.

Student: The intellect is part of the soul, which has to be a central topic in Aquinas' thought, as a Christian philosopher and theologian. What does he say about the soul?

Teacher: As for the soul, it contains five powers: vegetative, sensitive, appetitive, locomotive, and intellectual. The soul is the principle of intellectual operation, and it is not composed of matter, so it is spiritual. The intellect receives absolute forms since it is purely spiritual, while prime matter receives individual forms. Knowledge itself is considered a form of the soul. Aquinas appears to follow Augustine when he says that the one essence of the soul is constituted by the understanding or intellect, memory, and the will. But Aquinas also seems to believe that memory is not in the intellectual part of the soul.

Theological Dimensions of Spirit: The Holy Spirit

Student: We looked into the concept of spirit in medieval philosophy. Is there a connection with theology, and what is, properly speaking, a theological consideration of spirit, especially since most medieval Christian philosophers were also theologians?

Teacher: In the Christian tradition God is spiritual in the sense of being immaterial, not being apprehended by the senses, as pure intellect, and as infinite intellect and will. This view is shared by many medieval philosophers, regardless of their religious affiliation. Therefore God is wholly identified with his attributes. He is also, according to the Aristotelian tradition, purely active and not potential, potentiality being a characteristic which is often, though not always, associated with matter.

Student: What else can we say about spirit for medieval philosophers?

Teacher: Many medieval philosophers believe that God is purely spiritual, but for Christian philosophers and theologians there is a further dimension, which is essentially theological. While God as a whole is spirit and is purely spiritual, this view is reinforced by the dogma of the Holy Trinity, which affirms that God is one God but three persons, Father, Son, and Holy Spirit. God is spirit, generally speaking, and each of the three persons is spirit, but one person of the Trinity is the Holy Spirit, and this is its proper name. This dogma comes from scripture but it was developed in late Antiquity and also in the Middle Ages. The persons of the Trinity exist from all eternity and are mutually related by way of procession. The Son proceeds from the Father (and he incarnates in history as Jesus Christ), and the Spirit proceeds from the Father and (according to the Western tradition) also from the Son. The Holy Spirit is associated particularly with the revelation of scripture and with life, and it is the gift of grace to human beings. The Holy Spirit is the source of revelation. Spirit is also opposed to the material. Spirit is related to practical wisdom. For Aquinas, it is the Holy Spirit who forms matter, and shapes beings, creating their species.

Student: God is purely spiritual in the medieval philosophical tradition and it is clear how this connects with the Christian tradition. Can we speak of other intellectual substances in medieval philosophy?

Teacher: Other spiritual substances for medieval philosophers and theologians are the angels, and the human intellect is also spiritual in this sense.

Angels do not have a material body and do not need discursive knowledge. They know the essences of things without having to have empirical experience of them. However, they do not possess God's infinite knowledge either. They possess a will because they are intellectual beings, hence the distinction between good angels and fallen angels.

God is a spirit, and infinite spirit. In other philosophical traditions too, like the Jewish and Islamic, God is purely spiritual, as non-material and as intellect, but in Christian theology this is stressed by the affirmation of the Holy Spirit as the third person of the Trinity. These central dogmas would later have a decisive influence on Hegel, who claims that his notion of spirit, as absolute spirit and the culmination of the dialectical process, is the Holy Spirit of scripture, even though the way in which he interprets central Christian dogmas is a far cry from classical Christian theology.

As we have seen, in medieval philosophy we find the predominance of the Aristotelian and the Neoplatonic traditions which favor form (and spirit) over matter. In addition, they favor for the most part spiritual interpretations of God's nature, solving in this way some problems that had not been solved or had not been mentioned by Aristotle.

Student: I understand the preeminence of the spiritual over the material in medieval philosophy. How does God, who is purely spiritual, relate to matter?

Teacher: Medieval philosophers develop many notions that were not explicit in Aristotle's works. With regard to matter, it is considered by medieval philosophers as subsumed under form, and related to nonbeing and evil. In addition, existing beings are not considered as simply existing (including matter), but the efficient cause of their existence is examined. God is both creator of the world and its existing beings, and creator of matter. Matter itself remains an elusive notion which is contrasted with form, and the Aristotelian conception of matter as a pure abstraction is accepted, as well as the Neoplatonic view of matter as close to nonbeing.

In the medieval period we have a synthesis of Aristotelian and Neoplatonic thought fused with theology. Spirit is identified with God, explicitly in the Christian tradition and implicitly in other traditions. God is infinite spirit, from which everything spiritual proceeds. The concepts of form and intellect are convertible with spirit and they define reality. Aristotle had already stated that form and actuality, which goes hand in hand with form, precede matter and potency. The Christian dogma of God as creator of the world makes it even clearer that spirit precedes matter, because God precedes the world, and in this way intellect precedes matter.

In medieval philosophy we find the same understanding of spiritual realities, such as for instance God, the angels or celestial intellects, the human soul, and the ideas in God's mind (which include the forms of everything that comes into being). Independently of the particular ways in which medieval philosophers establish the connection and articulation between the spiritual and the natural and material world, it is the spiritual element which dominates the material world. Knowledge is of the universal and not of individual material beings. In the process of cognition there is a progression from the more material (sense perception, which deals with individual, material realities) to an increasing abstraction which culminates in knowledge of the first principles and the rules of logic. In ethics, morality is part of practical philosophy and it is based on the will, which is determined by the intellect. According to this reading, animals, not having an intellect, do not have a free will and consequently no morality. Since the will is dependent on the intellect it is also something primarily spiritual. The will has the good as its object, one of the four main transcendentals. However, the truth, which is the object of the intellect, is more general than the good, according to Aquinas.

At a more particular level, this means that the intellect within the soul is expected to dominate the lower faculties of the soul—such as sensation—which are more material, or, in other words, they are in closer and more direct contact with the body. This position had already been taken by Plato, namely the view that the intellect or the mind rules the lower parts of the soul, which are more closely related to the body and to its upkeep.

Student: We have seen that a spiritual view of reality according to these philosophers entails the preeminence of the intellect within the soul, in its relation to the body, and of the forms or ideas in relation to particular or material substances. How could we compare it to a view that was not spiritual?

Teacher: The view which highlights the dominance of the spiritual, stressed later by Hegel, predominates in ancient and medieval philosophy but is not the only one in the history of philosophy. We saw that the Presocratics looked for the material elements that explain the composition of bodies and natural phenomena. They often did away with religious or mythical explanations, relying primarily on the testimony of the senses. Later, Epicurus asserts that the only good is physical pleasure, or perhaps the absence of pain. Even the Stoics, for all their talk of a universal reason explaining reality, had clear materialistic elements in their philosophy, particularly their physics.

Other schools, such as the various editions of Plato's Academy, with their skepticism, resulting from a mistrust of the senses (which was already a feature of Plato's own philosophy), becomes a prominent trend and would resurface in the modern period.

Student: Returning to theology, is there an influence of the doctrine of the Holy Spirit on modern philosophers? I suppose that such an influence would also indicate a continuity between medieval and modern philosophy.

Teacher: Modern philosophers have also concerned themselves with religious and theological questions such as the proofs of God's existence and the immortality of the soul (in view of its immateriality), but there is one philosopher who directly takes up the question of the Holy Spirit. This is Hegel, who believes that the ultimate reality is spiritual and that the Absolute is a spirit, which he names the Absolute Spirit. He claims, as we have seen, that his view of the ultimate reality as an absolute spirit, which is a philosophical thesis, is equivalent to the Church's view on the Holy Spirit, who is God. He claims that his Absolute Spirit is the Holy Spirit.

Student: You mentioned that Hegel's conception of spirit is not necessarily in line with traditional Christian theology. Do theologians accept this identification of Absolute Spirit with the Holy Spirit of Christian dogma?

Teacher: In Hegel there is a conflation of theological and philosophical elements and the due distinctions between philosophy and theology are not observed. Some of Hegel's statements are clearly not in line with orthodox Christianity, Catholic or Protestant. Apart from a metaphorical reading of certain dogmas of Christianity, he prefers the view of God as spirit to the detriment of the other persons of the Trinity, namely the Father and the Son (which he takes as metaphorical expressions coming from the natural order of generation in the world). He also believes that there is an evolution in God (which would count, for orthodox theologians, against his perfection). Hegel defends the idea that God comes to know himself through human history and also that human beings come to know God in this life as God knows himself. He eschews the questions of the immortality of the soul and the resurrection of the body; or rather, in his metaphorical reading of Christian dogma and scripture, he claims that the absoluteness and infinitude of self-consciousness is equivalent to the doctrine of the immortality of the soul. He also identifies the Holy Spirit with the Church and the human community of believers. His stress on the Holy Spirit may have been influenced by the Joachimite tradition, mentioned explicitly by Hegel. According to Joachim of Flora, a medieval theologian, the three persons of the Trinity are each identified with a particular period in human and biblical history: the Father with the Old Testament, the Son with the New Testament, and the Holy Spirit with a new period which was about to start. This tradition was taken up by the spiritual Franciscans, and it challenged the hierarchy of the Church, for the era of the Spirit would not require the hierarchy of the Church.

Student: Does this interest in the spiritual Franciscans found in Hegel go hand in hand with an unorthodox approach to the Holy Spirit?

Teacher: Yes, because there is a focus on the person of the Holy Spirit to the detriment of the persons of the Father and the Son, and according to Christian dogma God is Father, Son, and Holy Spirit, one God and three Persons. In addition, Joachim of Flora understood that the age of the Holy Spirit meant a break from the institutional Church and that it implied an individual's relation to God in particular through the Holy Spirit.

Student: So Hegel's claim to the effect that his conception of spirit is tantamount to the Church's understanding of the Holy Spirit is not acceptable to theologians?

Teacher: Hegel's reading of Christian dogma was not accepted as orthodox by Protestant or by Catholic theologians because his conception of the Holy Spirit was not in line with traditional theology. And as we have seen, he claims that the notion of Father and Son in the Trinity derives from natural human relations. But this is not how the Church defines the relation, for the Creed states that the Son is begotten and not made—therefore not created or generated according to physical nature. Moreover, Hegel considers the Father and Son relationship in God as metaphorical and the true notion of God as more "abstract" (though this is not a term that he would use for his conception of God) than the one we find in scripture. However, we have seen that Christian theology accepts a variety of terms to describe human and divine reality and these terms often point to spiritual and transcendent realities. The Trinity is precisely something that cannot be comprehended by the human mind, but only partially understood, as was stated by Aquinas.

So in many respects Hegel's approach is not orthodox. At the same time, it cannot be denied that Christian theology had a decisive influence on his philosophy.

Chapter 3
Modern Philosophy

Student: In the Middle Ages, the intersection between philosophy and theology is quite clear, and we see a more systematic conception of spirit, deriving as it does from God as infinite spirit. Are there significant changes in the modern period with regard to philosophical views on knowledge and spirit?

Teacher: In the Renaissance, there is still a debate between the Neoplatonic and the Aristotelian trends in philosophy. There are certain philosophers keen on developing Neoplatonism, and commentaries on Aristotle's works are still being produced and studied. Therefore, notions of substance and form (and its counterpart, matter) still dominate the philosophical and scientific discourse, even though many aspects of Aristotle's philosophy come under attack. Therefore, the concept of substance dominates modern philosophical discussions, in spite of different interpretations of Aristotle's concept of substance. Substantial form, for instance, is gradually discarded as a kind of scientific explanation. Using substantial form means to assign an explanatory value to the essential quality of a substance, but in modern science, the focus is on quantity and measurability, and therefore qualities are rejected as explanatory models.

In the Renaissance, a return to the ancient Greek and Roman classics, culture, and philosophy as a whole, coupled with continuous developments in the scientific domain, mean that a gradual change takes place in science and philosophy. The focus in philosophy is now on human knowledge, on its origin, its characteristics, its remit and limits. There is correspondingly a focus on the human subject of knowledge over and above the object of knowledge. Although the nature of God is still debated, philosophical discussions center on the human process of knowledge.

Student: Can we say that there is a complete rejection of the medieval outlook?

Teacher: The modern period in philosophy, up to and including Kant, does not ignore previous notions, and many of the main themes of medieval philosophy continue to be debated, such as the question of the immortality of the soul. However, the focus of the debates shifts from theological questions, from the divine and from the celestial world, to the human intellect. Some principles inherited from the ancient and medieval periods are discarded. In particular the notion of substantial form, as we have seen, and the notion of a final cause as part of scientific explanation are discarded. Science becomes more closely based on mathematics, number, quantity, and measure rather than quality. In addition, the efficient or mechanical cause is preferred to the final cause, which does not always immediately precede its effect and is more difficult to observe in nature. In other words, natural phenomena are not explained by having recourse to the final cause or purpose, which seem rather vague notions, but to the agent.

With a new conception of science, there is a focus on the human intellect and the question of knowledge and certainty. Descartes, Spinoza, Locke, Leibniz, and Kant all wrote on the issue of the human intellect or reason. There is an emphasis on the limits of the intellect, and its ability to know nature and its objects. Theory of knowledge takes center stage in this period of the history of philosophy.

Student: If there is not a compete break with the past, what are the influences modern philosophers receive from ancient philosophy?

Teacher: The problem of skepticism is always in the background, sometimes becoming the focus of attention. This is very clear in Descartes, who initially doubts the data obtained through the senses, and claims that no certainty can be had from sense perception. This position arose in opposition to the medieval Aristotelian tradition, such as we find, for instance, in Aquinas. Many medieval philosophers considered the data obtained from sense perception as trustworthy. They held that knowledge started from sense perception and from an awareness of the data obtained through the senses, which were in direct contact with particular material objects. The reality of the objects perceived by the five senses was to be taken at face value. Descartes reacts against this tradition, stressing that first we can only be certain of our existence as mind or intellect. That is to say, we can be first certain that the human intellect exists, or rather, that we exist individually as intellectual beings. Subsequently, he goes on to prove the existence of spiritual beings, such as God, and only later the existence of objects that are not mental or spiritual. In this way, the intellect, and particularly the human intellect, becomes the basis of all reality. Within the context of scientific discoveries, the question of knowledge, certainty, and the origin of knowledge becomes central.

Student: It is clear that Descartes does not trust the senses and uses reason instead as a true guide to knowledge, a position that resembles that of Plato. Are there other positions which stress the use of the senses, or in other words a position on this issue which is closer to that of Aristotle?

Teacher: Epistemology dominates debates in modern philosophy, especially the question about the origin of knowledge, with opposing arguments between rationalists and empiricists, who stress respectively reason and sense perception as the source of knowledge.

Student: Does this mean that epistemology becomes the central focus of attention, to the detriment of metaphysics, which was clearly the central discipline in medieval philosophy? Is there still an interest in metaphysics in the modern period?

Teacher: There is an interest in metaphysics but it tends to be guided by a theory of knowledge. Some philosophers do offer a systematic view of the world, such as Spinoza, who appears to have been influenced by Stoicism. Like the Stoics, he believes that everything is determined, nothing in nature is contingent, and all events follow a law of necessity. In general, he holds that all reality can be described as God or nature, and that God and nature are two sides of the same coin—or rather, as he states, the two modes of God's existence that we can perceive in the world. This resulted in an accusation of pantheism, for a supposed theory that equates God with nature. Also, he claims that reason (and not the senses) is the best guide to knowledge in human beings. In addition, he is preoccupied with the practical consequences of philosophy, in particular the control of the emotions. This is a central topic in the 17th century, the study of the human passions, but it also recalls Stoic philosophy, which had a strong practical aspect, concerned with achieving the good life and happiness.

Again, when Spinoza speaks of God or nature we find the duality of spirit and matter, although spirit predominates—this is especially clear when it comes to ethics and the question of the good life in Spinoza.

Student: Is Spinoza the main metaphysician of this period, or are there other strong metaphysical views?

Teacher: Leibniz, for instance, views the universe as constituted by monads, discrete intellectual unities, and he strongly defends the idea of divine providence. It is with Kant, who opposed dogmatic metaphysics as expounded by Wolff, that metaphysics is especially called into question. This critique of metaphysics becomes problematic because the Enlightenment movement, which opposed authority, especially in the form of religious authority, had stressed reason and its capacity to understand reality and to search by itself for truth. Once Kant critiqued reason, it seemed that a new period of skepticism would follow. However, the German idealists found new faith in the human subject. Hegel has greater confidence in reason than Kant, and he believes that a return to Christian dogma when explaining religion, as is clear from his lectures on the philosophy of religion given at Berlin, will bear fruits for philosophy. Therefore, he departs from Kant in rejecting the latter's attacks on the power of reason and he criticizes the Enlightenment position which turns its back on Christian doctrine and medieval philosophy.

Student: With regard to theory of knowledge, you mentioned an empiricist and a rationalist position. Are these the main epistemological positions in the modern period?

Teacher: Yes, these were the two main positions concerning the origin of cognition. In the debate between the empiricists and the rationalists, Descartes belongs to the latter school, because he believes that one must search for knowledge by using reason and not sense perception. He believes that some ideas are not obtained from sense perception but are purely spiritual and mental. They must have always existed in the mind, and so they are innate. In other words, since these ideas do not follow from sense perception, they must be inborn in the mind. Such ideas are God, for instance, or the notion of one's existence as an intellect. Plato's ideas were innate, but he also held that the soul existed before the body, a claim that is not made by Descartes. As we have seen in his dialogue *Phaedrus*, Plato describes the soul as contemplating all forms in an ideal world, before coming down to the material world and becoming attached to a body (resulting in the birth of a newborn baby) and hence imprisoned in a body. The soul is akin to the forms and it prefers to be in that world which is composed of forms, so that it can always contemplate them. However, if the soul loses its attention in contemplation it comes down, as a punishment, and becomes united to a body, which is not its natural element. In fact, the body, being material, is the opposite of the soul. Given its needs it constitutes a great distraction for the soul and its activity, which consists in contemplating the truth, which is the forms or ideas.

Student: If Descartes, unlike Plato, does not accept that the soul exists before the body, how does he explain the origin of the soul?

Teacher: Following the Christian tradition, Descartes does not accept the existence of a soul before it animates the body but he still believes that the soul is born with certain ideas, obtained from God. Descartes defends the idea that it is God who creates the soul. He does not believe that sense perception is a sure guide to obtaining knowledge since the senses often deceive us. He follows a Platonic tendency in linking up ideas and the soul, as a response to others who believe in the trustworthiness of sense perception—a traditional Aristotelian position. Like many of his predecessors, he held that the essence of matter was extension. The essence of mind was considered to be thought, and the intellect had two basic operations, intellect and will, the latter being subordinated to the former. While matter is extended, thought is not, and matter does not think.

Student: Who are the philosophers who trust sense perception? Naturally, they would be reacting to Descartes' position.

Teacher: An empiricist like Locke believes that all knowledge comes from sense perception; even the most abstract ideas, for instance, mathematical principles and rules, derive from ideas that were initially obtained from sense perception. All knowledge starts from sense perception, and ideas gradually become more universal. It is because we use language that we have universal notions. When we see many individual objects which are alike, we find a common term for them, and the notion of the universal (such as a species or a genus) arises. So universal ideas result from using the same term to designate a plethora of individuals which are similar.

The debate surrounding the status of universal ideas is very old, as we know, given that it goes back at least to Plato and Aristotle. However, the debate as it takes place in the modern period is also related to developments in science. For instance, there is a greater use of mathematics in science, noticeable in Galileo and other modern scientists. This link between mathematics and physics becomes especially obvious with Newton. On the other hand, there was an added emphasis on experience and the experimentation process. Rationalism is clearly related to mathematics, and empiricism cannot be dissociated from an emphasis on experimentation.

Student: It is clear that reason and sense perception become central topics for the question of knowledge and the way in which it is acquired. How does the debate between the relative merits of reason and sense perception unfold for these modern philosophers?

Teacher: The respective domains of reason and sense perception are distinguished. For instance, an explicit distinction is made, by Locke, between primary and secondary qualities. The first are objective and measurable, such as extension, figure, and motion, and the secondary qualities are subjective and perceived by the senses, since they constitute what affects the senses, like color and taste.

Student: As you mentioned, the status of universal notions and the significance of reason and sense perception for cognition have been debated since the ancient world, so is there just a difference in focus in modern philosophy compared to ancient and medieval philosophy? What makes the discussion of these themes different other than the connection with the new science? Are the same themes presented in the same way as in the Middle Ages? And how are theological questions addressed?

Teacher: The focus of the philosophical debates, as we have seen, shifts towards the human intellect and the process of knowledge. Metaphysics and theology are still important but not as central as previously. We can say that metaphysics dominates in ancient philosophy and theological matters dominate in the Middle Ages, and these two subjects recede into the background, for philosophy, in the modern period. There are also important developments within theology which influence modern philosophical debates. The main development within theology is obviously the rise of the Reformation with its distinct theology (especially on the theological virtues, the sacraments, and the authority of the Church) from Catholic theology. In many European countries the Catholic Church no longer had the final say with regard to theological issues. With northern Europe predominantly following the Reformation and southern Europe retaining Catholicism, there is no longer one Church or one theology for all of western Europe. What counts as orthodox varies according to one's theology, and soon various Protestant churches emerge with their different theologies.

Student: It would seem that theology should become even more central in the Renaissance, so how does it come about that theology no longer dominates philosophical discussions?

Teacher: In the medieval period there were checks on what philosophers and theologians could say, since for the most part they worked under the supervision of the bishops and the Church authorities, and moreover philosophy was subordinate to theology. Aristotelianism appeared as a threat to church dogma, for instance with its affirmation of the eternity of the world. However, Aristotle's influence was gradually and selectively absorbed into Catholic theology itself, and the language of the Church came to use many Aristotelian terms and expressions, as we find in Aquinas. In addition, the hierarchy between theology and the other sciences was explicitly advocated by theologians such as Aquinas, who held that theology was superior to philosophy. His reasons are based on the view that reason is not a reliable source, as we have seen. But instead of avoiding metaphysical questions (as Kant later did), Aquinas holds that we have a sure guide to knowledge of these issues in scripture, which is God's word revealed to us. Scripture and sacred doctrine (which could be identified with theology) are God's own knowledge revealed to us, and so a more direct way to knowledge of sacred things. Therefore theology, which had its foundation in scripture, was considered more reliable than philosophy and the other sciences, based as they were on human reason, which was considered finite and limited. By contrast, God's knowledge was infinite.

Student: What were the other implications of the structure of Church hierarchy? Was it also observable at the social or educational level?

Teacher: This hierarchy was reflected in the structure of medieval universities and medieval curricula, where the study of philosophy was preparatory for the study of theology, and theology held pride of place among the various disciplines studied at European universities.

In the modern period, after the scientific discoveries of the Renaissance and the rise of the Reformation, theological issues are still important but there is not a uniform control of ideas and new theories, as was the case in the Middle Ages. This allows for a variety of views, and the Reformation implies a variety of positions on theological matters too, in particular with regard to the sacraments and the Church hierarchy, as we have seen. While some theological themes remain, the views proposed by the philosophers vary widely, though central tenets are still maintained by the majority of philosophers, especially on the issue of God's existence and the immortality of the soul.

Student: I understand that these are the two central theological issues discussed by modern philosophers. Are there other theological aspects to their work?

Teacher: Morality and ethics are very much discussed in modern philosophy. For instance, Spinoza's magnum opus, published posthumously, is titled *Ethics*. These philosophers are interested in studying questions of morality as well as theory of knowledge and the human intellect. Other topics include God's providence.

Student: I understand how the variety of new theological positions influences the relative standing between theology and philosophy, starting from the Renaissance. Are there other ways in which the new theologies influenced philosophical reflection?

Teacher: Later, many aspects of the Reformation would influence Hegel, for example the need to seek a direct connection with God, instead of using the mediation of the Church hierarchy. In this sense, the emphasis on subjectivity and on the human intellect may have arisen in large part from the different kinds of theology which were born during the Renaissance, because the Reformation placed a great emphasis on one's personal relationship with God, and on the authority of the individual human conscience.

Student: Do the modern philosophers who defend theological principles, such as the immortality of the soul and God's providence, explain those principles from a philosophical perspective?

Teacher: Some modern philosophers strongly defend the notion of God's providence from a philosophical perspective, such as Leibniz, who holds that this is the best of all possible worlds. He also furnishes an ontological proof of God's existence, expanding on Descartes' argument for God's existence. Others, like Berkeley, develop their views as a defense of religion, in particular the belief in God's existence and the immortality of the soul. These principles are in this way defended on the basis of human reason, and not primarily on the basis of scripture. This procedure comes from the new emphasis on the human intellect and the scrutiny which the human intellect goes through in this period.

Student: Given the focus on the human intellect and in spite of its perceived limits in obtaining knowledge, can we say that the human intellect is the most significant expression of spirit in the modern period of the history of philosophy?

Teacher: Yes, the human intellect lies at the center of what we can call spiritual in the modern period. The questions regarding nature or creation and the nature of God are still discussed, and we find some of the same themes as in the Middle Ages, such as God's attributes and the human soul. But the emphasis is squarely on the human intellect or mind.

Student: In that case, what is specifically spiritual in the modern period?

Teacher: The question surrounding knowledge is spiritual. For most modern philosophers, as for Aristotle, knowledge is still of the universals and cannot be regarded as something material. It is worth invoking Aristotle's principle which states that the object of knowledge (especially if it is a material individual substance) is not in the head, but only an image of it is. For example, when we perceive a stone, we have the mental picture or image (or the form) of the stone and not the stone itself in our minds, as Aristotle states. So knowledge is always something spiritual and intellectual, and not something material. Naturally, the senses are closer to materiality since they have direct experience of material objects, but once the information is conveyed to the imagination and the intellect, which is the proper subject of knowledge, the traces of materiality disappear.

Student: I understand that the predominant view points towards a spiritual reading of knowledge and reality. Are there materialist philosophers in the modern period?

Teacher: We do find materialists philosophers in the modern period who, for instance, question or deny the immortality of the soul, but the majority of philosophers defend these spiritual principles which are later stressed by Hegel, in whom the metaphysical tradition culminates. Perhaps these materialistic tendencies are more evident in modern philosophy, for instance with certain philosophers of the Enlightenment (such as La Mettrie), but they also existed, to a lesser extent, as we have seen, in ancient philosophy, and even in the Middle Ages.

Student: How are these ideas, such as God's existence and the immortality of the soul, defended in the modern period, when philosophy becomes more independent from theology?

Teacher: Philosophers still appeal to theological or scriptural principles. Descartes, for instance, seeks to show that his views on God and the soul are not contrary to those of the Catholic Church. Berkeley is an important philosopher in this regard because he seeks to stay true to Christian doctrine, especially when it comes to God's existence. In order to prove these principles, he strongly defends the notion of spirit to the point of denying the existence of matter, in an attempt to take the ground from underneath the feet of materialists who defend the principle of atheism by rejecting the existence of a spiritual reality. His goal is to prove God's existence and God's immateriality, as well as the immortality of the soul. Other philosophers, such as Descartes, Locke, and Leibniz, had clearly defended God's existence. Berkeley takes a step further and denies the existence of matter, which for him was a stumbling block to the full affirmation of God's existence and the immortality of the soul. The affirmation of the existence of matter could be the slippery slope which led to a gradual or complete materialism, leading ultimately to atheism. Once matter is denied, the materialists' positions are defeated and there can be no objection to God's existence, a thesis which also justifies the immortality of the soul, and which grounds human morality and ethics.

Student: How does Berkeley undertake to prove God's existence and the immortality of the soul, and how does the rejection of matter help in attaining this goal?

Teacher: Like other philosophers before him, such as Aquinas, and after him, such as Kant, he believes that the human faculties of the soul are weak, but he also accepts that it is possible to prove in principle, rationally, both God's existence and immateriality, and the immortality of the soul. He defends the existence of spirit versus matter—denying altogether the existence of matter, by defending a specific theory of knowledge.

Student: How does Berkeley's theory of knowledge serve to prove God's existence?

Teacher: Berkeley holds that the object of knowledge is not a material object that we see or hear. The object of knowledge, in its various forms, can be obtained through sensation or sense perception, imagination, or the intellect; however, the object of these faculties is always the idea which comes from sensation, the imagination, or reason. According to Berkeley, if something exists it has been seen, heard, felt, or perceived in some way, so he identifies existence with being perceived. His famous principle reads: to be, or to exist, is to be perceived. He related any ideas to sensation and being perceived, hence his rejection of abstract ideas, which are completely divorced from the senses. Abstract ideas, according to Berkeley, give us the wrong impression that ideas that are thought are separate from the way in which we perceive them. Although Berkeley accepts the existence of general ideas, these are not completely divorced from sensation, and thus they are not truly abstract. These general ideas apply to several particular things but they are not abstract. Whatever the content of our knowledge or sensation, it does not exist independently from being perceived in some way by some mind, so the spiritual principle, or, we could even say, the principle of subjectivity, is always preserved.

Student: If abstract ideas do not exist, does this mean that knowledge is of the particular for Berkeley?

Teacher: No, knowledge and demonstration are of the universal, based on general, though not abstract, ideas.

The mind thinks, perceives, wills, and no object is separate from the way it is perceived, so that everything that exists is related to a thinking spirit and in this way always has a purely spiritual existence. Equally, Berkeley does not make a major distinction between sense perception and thinking.

Student: This conflation of sense perception and thinking is not very common, or is it?

Teacher: No, most philosophers draw a clear line between sensation and thinking. Aristotle, for instance, setting the tone for a predominant tendency in epistemology, holds that sense perception deals with material and particular objects that are by definition outside the mind and the body, and therefore are external objects. According to Aristotle the senses perceive external, material objects. Subsequently, the other faculties of the soul, such as imagination and finally thought, extract the formal aspect within the object, or divest it from its material aspect, in order to reach a form which is a universal. Berkeley, on the other hand, does not believe in abstract ideas, or in a great difference between thinking and sensing, and in this way the notion of an external object is discarded. In other words, thinking or sensing are both kinds of perception, and any perception for Berkeley is purely spiritual. Consequently, all the things in nature that we perceive as external objects are in reality ideal objects in the mind. The mind perceives knowledge or sensation, not the objects themselves, whose external existence can thus be rejected. Therefore nothing exists without or outside a mind, as Berkeley states in his *A Treatise Concerning the Principles of Human Knowledge*. Later, Bradley, a British idealist, also holds that there is no reality outside of knowledge. Therefore, for Berkeley existence is made up of feeling, thought, and volition, and will and feeling are included in thought.

Student: Berkeley is then considered to be an idealist philosopher?

Teacher: Yes, but in his *Three Dialogues between Hylas and Philonous*, he calls his doctrine immaterialism. According to him, we do not perceive anything outside the mind; we only perceive what is in the mind. Therefore, there can never be a proof of an external thing which is not spiritual, and the content of mind or the intellect is the only reality we know. This is because Berkeley does not make a stark distinction between intellect and sensation or imagination. He also explicitly holds that only spirit and their objects, which are ideas, exist.

Student: How does he justify this immaterialist position?

Teacher: Berkeley holds that everything only exists if it is perceived, that is, if it is thought by a mind. We subsequently discover that this does not necessarily have to be a human, finite mind. Ultimately, the divine or infinite mind is the source of all ideas, and thinks all ideas. Berkeley clearly holds the intellect or the mind to be something spiritual, akin to the spiritual ideas it thinks. Therefore, forms or ideas (and perceptions and sensations, as we have seen) are spiritual, and the mind (finite and human, or infinite and divine) is also purely spiritual. Minds or spirits and ideas both belong to the realm of spiritual things or realities, even though a distinction is drawn between them, for spirits are active and ideas are passive. Berkeley does not believe that the senses point to something existing outside the mind.

He also does not believe in a strong difference between primary and secondary qualities, as defined by Locke, and so no qualities are independent of a spirit. And he argues that the concept of matter involves many contradictions.

Student: What are the contradictions involved in the concept of matter?

Teacher: In his *Three Dialogues*, Berkeley explains that matter is considered by philosophers to be a cause or an occasion, and therefore to have some kind of efficiency. At the same time, however, it is described by the same philosophers as passive and inert, which is to say that it is a cause and at the same time not a cause.

Student: And this criticism is based on Aristotle's views on matter?

Teacher: Yes, the implication is that the contradiction goes back to Aristotle. We saw that in Aristotle matter only becomes actual, and perceptible, when united with form. Without form, matter is purely potential. What we perceive, then, is not prime matter, or pure matter, but informed matter, which has one or more specific forms. So matter only actually comes to exist through form and does not have an independent actual existence. This means that it is only perceived if it contains its contrary, the spiritual, in the guise of the form or forms. Prime matter does not exist by itself; it is a mere abstraction or mental entity, as we have seen. While we usually ascribe hardness and extension to matter, this is only the case when it possesses forms, such as a genus or a species, or accidents. We tend to think of matter as that which is perceived by the senses—while the spiritual is perceived by the mind, as the content of the mind—but again this is only the case when matter possesses certain qualities or forms. In this way, Berkeley points out the contradictions involved in the concept of matter, explaining why matter remains an elusive concept which we cannot fully understand or comprehend. For Berkeley matter is one of those abstract ideas which are unclear and do not correspond to anything real outside the mind. Since we cannot perceive matter with either the senses or reason, and it is a contradictory concept, we have to deny its existence.

Student: I understand that Aristotle's conception of matter is quite complex and could be challenged, but does Berkeley explicitly mention Aristotle's views on matter?

Teacher: In *A Treatise Concerning the Principles of Human Knowledge* he states that contemporary views on matter resemble Aristotle's understanding of prime matter.

Student: If Berkeley defends immaterialism, does this make him an idealist?

Teacher: It is clear that for Berkeley only spirits and ideas exist, so he focuses on ideal existence rather than physical existence. Something only exists for him, as we have seen, if it exists for a mind. Berkeley believes that the idea of being is the most abstract of all, a thesis that Hegel would take up later. We know that we are affected by ideas and have these ideas, but we cannot prove their connection to anything outside the mind. We also cannot explain the connection between the immaterial and the material, so we only accept the existence of the immaterial. Another reason for this position is the awareness that only spirit is active, and matter, if it existed, would be purely passive. But matter is an impossibility given that the very concept of matter is a contradiction in terms. The view that existence comes from form (or, we could say, from spirit) is not dissimilar to Plato's and Aristotle's positions. Plato holds that the forms are responsible for both existence and existing things, and Aristotle also believes that form renders the things intelligible, and actually existing. We also saw that, in Aristotle, the other causes, final and efficient, can in a certain way be identified with the formal cause. These three causes form a coherent set vis-à-vis the material cause, which stands apart since it cannot be reduced to, or united with, the other three causes. In addition, for Aristotle these spiritual causes produce existing things while matter on its own is purely passive. We saw that in the medieval period most philosophers held that God is the foremost efficient, final, and formal cause. For God has the forms in his intellect, and he is the beginning and end of creation.

Student: It is clear that Berkeley had a thorough knowledge of ancient as well as medieval and modern philosophy.

Teacher: Yes, he had a good knowledge of philosophy and science. Aristotelian science was under strong criticism from the Renaissance onwards, and the differentiation between primary and secondary qualities clearly aims at speaking of matter in a modern and scientific way. Primary qualities were more closely tied to the new science, since they seemed to be objective and measurable. Primary qualities were properly speaking the object of science, such as mathematics and physics, while secondary qualities could be differently perceived by different knowing subjects. The influence of Aristotle, though, was still observable in views about matter, since even primary qualities, according to Berkeley, are not truly objective and are still based on an obscure notion of matter. In his criticism of the concept of matter, which still influences modern philosophers, he probably had in mind Descartes' difficulties in explaining the interrelation between the body and the soul. Berkeley says that it is not possible to give a convincing account of the connection between the mind and the body, and between the spiritual and the material. He certainly does not believe that something material and passive can affect something active like spirit. Doing away with matter altogether solves the problem in Berkeley's view.

Student: Does this mean that he solves the problem of the connection between the spiritual and the material by rejecting the latter?

Teacher: He attempts to solve it by doing away with the material, so that the problem of the connection between matter and spirit ceases to exist. Even if there were external bodies, it would be impossible for us to know them. However, towards the end of his *Three Dialogues* he concedes that it is possible to speak of material objects and before that he speaks of bodies and movement, so it is not really clear that it is possible or practical to do away completely with matter. Berkeley sometimes speaks of ideas as if they had material qualities, such as movement, which defeats the purpose of denying matter.

Student: What are Berkeley's views on the mind?

Teacher: Berkeley holds that the mind is active and the ideas it thinks are passive, without an effective power. Therefore the ideas are caused by a spirit. The object of spirit is the ideas, and the will and mind are active, and are not ideas.

Student: Does Berkeley deny the reality of the things we perceive?

Teacher: No, he affirms their reality as ideas. They are real but not material. All that exists is spirits or ideas. Our ideas come initially from the divine mind, and those ideas which proceed from God are more vivid—more keenly perceived by our minds—than the ideas we have by the imagination, which are based on the ideas obtained from sense perception. We perceive ideas rather than things, which is a more general term than "idea." God creates the ideas of sensible things we perceive, or rather creates the sensible ideas, from which all other ideas derive. In doing away with matter, Berkeley also discards the notion of substance or substrate and accidents, and the notion of subject and attributes.

Student: How does Berkeley justify his denial of the existence of matter in view of modern science, which presupposes the existence of matter?

Teacher: He believes that his view does not prevent scientific discovery, since at any rate there is a coherence between the ideas in our minds, and we can say that science is based on what we perceive with the senses. He claims that the laws of nature show the connections between our ideas, instead of the connection between material things. In addition, he holds that spirit, goodness, and wisdom account for everything that we perceive. As the outcome of his views on matter, he holds that there are no material substances, and the only existing things are ideas and spirits; spirits are active and invisible substances, and ideas are inert. If scripture describes things that appear to be material it is only as a concession to common language. Certainly, in his view, there is no trace of a philosophical or abstract conception of matter in scripture.

The aim and corollary of this refutation of matter is to refute skepticism and materialism, as well as atheism and idolatry. Ultimately, all the ideas come from God and the existence of ideas in our mind is the very proof of his existence.

Student: In spite of Berkeley's arguments, some philosophers still felt attracted to skepticism?

Teacher: Skepticism has a strong presence in Descartes before Berkeley, and it is still an important influence for Kant, prompted by his reading of Hume, a British empiricist. In Kant, skepticism is not directed at sense perception; rather, it implies placing limits on what reason can know. It also affects his position with regard to traditional natural theology as propounded by Wolff, concerning the proofs for God's existence and the immortality of the soul. Kant believes that given that our reason is limited—whereas the scope of the understanding is well defined and reliable, working as it does with sense data—the thing in itself is always something beyond reason, in other words, something which we cannot know but remains beyond our knowledge. His critical project consists in assessing the limits of reason—pure or theoretical and practical reason, a project which Hegel would later criticize. Kant follows in the tradition of the studies on the human intellect, which explains his critical project, and the focus on the human subject, together with the question of knowledge and its limits. He finds that practical reason is better suited to deal with religious or theological questions, such as the existence of God, which cannot be proved by pure reason.

Student: Why does Kant claim that reason cannot prove God's existence?

Teacher: In the *Critique of Pure Reason* he analyzes Saint Anselm's proof of God's existence, which he calls the ontological proof. Anselm holds that the mind has an idea of a perfect being, greater than which nothing can be conceived. He adds that a perfect being has all the perfections. If this perfect being did not have existence, it would not be perfect, since it would lack a perfection that many finite and imperfect beings possess. Accordingly God must exist, and this constitutes the proof of his existence. Kant, however, points out that existence is not a predicate like other predicates. It is not a predicate that we simply add to a subject.

Student: This criticism on the part of Kant is well known, but is it the first time that the question of existence as an attribute is explicitly raised? Are there precedents for this question in ancient or medieval philosophy?

Teacher: Naturally, the question of existence and essence is central to philosophy and particularly metaphysics. One could say that it is the central question of metaphysics, given that this discipline studies being, and existence is closely related to being. It is natural to assume that the question of the relation between essence and existence goes back to ancient philosophy. However, this distinction was not explicitly articulated by Aristotle, although it is mentioned by him. He states, in the *Posterior Analytics*, that asking what a thing is and whether it exists are two different questions. It is in the Middle Ages, when the theme of divine creation becomes central, that the differences between essence and existence become more evident. Avicenna, for instance, holds that existence is an accident, while Averroes, in a more Aristotelian vein, denies that this is the case. And in this way we have the tone set for the debate that would ensue in the medieval period and into the modern period.

Student: I understand how the distinction between essence and existence becomes particularly evident with regard to the proofs of God's existence. It is also natural that Kant's approach should vary widely from that of medieval philosophers.

Teacher: Kant rejects the ontological proof given his position on the limitations of human reason. In the *Critique of Pure Reason*, he presents his antinomies of human reason, which consist in contrary positions on perennial problems of philosophy (for instance, determinism versus free will). These antinomies cannot, according to Kant, be truly and satisfactorily solved, and they are final proof that human reason has certain limits and cannot reach the thing in itself. The focus on the human subject remains present in post-Kantian philosophy and is clearly observable in the German idealists.

This focus reaches its culmination in German idealism, with Fichte's emphasis on the "I," and subjectivity, which is the leading theme of his philosophy, and it continues with Schelling, who follows in Fichte's footsteps. Both philosophers, as well as Hegel, inherit and seek to solve Kant's problems with regard to the possibilities of knowledge. The human subject and intellect stand at the center of German idealism, and these are forms of spirit, as it becomes abundantly clear with Hegel.

Student: The question regarding the limits of human reason must have been uppermost in the minds of the German idealists. How does Hegel approach the problem of the limitations of human reason as posed by Kant?

Teacher: To cut a long story short, Hegel does not believe in the limits of human reason, but for it to reach absolute knowing it has to undergo a long process through various stages, until it finally, as it were, becomes one with the divine spirit which is the absolute spirit which possesses absolute knowing.

Student: Does Hegel reject Kant's critical project?

Teacher: Hegel holds that Kant's analysis of human reason contains a fallacy, or rather, a vicious circle, in that it begs the question. The object which is being studied and examined is reason. The subject carrying out this theoretical experiment, to determine the extent and remit of reason, is also the human intellect or reason. In this process, reason is the subject, the object, and the means of the intellectual experiment. In other words, reason analyzes itself. Consequently, if there were a problem with the instrument, the outcome of the assessment would be flawed, unbeknownst to us. An independent faculty would have to analyze reason and this is not possible. The implication is that reason cannot analyze itself, and there is nothing which can analyze it because it stands at the top of the human faculties of knowing. There is not another faculty which is independent and which can analyze reason. In this way Hegel believes that Kant has make a fundamental mistake with respect to his critical philosophy, and he dismisses, in a few pages in the introduction to the *Phenomenology of Spirit*, Kant's entire critical project. Hegel himself believes that the learning process must be undertaken gradually, and it involves direct experience of the object studied. One learns by learning, so to speak, and reason learns about itself in this process. It is not possible to learn about reason before seeking to understand the object of reason, or to learn about reason independently of the object of reason. He illustrates this paradox by giving a clear example of someone who wanted to learn how to swim before diving into the water.

Hegel

Student: Spirit is the explicit object of the *Phenomenology of Spirit*. How does spirit feature in Hegel's philosophy?

Teacher: We have seen that Hegel is the philosopher who makes spirit the central theme of his philosophical project. Accordingly, spirit is the central question of Hegel's first main work—and according to some scholars his best work—the *Phenomenology of Spirit*. This work consists in the study of the various stages of the appearance of spirit in its process of learning, which culminates in absolute knowing. The *Phenomenology of Spirit* contains the main elements of Hegel's philosophy as they appear in later works. The goal is to examine spirit as it proceeds from sensation and sense perception, understanding and reason, through to universal knowledge. It describes the process of knowledge, and as such it is a work of epistemology. However, Hegel does not just give us the perspective of an individual human subject as he or she obtains knowledge by going from the particular to the universal. Rather, he describes the various kinds (and faculties) of knowing, and the subject of the process of cognition is always spirit. Some kinds of knowing and states of this spirit are identified with particular schools of philosophy or historical moments. Therefore, this is not just an individual undertaking but the subject is a spirit which embodies history, particularly European history and the history of ideas, as well as theological themes, such as faith, for instance.

Student: I assume that by linking up the history of ideas and European history he shows how epistemology and metaphysics go hand in hand.

Teacher: Yes, for Hegel theory of knowledge and metaphysics are two sides of the same coin. He holds that the real is rational and the rational is real, as we have seen, and also that knowledge reflects the actual state of affairs. In addition, we find in the *Phenomenology of Spirit* two important movements: our observation of this spirit, and the spirit's own voyage of discovery.

Student: Is there a religious dimension of spirit in the *Phenomenology of Spirit*?

Teacher: Yes, and one of the striking aspects of Hegel's philosophy, as we have seen, is the explicit incorporation of Christian themes (such as the theme of reconciliation—between the human and the divine, after the fall which original sin represented) into his philosophy. This does not mean, as we saw, that he always follows an orthodox reading of these themes, but his reflection on them, and the way he integrates them into his philosophy, are quite striking. For him, belief is a kind of knowledge. In addition, he believes that representation—which is a type of religious thinking, or the kind of thinking that is typical of religion—is a way of thinking, and thinking is knowing, or an immediate kind of knowing. He believes that Christian theology is philosophy, and he endeavors to bring together both disciplines.

Student: What is distinctive about Hegel's understanding of spirit? I mean, why does he use the term "spirit" in the context of theory of knowledge, and not other terms to describe the human ability to know?

Teacher: He differs from his predecessors because he does not primarily talk about the intellect, or human reason, or even the human subject, and he does not focus just on the two main intellectual faculties, understanding and reason. He does distinguish between these two faculties, as we will see. But in his endeavor to show the progress of spirit towards absolute knowing—which is infinite knowledge—intellect, or reason, and understanding are too limited for Hegel's purpose, for absolute knowing surpasses merely finite understanding or reason. Indeed the spirit takes on these shapes and all the shapes and guises of human knowledge and faculties, but spirit is a more comprehensive and far-reaching term than any specific human faculty. Spirit for Hegel includes understanding and reason, and even simpler faculties such as the imagination and sense perception, and consciousness generally speaking, but it surpasses them. Spirit is a broader and more encompassing concept, since in the end we are not talking about human knowledge but also divine knowledge. Spirit is related to thought and thinking, science and wisdom, as well as the human faculties of understanding and reason.

Student: It is clear that for Hegel spirit has a theological as well as a philosophical dimension.

Teacher: Spirit is a rich, multifaceted concept, containing the theological overtones which Hegel highlights in the context of his search for absolute knowing. The possibility of attaining absolute knowledge is an essential aspect of his trust in human reason. In this respect, the connection between philosophy and theology plays an important role. We have seen that Hegel takes into account the main themes in Christian theology and dogma, in a unity of reason and dogma—for Hegel believes that it is important to consider seriously and rationally the dogmas of Christianity. Some of these themes ensure the possibility of attaining absolute knowledge. In particular, for Hegel, it is important to seek to bridge the gap between the human and divine, a project which he discerns in Christianity's dogma of the Incarnation, in which God, specifically the Son, the second person of the Trinity, took on a human shape and became man. It is the Incarnation, according to Hegel, which enables the revelation of God as Spirit.

Another important point in Hegel's project, set out in the preface to the *Phenomenology of Spirit*, is the hegemony of spirit, and the way in which everything is related to spirit. He rejects a metaphysics of the substance, based on particular things or objects as the primary elements of reality, which could potentially lead to a materialist position. He admires Spinoza's philosophy, which was a great inspiration to German idealists in general. He admires for instance its monism, with the implication that there is only one substance, of which we perceive two modes, thought and matter, or God and nature—which are two aspects of the same reality. However, Hegel favors a closer connection between substance and thought, stating that the substance is subject. This is a way of ultimately reducing everything to thought or spirit, more so even than in Spinoza.

Student: I understand that Hegel was attracted to the idea of one single spiritual principle of reality. Does Hegel accept other aspects of Spinoza's philosophy?

Teacher: There is a sense in which for Hegel there is only one substance. This means that thought, the activity of spirit, is the main element of reality. The other element, nature, is not equivalent to spirit, it differs from spirit, but it can be seen to be subsumed under it. In addition, and in order to stress this idea, Hegel states that the substance is subject, so all reality is animated by thought or spirit. He also admires in Spinoza the principle according to which negativity is an essential element in determining something—stating that every determination is a negation.

Student: Does the principle that thought is the main element of reality, defended by Hegel, make him an idealist?

Teacher: This depends on how we define idealism. Usually idealism is defined as the theory according to which things only exist in so far as they exist for a mind, or insofar as they are perceived. According to this definition, Berkeley would be considered an idealist, for he states that to be is to be perceived. Some philosophers would say that idealism means that we cannot go beyond our perceptions even if there is something beyond them, a thing in itself, which we cannot grasp. Kant believes that there is something beyond our understanding which we cannot grasp. Idealism can also mean that only ideas and minds or spirits exist, or at least that they are the determinant factors of reality. Hegel seems to be closer to Berkeley in this sense, because he thinks that there is nothing outside thought, as we will see, for he believes that being is thought. Some have termed his idealism an absolute idealism, as opposed to a subjective idealism, which focuses on the subject, particularly the human subject, whose intellective powers are limited.

Student: You mentioned that in the *Phenomenology of Spirit* the subject goes through and is identified with various shapes of spirit; I wonder what these shapes are?

Teacher: Hegel states in the introduction to this work that it traces the path of consciousness towards absolute knowing. In this work he argues that consciousness becomes gradually more universal, becoming understanding and reason, and finally spirit. All these latter stages include consciousness, so consciousness is included in understanding, reason, and spirit. Self-consciousness is also an important stage and it accompanies reason and spirit. Consciousness implies a knowing awareness of spirit in relation to its object, and self-consciousness means for the subject an awareness of itself.

Student: In this sense, for Hegel spirit is also synonymous with consciousness?

Teacher: Yes, spirit implies consciousness, certainly if we speak of subjective spirit. The first stage of consciousness is sense certainty, and this is an immediate approach to the object of consciousness. We are always observing the point of view of the subject in this work, and the first stages of this process consist in an immediate, sensible apprehension of the object of consciousness by the human subject. The subject is aware of the existence of the object, the thing before it. At this stage, the object is independent of consciousness or the subject. The subject here is the "I," which is not a particular subject but is taken to represent any human subject. Hegel explains that sense certainty has many limitations, in this way going against the empiricist position which bases all knowledge on sense perception. Since sensible reality keeps changing, an immediate apprehension of it in itself is not a sure guide to knowledge. And the use of language necessarily involves universal concepts, which means that it is not possible to take the sensible immediately by itself as a source of certainty and scientific thinking.

Student: Does the rejection of sense certainty as a sufficient guide to knowledge mean a denial of empiricism on the part of Hegel?

Teacher: For Hegel, empiricism is a necessary stage in the path towards absolute knowing. He says that the empirical perspective has to be taken into account by philosophy, initially, and that empiricism is the normal procedure of the sciences, in the sense that metaphysical empiricism is the basis for the sciences. He does not consider the distinction between empiricism and rationalism as an irreconcilable difference, for in reality these two positions require one another. While empiricism seeks to discover the laws of nature, rationalism takes into account aspects from experience, which means that they are interrelated. It is also important to stress that, according to Hegel, each philosophical school within the history of philosophy contains at least a grain of truth. Therefore, all theories and systems contain some truth, although some of them are closer to the final or absolute truth than others.

Student: What is the position of the mind and the subject with regard to these limitations of sense certainty?

Teacher: The mind comes to know itself through its learning experiences, and in this way there is an affirmation of the "I" in the process of learning. From sense certainty we progress to perception, which apprehends the properties of a certain thing. In perception, the subject distinguishes the thing from its properties, which is one with respect to its many properties. The subject begins to think of a universal, which differs from the kind of thinking typical of common sense. At this point the subject reaches the level of understanding in its grasp of nature.

Student: Does Hegel identify this stage with a particular branch of knowledge?

Teacher: For Hegel this corresponds to modern physics, with its further level of abstraction in relation to sense certainty and perception. Naturally, the understanding goes beyond sense data and understands what the senses do not immediately perceive. There is here a distinction between the sensible and that which is beyond the sensible, appearance and the thing in itself. Other than going beyond appearances, the role of the understanding is also to discover and formulate the laws of nature, which are multiple rather than just one. The question of the nature of knowledge becomes central with the focus on the understanding, and in this way consciousness becomes self-consciousness.

Student: How is this shift from perception to understanding reflected in the various disciplines of knowledge?

Teacher: The theme of understanding introduces the question of the modern sciences and their relation to other disciplines of knowing. Hegel clearly believes in a hierarchy of the sciences, and this is noticeable in the *Phenomenology of Spirit* and also in the *Encyclopedia of the Philosophical Sciences*, a later work. In the *Phenomenology of Spirit*, the various sciences feature as modes of knowing (as do specific philosophical schools and periods of history), and they show a progression towards absolute knowing. The closer to absolute knowing, the more complex the discipline in question. More specifically, human forms of knowledge (such as ethics) are discussed later in the *Phenomenology of Spirit*.

Student: Does this mean that Hegel favors the humanities over the natural sciences as forms of knowledge?

Teacher: It is clear that for Hegel the humanities are more complex and reveal a higher stage of knowing than do the natural sciences. The natural sciences—physics, for instance, and also mathematics—tend to study their object in an abstract way. For him, knowledge should be concrete in the sense that it should encompass the singular, which unites the particular and the universal. Abstract knowledge does not look at reality as a whole. Abstract means that we consider something without taking into account all the related aspects, or that we consider the object in isolation, and for him this is not the best kind of approach. Hegel stresses that "abstract" means separated, and isolated, leading to the consideration of something in a simplistic way. The universal for Hegel is not the same as the abstract. Therefore it is natural to see that within the natural sciences he favors biology over physics in his works, and physics over mathematics, for biology is more concrete than physics, and physics is more concrete than mathematics. The concrete encompasses both the particular, which is limited if taken in isolation, and the universal, which is limited without the particular. It is interesting to note that, according to Hegel, in physics the central human faculty is the understanding, which makes distinctions, while biology is studied at a higher level, by reason, a faculty which is able to make connections between all the elements studied. Aristotle also raised metaphysics over the more particular sciences such as physics or biology, so Hegel's position is not really something novel. In this sense, spirit is associated with life and activity.

Therefore, when in the *Phenomenology of Spirit* consciousness advances towards ever more complex forms and shapes of cognition, the human and spiritual element becomes more obvious and explicit. Spirit as such begins with the section on ethics. Subsequently, the forms of knowledge that precede absolute knowing are art and religion, and finally philosophy. But more on that later.

Student: Hegel makes a distinction between consciousness and self-consciousness, although they are related. Which forms of consciousness do we encounter as part of self-consciousness?

Teacher: Self-consciousness means that consciousness turns from an external object to itself. It becomes its own object of cognizance and study. It also learns about the separate object's independence. It contrasts itself with the separate object. Here the concept of life emerges. Life implies a certain independence and autonomy, and it implies consciousness. Human consciousness, by looking into itself, becomes aware of other consciousnesses and human lives. The question of mutual awareness is illustrated in the famous section on lordship and servitude in which two self-consciousnesses face each other and expect recognition from each other.

Student: I understand that certain structures or themes are reproduced at different stages of knowing in the *Phenomenology of Spirit*. Does the section on lordship and bondage reflect an earlier theme in the section on understanding?

Teacher: The competition between the two consciousnesses mirrors the combat between two forces in the section on understanding, except that these forces were forces of nature, not human subjects. The standoff between master and servant becomes a struggle for life, and a question of life and death. Life is clearly an essential aspect of self-consciousness. Paradoxically, self-consciousness becomes free as a subject by spurning life and not being afraid of death. This disinterested contemplation of existence turns into other forms of consciousness which happen to coincide with particular schools of philosophy in antiquity, namely Stoicism and Skepticism, followed by the unhappy consciousness, which some scholars associate with the medieval period and a certain type of religious consciousness.

Student: I see that in terms of history and the history of philosophy and ideas the narrative of the *Phenomenology of Spirit* goes back and forth. What does Stoicism mean in this context and how does it fit Hegel's purpose of explaining self-consciousness?

Teacher: In Stoicism consciousness moves in the element of universality, and there is not a regard for the particular. There is also an indifference towards natural existence, and the mind is occupied with universal ideas, such as the good and the true. This indifference towards the world that is external to the mind becomes so acute that this position turns into skepticism, which denies that any certain knowledge is possible.

Student: We saw that skepticism goes back to ancient philosophy.

Teacher: It is important to bear in mind that the first forms of skepticism originate from within Plato's Academy, the school which he founded and which continued at the hands of his successors.

Student: You mentioned how the Academy became a platform for skepticism, in spite of the fact that Plato emphasizes the possibility of certain knowledge and shuns any kind of relativism.

Teacher: This skeptical vein resulted from an important aspect in Plato's philosophy, a mistrust of the senses. This mistrust became generalized, extending to knowledge in general, which is why the Academy became a byword for skepticism. Returning to Hegel, at this stage, namely skepticism, the testimony of the senses is annulled. Consciousness focuses on itself and identifies itself with the unchangeable versus the changeable, that is, it tends towards the divine, passing into a stage described by Hegel as the unhappy consciousness. Then it passes over into reason.

Student: How is the passage from self-consciousness into reason effected? How is it justified?

Teacher: Since the unhappy consciousness gives up its individuality and wishes to be united with the unchangeable, it becomes united to the universal, which is a hallmark of reason. As such, consciousness becomes the focus of knowledge, and this constitutes a kind of idealism. The world exists according to its understanding of it, and reason is conscious and certain of being all reality; the world truly exists for it and follows the rules of reason. The object is as "I" is for consciousness or reason, so this is no empty idealism, according to Hegel, for it does not state that everything is simply sensations or ideas. Reason is the very essence of things, and it apprehends things in an intellectual way, as concepts.

Student: What are the applications of reason for Hegel at this stage of the development of consciousness?

Teacher: Reason observes nature but does not just rely on the senses. It extracts the universal from natural phenomena and objects, such as the concepts of genus and species, and it formulates the laws of nature and tests them with experiments. In this approach, which pertains to biology, it unites the particular and the universal. Moreover, reason here makes a distinction between organic and inorganic nature. Reason is rather self-consciousness and not mere consciousness, since it identifies itself with reality, and with the laws of nature. In this section Hegel focuses primarily on biology, including the notion of teleology which he takes up from Aristotle. We see that while the understanding dealt with mathematics and physics, it is reason which studies biology.

From studying nature, reason proceeds to studying the laws of thought and the human mind according to psychology. Hegel affirms human freedom versus the biological necessity to be observed in nature, and he relates spirit to intention. He also dissociates here ethical action from biological determinations, or external features.

Student: And at this stage Hegel turns to ethical questions?

Teacher: Yes, he turns to ethics and morality, and practical questions. He also contemplates virtue, which pertains to the domain of the human individual. Naturally for Hegel, the notion of spirit has strong links with the ethical. When it comes to the individual, Hegel also mentions culture as a further development of the human mind towards spirit. In fact, it is ethics which marks the passage from reason to spirit.

Student: Which shapes of thought do we find in the context of the section which deals with spirit in its explicit form?

Teacher: In connection with spirit, other shapes of consciousness arise, one of them being the Enlightenment, which is set up against faith. Hegel is critical of this view which shuns theology and religious culture. He does not believe that religion should be left out of the various shapes of consciousness. We will see that religion, in the schema of the *Phenomenology of Spirit*, occupies one of the higher places among the shapes of consciousness, coming second only to philosophy in the path towards absolute knowing. Religion is a subject that Hegel takes very seriously at all stages of his philosophical work, as we see also from the extended lectures on the philosophy of religion which he delivers later in life at Berlin. We can also confirm his admiration for religion in the *Phenomenology of Spirit*, from a cognitive perspective. Religion is placed towards the end within the section on spirit, whereas the Enlightenment is placed well before religion, at a much lower level from among the shapes of consciousness.

Student: How is the passage into the next stage, and religion, effected?

Teacher: Because at this stage spirit and consciousness are not satisfied in this world, there is a passage into a further realm. The previous stages of consciousness dealt either with nature or with the human realm. We saw that spirit makes its explicit appearance first within the human sphere of action and interrelations, but there is a further dimension which must not be neglected, which is religion, and the domain of the divine.

Student: Does Hegel approach the concept of religion in a general way or does he distinguish different stages within religion in the *Phenomenology of Spirit*?

Teacher: He does distinguish different stages within religion, and given the central place of history in the *Phenomenology of Spirit*, he follows a chronological order, starting with natural religion, then religion of art, and finally, revealed religion, which he identifies as Christianity. In the *Lectures on Philosophy of Religion* he also designates Christianity as the consummate concept of religion. In these lectures, Christianity is preceded by other religions, which are considered to be particular, or to show partial aspects of the divine, while Christianity contains the revelation of God himself to human beings.

Student: In his treatment of religion, does Hegel offer a broad approach to the topic, or does he follow a phenomenological perspective, taking into account the human conception of God?

Teacher: He takes into account a human perspective, but the novelty of his approach is quite striking. While modern philosophers speak of proofs of God's existence, and human knowledge of God, he aims at presenting God's own perspective, or speaking of God as subject and not merely as object of human cognition and aspirations. One could argue that this approach is not radically different from Aquinas' views on sacred doctrine. In Aquinas' writings, theology should not be understood as the sum of our theories about God. Instead, sacred doctrine is God's revelation to us, and the revelation of God's own knowledge which he shares with us. However, Aquinas does not assume that we ever attain God's full knowledge of himself, whether in this life or in the next. Hegel's approach is in line with the project he presents in the preface to the *Phenomenology of Spirit*, to the effect that it is important to present the substance as subject, or spirit itself as subject, and not merely as object. He speaks of God as self-consciousness. This is also in line with later writings on the different aspects of spirit, including subjective and objective spirit.

Student: You said that Hegel differentiates between different kinds of religion. What do the different shapes or aspects of religion mean?

Teacher: In the *Phenomenology of Spirit* Hegel distinguishes first natural forms of religion, which is the stage when the deity is identified with a natural element or force, such as fire, or the sun, and specific animals. The religion of art, which is more developed, has a further ethical element lacking in the religion of nature. Within the religious work of art we find abstract art, and the living work of art, which is identified with tragedy and Greek and Roman religion in the ancient world. Nevertheless, it is in revealed religion that the divine is known as spirit, according to Hegel. This is based on the fact that in Christianity God becomes man, and in this way the divine nature is revealed to humankind.

Student: Is religion identified with the last stage of the process culminating in absolute knowing, or is there another stage beyond religion?

Teacher: There is a final stage which is absolute knowing, and it is identified with philosophy. We therefore move from representation, which is characteristic of religion and implies the use of images and imagery, to thought and concept, which are identified with philosophy and which Hegel considers to be more universal than religion. One could argue that Hegel shows here a tendency for abstraction—although he prefers to use the term "concrete" or even "singular"—because he thinks that the universal is the most real and the most concrete, while the particular is partial and truncated. For instance, he uses the term "God," but he holds that this is a proper name, and so he prefers to say "Being" or the "One."

Student: Perhaps Hegel does not manage to avoid the kind of abstractions that he critiques in other philosophers?

Teacher: That is true, and in reality perhaps the particular deserves more attention, especially when dealing with religious forms of knowing.

At the end of the *Phenomenology of Spirit*, we finally have the unity of thought and being, meaning that there is complete knowledge of all reality. We definitely move from substance to spirit as subject. Generally speaking, Hegel identifies being with thought, which means that there is nothing outside thought. This may be considered to be a kind of idealism, but not in any way that limits what can be known. Therefore what we find in Hegel is objective idealism, or absolute idealism. Nothing is beyond the absolute consciousness, but we can state this principle in a different way: nothing that is remains unknown. Hegel defines idealism as the stage when the object of knowing is all reality.

To sum up, in the *Phenomenology of Spirit* Hegel thinks of the advancement of spirit as consciousness and self-consciousness, through understanding and reason to spirit. Thought is related to consciousness in the sense that both involve a subject which perceives an object. Thought implies consciousness, which generally speaking means any kind of mental awareness. Consciousness is also associated with sense certainty, perception, the understanding, whose object is the universal, and also with life. Spirit, which is also consciousness, goes hand in hand with morality and ethics, rather than nature or the senses.

Student: Spirit, as you have mentioned, has many different aspects, including rationality. What other associated aspects does Hegel bring up in this context? Does he mention the connection between language and rationality?

Teacher: Language is an expression of the universal and of self-consciousness, as something existing for others. With regard to other aspects of spirit, spirit is further divided into theoretical and practical, the first being related to individual forms and with the notions of genus and truth, while the practical aspect of spirit is related to the notion of useful.

Student: In addition to its connection with consciousness and thought, are there other ways of understanding the meaning of spirit? Does Hegel contrast spirit and matter, as the ancient philosophers do?

Teacher: For Hegel, spirit cannot be seen or touched, so it is not attainable by the senses. When it comes to matter, Hegel has a surprisingly close position to Aristotle's in that he does not believe that it can be perceived. We perceive the qualities of material objects, but not matter itself. We must abstract from what we see, feel, and touch in order to reach some notion of matter. He also holds that matter is the poorest mode of determinate being.

Student: It is clear that spirit is the main subject of the *Phenomenology of Spirit*, but how does he address this topic in his other works?

Teacher: Hegel's notion of spirit also appears in his *Science of Logic*, his next great work, and in it he again asserts that reason is a form of spirit which is higher than understanding. He sees spirit also as feeling and imagination, above which is cognition. The soul is also spiritual.

The *Encyclopedia of the Philosophical Sciences* consists in the *Logic*, the *Philosophy of Nature*, and the *Philosophy of Spirit*, in analogy with the ancient order of the philosophical disciplines, which started with logic, and was followed by philosophy of nature, and then metaphysics. In the *Encyclopedia of the Philosophical Sciences* Hegel opposes the sensible and the spiritual.

Student: Does the opposition between the sensible and the spiritual imply an opposition between spirit and matter?

Teacher: Yes, there is a connection between the two kinds of opposition, but the clearest contrast in Hegel is that between spirit and nature. Nature is the other of spirit for Hegel. In some passages he seems close to adopting the position which asserts that matter does not exist, but elsewhere he accepts the existence of matter, and seems to hold a similar conception to that of Aristotle, as we have seen. In the end, however, everything is subsumed under spirit, including nature, and nature is the creation of spirit, which in turn is created by God. Spirit is implicit in nature. He believes that nature is rational and divine, and represents the Idea. It is nature that comes from spirit and not the other way around, because thought does not come from something other than thought, so it cannot be produced by something material. We observe the presence of spirit in nature, for instance in the laws of nature, which are rational, and also in the notion of teleology or a purpose in nature, which Hegel adopts from the ancients. He contrasts a teleological approach to modern scientific conceptions, which are purely mechanistic (and in this way take into account only Aristotle's efficient cause, disregarding the final cause or purpose).

Student: You have mentioned that for Hegel the rational is real and the real is rational. Does this mean that spirit is equivalent to being?

Teacher: In a certain sense, spirit and being are the same, because true being or reality is at bottom spiritual. However, it is important to note that for Hegel, spirit or thought is a much richer concept than being. The notion of being has to be qualified in order to become concrete, but spirit immediately evokes many different aspects and qualities, even though in the *Phenomenology of Spirit* a lengthy process is required in order for spirit to know itself as infinite spirit, which leads to the full and ultimate meaning of spirit. Generally speaking, one can say that in the relation between spirit and being, spirit is the truth of being, given that spirit is the more concrete reality. And in identifying spirit with God, Hegel highlights subjective or active spirit, and not objective or passive spirit. Spirit is also active in human beings, and this aspect becomes especially noticeable when it comes to practical philosophy.

Student: It is clear that there is an infinite dimension of spirit, and it is identified with the divine spirit. However, what does spirit mean in a specifically human context?

Teacher: Hegel explains the differences between what previous philosophers termed the faculties of the soul in a more systematic way in the *Encyclopedia of the Philo-*

sophical Sciences, which was published after the *Phenomenology of Spirit*. With regard to the different faculties of the soul, he grounds feeling, perception, intuition, representation, conception, and will in thought, and thought itself leads to cognition. In addition, we find a progression towards the universal in the various faculties of the human mind or soul (starting with feeling). Equally, the distinction between subject and object is not clear initially, whereas it becomes clearer for consciousness. Sensibility, or sensation, and feeling (such as pleasure, joy, or hope) are still immediate and particular. A kind of universal knowledge only comes into being later.

Student: Speaking of universals, idea is a concept which is related to spirit. What does idea mean for Hegel?

Teacher: Sometimes he speaks of idea in the sense of Plato or Aristotle, respectively as universal qualities or thoughts within the mind, but sometimes he equates it with spirit, relating idea to life, subjectivity, and knowledge, that is to say, with subjective spirit. He also associates it with the objective world as well as knowledge. He identifies it with the notion of thought thinking itself, which is the expression used by Aristotle to describe God. The absolute idea thinks itself, so it is not just the object of thought, hence its similarity with spirit and the notion of life. He also identifies the idea with the work of reason, and with the will. Ideas are also concepts. Finite concepts exist in the universal divine Idea, which means that ideas are not confined to our minds.

Student: With regard to the faculties of human cognition, how does Hegel describe intuition?

Teacher: He holds that we have intuition when faced with a single, material object. Intuition is preceded by sensation (of the immediate material object) and attention (to the object); and finally, intuition considers the object as external. Therefore intuition is the first part of the learning process, and is a kind of singular knowing, although it deals with a totality, while universal knowing as such is called thinking. Empirical knowledge is an immediate kind of knowledge.

Student: After intuition, what is the following stage in the process of cognition?

Teacher: A second stage of intelligence, which is representation, comprises recollection, imagination, and memory (where he distinguishes a reproductive imagination from a creative imagination). These are followed by the third stage of knowing, which is thought, and which comprises understanding (including categories such as species, genera, laws, forces), judgment, and reason (which produces the identity of differences). At the level of thought we have intelligence and the awareness that thought is being, that thought is the reality. When intelligence determines the content, it becomes will.

As we know, in the *Encyclopedia of the Philosophical Sciences*, Hegel seeks to present the content in a more systematic way, and he does not include all the histori-cal elements present in the *Phenomenology of Spirit*. This latter work combines as-pects of world history, especially European history, with the history of philosophy, with a focus on Western philosophy, as we have seen. The *Phenomenology of Spirit* offers a philosophical perspective on the classical world, and it also mentions aspects of religious life in the Middle Ages and in the modern period, and takes into account the French Revolution. Among the philosophical schools he mentions are Stoicism, Skepticism, and the Enlightenment, as we have seen. In the *Encyclopedia of the Phil-osophical Sciences* he treats the different subjects following the classical curriculum, ranging from ethics to the philosophy of mind or spirit, and including the philosophy of nature. The latter addresses questions pertaining to the philosophy of the particular sciences, namely, mathematics, physics, and biology.

Student: We have spoken about the significance of consciousness for Hegel. Does he actually define consciousness?

Teacher: There appear to be two somewhat different conceptions of consciousness in the *Phenomenology of Spirit* and in the *Encyclopedia of the Philosophical Sciences*. In the former, any perception, including sense perception, is a form of consciousness, which is a broader conception of consciousness. In the section on logic of the latter, however, it is when the soul becomes a thinker and a subject that it becomes con-sciousness. Hegel also then states that reason is included in consciousness and self-consciousness (which is the truth of consciousness). Here we have a narrower and more rationalistic understanding of consciousness, and Hegel speaks of an intellectual consciousness. Each later stage comprises the former, which means that for Hegel spirit is the truth of soul and of consciousness, and that spirit is the likeness of God.

In the third part of the *Encyclopedia of the Philosophical Sciences*, on spirit, he mentions subjective, objective, and absolute spirit and provides us with a more de-tailed description of the various faculties of the soul. He considers the soul to be a particularization of spirit. This means that spirit is a broader concept than soul. Every soul implies spirit but not every spirit is necessarily a soul. This resonates with the medieval position to the effect that God is a spirit but does not have a soul, since the soul is closely related to the body, and God does not have a body.

Student: Given that Hegel mentions the faculties of the soul which for him are not static but develop in a seamless way, how does he relate the intellect and the will?

Teacher: Spirit can be divided into theoretical and practical. The former is related to the intellect and the latter to the will, which he considers to be more limited than intelligence or intellect. The latter involves a sense of universality, although it includes feeling and intuiting. Finally, spirit is considered as a universal substance, which is self and consciousness.

Student: What of his other works, with regard to spirit?

Teacher: In the *Lectures on Philosophy of Religion*, a later work, he states that spirit is active, and that it is knowledge, and that it is essentially consciousness. In the *Lectures on the Philosophy of Spirit* he organizes his examination of spirit into subjective spirit, objective spirit, and absolute spirit. Subjective spirit refers to the individual human soul or mind, while objective spirit is identified with society and its customs, laws, and rules. Objective spirit includes concepts pertaining to society, such as contract, property, family, and the state, so it has a practical or political dimension, and even a collective aspect which is lacking in subjective spirit. Objective spirit, unlike subjective spirit, has a strong social dimension. This is particularly clear in Hegel's later works, in his philosophy of right, and also in his lectures on philosophy of religion. Subjective spirit is treated in greater detail in the field of epistemology, while objective spirit displays a strong political aspect.

Student: It appears that Hegel considers objective spirit as a collective entity in these works, while subjective spirit tends to be rather particular or individual.

Teacher: Subjective spirit is not necessarily particular or individual, since different human subjects perceive reality in much the same way. Therefore, there is no hint of solipsism in Hegel, that is, the view that the true is what appears as such to one individually. What is said about subjective spirit is valid for each human being or each knowing subject. Objective spirit involves collective forms of thinking, and the practical consequences are paramount.

Student: What is the connection between subjective and objective spirit?

Teacher: Subjective spirit passes over into objective spirit, and absolute spirit re-unites both, although the term can also be used to describe the divine spirit. Absolute spirit comprises art, religion, and philosophy, and it is infinite. Hegel also mentions in his works a world-spirit, which consists in the historical revelation of spirit, and the spirit of an age. He also speaks of the spirit of a nation.

Student: Does Hegel continue to oppose nature and spirit in these later works?

Teacher: Yes, Hegel tends to talk more about nature as the opposite of spirit than about matter, and therefore for him materialism means naturalism. Spirit and nature are not, however, completely dissociated from one another in his view. The soul represents the closest synthesis we can find between spirit and nature—an apparent endorsement of ancient conceptions about the soul—and the soul is the first mode of the spirit. Hegel describes it as a slumbering spirit. After the soul comes the "I." Spirit is also soul, and soul is spirit. Reason is spirit that knows itself, for spirit is termed intelligence, which is also related to feeling, as knowing. Intelligence is the form of consciousness as awareness and attention. Notwithstanding his emphasis on spirit, we have seen that Hegel does not deny the existence of matter.

Student: In your view, why does he focus on nature rather than on matter as the counterpart of spirit?

Teacher: Hegel accepts the existence of matter, but he equally holds that everything is pervaded by spirit, and ultimately by the divine spirit. Nature is the other of spirit but it seems more apt to being turned into spirit than is matter. Matter appears to be a more irreducible and inexplicable concept than is nature, even though Hegel believes that matter is not an independent reality standing alone from form. In opposing nature to spirit Hegel seeks to reinforce the role of spirit and to show its pervasiveness. Also, the question of a philosophy of nature was being debated by other influential philosophers, such as Schelling, and therefore the emphasis on nature could be the outcome of an influence of contemporary philosophical debates.

Student: Going back to the question of idealism, can we say that Hegel is an idealist, since he focuses more on the reality of spirit and ideas, and defends the notion that spirit pervades everything?

Teacher: He certainly defends the idea that anything exists only in so far as it is thought, and that what is thought is the very thing, reality. He believes that being is thought, in the sense that spirit is the only true reality, and also that reality is known to us. Once we investigate being, we observe that it cannot be dissociated from thought. Consequently, there is nothing beyond thought. But this is not subjective idealism, as we have seen, given that he holds that thought, human and especially divine, embraces all reality. Ultimately there is nothing which escapes thought. The implication in Hegel's philosophy is that human thought can become all-knowing in alliance with divine thought. In that sense, Hegel can be considered a rationalist since reason and knowing pervade everything, and human reason appears to be almost unlimited in connection with divine knowing. This kind of idealism does not deny any external reality that we can perceive with the senses or the imagination, nor does it deny matter or the existence of material beings. It even accepts an empirical position in some cases, but it does hold that everything is pervaded by thought, in the sense that it is known by a human or the divine intelligence, or both, and nature is surpassed by, and subsumed under, spirit. Hence we could speak of an absolute idealism, or even a realist position. Nothing exists which is not known by some mind, and therefore everything is enveloped by spirit and can be reduced to spirit, which expresses itself in ideas.

Student: Naturally, for Hegel, spirit is God? Or one might say that the essence of spirit is God?

Teacher: God is the absolute spirit and it is the foremost expression of spirit. God is also the cause of other spirits and of all that is spiritual. Medieval philosophers and Hegel have different ways of explaining the relation between spirit and God, but for both, God is the ultimate expression of spirit and the cause of all that is spiritual. We have seen that for medieval philosophers God is the foremost final, formal, and efficient cause. God is cause by virtue of his ideas, by which he creates, and he is the cause of the forms and the cause of the intelligences. This is what it means to say that God is the exemplar cause of all, as stated by Aquinas. And since spirit precedes matter, which is created, spirit is the cause of matter, and God is the cause of both spirit and matter. Medieval philosophers stress the fact that spirit precedes matter and causes matter.

Student: How do Hegel's views on spirit differ from those of medieval philosophers?

Teacher: According to Hegel, it is the same spirit that begins as subjective spirit and then evolves into objective spirit and absolute spirit. It is always the same spirit which takes on natural traits and transforms itself into nature and then returns to itself as absolute spirit. Hegel bases this view of one single spirit on the principle that the infinite cannot exclude the finite, on pain of finitizing itself. The infinite must embrace everything. However, as it becomes clear, this position eliminates the difference or differences between finite and infinite spirit. Human spirit becomes one with divine spirit, if we follow this thinking into its final implications. Aquinas and other medieval philosophers, on the other hand, stress the difference between the various kinds of intellect, human, angelic, and divine, in order to maintain divine transcendence.

Student: Is there a precedent for an identification between the human and the divine spirit?

Teacher: In the Middle Ages, some philosophers advocate a closeness between the human and the divine intellect, for instance in mystic literature. Another example, condemned by medieval Christian theologians, is the proposed union between the human and the active intellect, defended by Averroes, as we have seen. However, Averroes does not advocate a union between the human and the divine intellect, which is different from the active intellect. This is in line with his efforts to preserve divine transcendence.

Student: Does this view of the precedence of spirit over matter, which is very obvious in Hegel, go back to Aristotle?

Teacher: Yes, in the sense that form for Aristotle precedes matter, or rather, renders matter active and visible. Matter is passive while form is active. Form is the spiritual aspect of an individual substance, or a universal. Matter stands alone as a cause that is passive and inert, while the other three causes can be considered as a unity and to constitute a whole. Matter is not truly reducible to the other three kinds of forms. The idea that the final cause precedes the efficient cause illustrates this point. Before the carpenter makes a table, he or she has to have the idea (or form) of table in his or her mind. Therefore, the form and the intention (final cause) of the table actually precede the table. In addition, we should bear in mind that the efficient cause is active by imposing form, which makes everything both existent and intelligible. Aristotle's notion of the final cause and the defense of teleology in nature also reinforces the notion that spirit dominates, because form (as intention) dominates and leads nature. He did not have a conception of divine providence, as we have seen, because according to him the gods are above concerning themselves with us. However, his idea of teleology in nature and the preponderance of the final cause—which, as Avicenna often notes, is the efficient cause of the efficient cause—goes hand in hand with the predominance of spirit.

Student: Do philosophers agree that God is spirit, the foremost spirit, and that he ensures the preeminence of spirit in philosophy and in reality?

Teacher: The majority of philosophers, and certainly those in the Aristotelian tradition, say that God is spirit, and that the foremost spirit is God. They may name God the One, or the First, which are philosophical rather than theological terms (by referring to a transcendental or other attributes to designate God), but there is a notion of a supreme spirit, and this is identified with God.

Hegel states that "God" is a proper name, as we have seen, and he sometimes prefers to use other terms to designate the supreme spirit, such as "being," "one," or "subject." For Hegel, it is certain that spirit is God and God is spirit. Hegel's philosophy represents the culmination of a tradition, which we may call metaphysical, that privileges the spiritual. In particular, it privileges the spiritual over the material. With regard to theology, we have seen that he does not shy away from the opportunity to discuss theological themes such as original sin, the Trinity, and the Incarnation. And although he sometimes interprets them in a manner that is not orthodox by any means (preferring as he does a more metaphorical and philosophical reading of scripture than a literal one), these themes are still determinant in his philosophy, as an inspiration. Hegel praises the Incarnation and states that God revealed himself to us most explicitly in Christianity with the incarnation of Jesus Christ, and in this way he considers Christianity to be the revealed religion.

Chapter 4
Contemporary Philosophy

Student: After Hegel, which developments do we find in connection with spirit?

Teacher: After Hegel, there is a split between Left Hegelians and Right Hegelians. This split turned on the question of religion and its significance within Hegel's philosophy. This shows how important the question of religion was to the debates concerning the nature of Hegel's philosophy. The Right Hegelians affirmed Hegel's religious orthodoxy and the continuity of Hegel's philosophy with the previous philosophical tradition, but the Left Hegelians challenged this view.

Student: You mentioned that the orthodoxy of Hegel's philosophy, in matters of religion, was called into question.

Teacher: Already in Hegel's lifetime there was a debate about his religious convictions, and an accusation of pantheism was leveled at Hegel during his stay at Berlin. The question of religious allegiance was significant during this period. Fichte had to renounce his philosophy post at Jena due to accusations of irreligion. Therefore, the old charge of irreligion against philosophers, which had been around since the time of Socrates (and Anaxagoras before him), was very much alive. Naturally, Hegel defended himself against this charge. In the *Lectures on the Philosophy of Religion*, which date from his tenure at Berlin, he explains the concept of pantheism, defining it in a narrow way. He claims that true pantheism would be to state that everything is God, including, for instance, this sheet of paper. In this way, by belittling pantheism, he renders the charge of pantheism much more difficult to level at philosophers.

Student: Why was the charge of pantheism so serious?

Teacher: Because by identifying God and nature, like Spinoza (who was a major influence for German idealist philosophers), those who held this position could be seen as rendering God material or at least not transcendent, since God would be at the level of nature. This position could be construed as a divinization of nature, or a diminishing of God's transcendence, by identifying him with nature.

Student: Did Hegel defend himself convincingly?

Teacher: Like other German idealists, he was an admirer of Spinoza's philosophy, but as we have seen, he does take care to comment on Christian dogma from a philosophical perspective. And some of his main philosophical theses are influenced by

Christian dogma. Therefore he clearly did not consider himself a pantheist or an atheist, and he took religion very seriously. Nor should we assume that he is not sincere in his writings about religion—which changed over the course of his life. His initial interest in religion came from his belief that it promoted morality. At the same time, the young Hegel rejected what he called the positivity of religion, that is to say, external aspects of religion, such as miracles, and any literalism in reading scripture. Later on he takes dogma more seriously into account. It is difficult to believe that he would have supported atheism. We would have to accept a Straussian reading of his work, as though Hegel had to conceal his true positions on religion in order to keep his standing in German society. Leo Strauss claims that some of the medieval philosophers supposedly hid their true views on religion in order to defend themselves against charges of unorthodoxy. This may have happened in some cases, but it cannot be generalized. Moreover, it is obvious that Hegel's interpretations of scripture are not entirely orthodox, so it is clear that he was not trying to conceal his true views on religion.

At any rate, Right Hegelians stress the religious aspect in Hegel's thought.

Student: And how are the Left Hegelians to be distinguished from the Right Hegelians?

Teacher: Left Hegelians, who came to be rather more influential than Right Hegelians, critique the religious aspect of Hegel's thought, sometimes denying it altogether and consequently denying the more spiritual aspects of Hegel's philosophy. They were bent on a materialist and truncated reading of Hegel which takes up Hegel's dialectics more than anything else in Hegel's systematic philosophy.

Student: Were there other kinds of response to Hegel's philosophy?

Teacher: The division between Right and Left Hegelians constitutes an immediate and direct response to Hegel's work and legacy. Many other philosophical movements emerge at least partially in response to Hegel's philosophy. Thus other movements, in addition to Right and Left Hegelianism, develop, for instance existentialism, which, with Kierkegaard as its earliest exponent, arises in part as a reaction to Hegel's philosophy. Another movement, phenomenology, is more closely related to Kant's thought in its analysis of the attending circumstances of the act and process of cognition. Phenomenology centers its attention on the theory of knowledge.

Some branches of analytic philosophy also develop in reaction to Hegel's philosophy, or rather to Hegel's influence on philosophy; in particular, there is a strong reaction, in the Anglo-Saxon tradition, against the inheritors of Hegel's philosophy, the British idealists. Prominent early philosophers in the analytic tradition, such as Bertrand Russell, were themselves initially idealists. Currently, analytic philosophy can be seen to form one big branch of philosophy, and continental philosophy is a term used by analytic philosophers to designate contemporary non-analytic branches of philosophy, such as existentialism and phenomenology.

Student: I understand how Hegel profoundly influenced contemporary philosophy in the way that recent philosophical movements arise as a response to Hegelianism. With regard to current movements, how can we distinguish continental from analytic philosophy?

Teacher: We could see the distinctions between them in different ways. On the one hand, analytic philosophy is closer to science and also to philosophy of science. Analytic philosophy also centers its attention more on philosophical problems and arguments than on the history of philosophy. Even when it studies the history of philosophy, it often focuses on specific problems in the works of past philosophers.

Continental (European) philosophy, in turn, is closer to the humanities and the arts. When it comes to the history of philosophy it pays close attention to the historical and linguistic context in which the works were composed. The split between continental and analytic philosophy is linked to the distinction between the "two cultures," that is to say, between the sciences and the arts.

There is another difference in perspective when looking at the history of philosophy from an analytic or continental perspective. Analytic philosophy sees the history of philosophy as a progressive evolution in the discovery of truth, much like the sciences see themselves. According to this interpretation, philosophy makes progress by discarding certain views and adopting others which become established positions.

Continental philosophers, on the other hand, study solutions to the same perennial problems that do not appear to have a definitive solution.

Student: What kinds of perennial problems do these philosophers study?

Teacher: One of these perennial problems is, for instance, the question of free will in view of unchanging laws of nature. The question is whether we have free will and therefore responsibility for our actions, or whether all our actions are determined by the laws of nature. This problem is expounded by Kant as the third antinomy of pure reason, as we have seen.

Moreover, continental philosophy looks at each philosopher or philosophy as a self-contained system. The truth of the system is studied on the basis of its internal coherence and judged on that basis, rather than by an external criterion. It is more important to understand the views of each philosopher from his or her own perspective than to judge its validity. This different approach to the history of philosophy is perhaps due to the fact that analytic philosophy is more aligned with the natural sciences and continental philosophy is closer to the humanities, including literature. Therefore, in reading philosophical texts, analytic philosophy concentrates on logic and the validity of arguments while continental philosophy looks at the coherence and the meaning of the ideas conveyed in philosophical texts.

Student: We have seen that analytic philosophy studies the sciences and prefers to model itself on the sciences, while continental philosophy, especially if we think about phenomenology, studies the thinking subject and the way in which it is affected by the objects surrounding it. Could we say, in an analogy with a particular theme in modern philosophy, that analytic philosophy analyzes the primary qualities of perception, which are also studied by the natural sciences, while phenomenology studies the secondary qualities, which say more about the subject of perception than about its object?

Teacher: That is certainly a way of looking at the difference between analytic and continental philosophy, if the latter is seen to be especially represented by phenomenology.

In addition, questions concerning sense perception, attention, and intention in human perception are still an important part of phenomenology, perhaps because they have been in a certain way disregarded by the sciences and by other philosophical schools. Within analytic philosophy and continental philosophy we find different approaches to the various aspects of philosophy and the philosophical disciplines.

Student: In spite of their differences, is there something in common between the analytic and the continental tradition with regard to spirit?

Teacher: Both contemporary schools initially followed Kant's judgment concerning the end of metaphysics and disregarded the metaphysical tradition that goes back to

Aristotle, Plato, and the Presocratics. In some cases, there has been a return to metaphysics. However this is primarily a return to ontology and not a return to theology, the other part of metaphysics, even though some groups have tried to tackle this branch of metaphysics, both in the continental and in the analytic tradition.

Given the rejection of metaphysics, and particularly its spiritual aspect—which means a rejection of a truly spiritual reality—we must turn to Hegel for inspiration on this topic, without disregarding his predecessors, particularly Saint Thomas Aquinas, who integrates philosophy and theology and builds a bridge between Christianity and Aristotle's philosophy.

Student: Are there exceptions to the contemporary rejection of metaphysics?

Teacher: A notable exception to this trend is modern Thomism, or Neo-Thomism, which is based on, and consists in a modern revival of, the philosophy of Saint Thomas Aquinas.

Student: Does Neo-Thomism mean a strict adherence to the philosophy of Saint Thomas Aquinas?

Teacher: Some Neo-Thomistic philosophers attempt to combine the philosophy of Saint Thomas Aquinas with contemporary philosophy. For example, Edith Stein seeks to harmonize the philosophy of her teacher, Husserl, that is, phenomenology, with Thomism. She also speaks of spirit, and of spirit in Aquinas, for instance in her work *Potency and Act*. She holds that the ideal and spiritual in Aquinas is what Aquinas calls "intelligible" in his work. She does not believe in the purely material but identifies the spiritual in the material, and stresses the spiritual origin of the material. She holds that form is being and imparts being. She distinguishes between sensible and intelligible species.

In addition, Edith Stein speaks of subjective and objective spirit. The former incorporates the understanding and the will as essential attributes. Objective spirit points to the world of objects as dependent on subjective spirit. For her, subjective spirit is constituted by God and by the other spirits, which are finite. Furthermore, objective spirit is constituted by the form or species. Subjective spirit can be objectified, or studied as objective spirit. She holds that the spiritual life is intentional, and that for Aquinas ideas are archetypes in the divine mind. For her, God is pure intellect, and not a soul, following a traditional view in medieval philosophy, as we have seen, although the soul is also a kind of spirit. She stresses that God is spirit in the most perfect sense. If we speak of mind as spirit we are referring to the intellect.

Student: I can see how Neo-Thomism combines modern, medieval, and ancient philosophy. This philosophical school clearly seeks continuity rather than a break with tradition. Hegel also seeks continuity rather than a rupture with tradition.

Teacher: Yes, Hegel seeks continuity and therefore it is ironic that Left Hegelianism should be the most influential movement to be inspired by Hegel's philosophy, since Left Hegelians were clearly breaking with the philosophical and the metaphysical tradition.

Student: There are many points of contact between Aquinas and Hegel too, are there not?

Teacher: Yes, one can find many similarities between the philosophy of Aquinas and that of Hegel. Although the latter develops his philosophical activity in the aftermath of the Enlightenment, which rejects any kind of religious authority, he is keen on discussing Christian dogmas and he is not averse to discussing and accepting religious authority in the form of scripture. His emphasis on spirit brings him closer to the classical metaphysical tradition. At the same time, he develops that tradition with an emphasis on absolute idealism and he does not strictly follow the previous philosophical tradition, since he does not accept a metaphysics of the substance. Or rather, as we have seen from his approach to Spinoza, the substance must also be subject and it must be spirit. We do not find in him a metaphysics of individual substances, as in Aristotle, or a metaphysics of a single substance, as we find in Spinoza, but rather a metaphysics of the spirit, which implies that substance is ultimately spirit.

Student: And Hegel's philosophy is true to the history of philosophy, it seems to me.

Teacher: Yes, Hegel's philosophy constitutes a bridge between ancient philosophy, in particular Plato's and Aristotle's, and modern philosophy. One can already find many traces of medieval philosophy in modern philosophy, not least in Descartes, Leibniz, and Berkeley, as 20th-century Neo-Thomists emphasized, but Hegel has revived certain aspects of medieval philosophy, not least with his emphasis on Christianity and his reading of Christian theology.

Student: How does Hegel view medieval philosophy?

Teacher: It is no accident that Hegel so much admires medieval philosophy, particularly Scholasticism. Given his confidence in reason and its ability to fathom the ultimate reality, he admires the schoolmen's attempt to understand and explain rationally the dogmas of the Church. Hegel himself believes in the rationality of Christian dogmas, in contrast to his contemporaries' approach to religion. They stressed the sentimental aspects of religion and the centrality of religious feeling, which was a hallmark of Lutheran theology in Germany during Hegel's time. Hegel also believes that human reason through philosophy can attain the ultimate reality, and this reality is spiritual. He follows in the footsteps of philosophers who place the spiritual above the material, and these represent the predominant philosophical tradition up to Hegel, starting with Plato and Aristotle. Hence the need to concentrate on Hegel and the previous tradition rather than on philosophical developments which arose after Hegel if we are to understand the notion of spirit in philosophy. That is not to say that Hegel is simply synthesizing the tradition that comes before him. In fact he is extremely innovative, and, as we have seen, his philosophy gave rise to several different philosophical movements, either as an inspiration or as a cause for change in a different direction.

Hence when we analyze the notion of spirit in the various philosophical disciplines we will follow Hegel and the philosophical tradition that goes before him rather than later philosophers.

Student: We saw that according to Hegel the foremost disciplines of knowledge are religion and philosophy. Is it possible that his interest in spirit is connected with his emphasis on philosophy and religion?

Teacher: We have observed that spirit as such is studied and discussed primarily in philosophy and in theology or religion. Other disciplines may use the term, but spirit is truly defined in philosophy or in theology and religion. The natural or empirical sciences cannot, by definition, tackle the question of spirit, since this is a concept that cannot be empirically verified, that is to say, by means of experience or experiments. In other words, spirit is not subject to material verification, since matter is the opposite of spirit, and the empirical sciences, including physics and biology, require experimental and material confirmation of their theories. In addition, these disciplines, although they originally formed part of philosophy, became independent of philosophy in the modern period, with the development of experimentation techniques and scientific technology.

However, it is possible to speak of spirit in philosophical disciplines related to the empirical sciences, as we shall see, such as philosophy of physics or philosophy of biology. This is why the question of spirit is specifically philosophical, and especially metaphysical as well as theological and religious.

Student: Is it possible to include other disciplines as tackling spirit directly?

Teacher: Yes, if we think of the term "spirit" generally, as Hegel does, we may include the social sciences (sociology and anthropology) and psychology, all of which study individual and collective aspects of the human soul or mind, as well as the humanities in general, under the rubric of the sciences of the spirit ('Geisteswissenchaften'). In his lectures on philosophy of spirit, Hegel includes aspects of anthropology and psychology. He also includes phenomenology as pertaining to the study of spirit, although, as we have seen, this is different from the movement which appeared later and was developed by Husserl. Speaking of the "sciences of the spirit," Dilthey, for instance, holds that the sciences of the spirit deal with historical and social reality, although natural facts may be included.

Therefore, philosophy and religion or theology must be the center of our discussion. Subsequently, by taking account of the fact that most of the areas of knowledge initially came under the umbrella of philosophy, other ancient disciplines, such as physics or logic, should be considered in our study. This means that up to the modern period the question of spirit is part of philosophy, while philosophy also embraced the natural sciences. This is illustrated by the hierarchy of sciences, which was clearly defined in ancient and medieval philosophy. One of the main principles pertaining to the hierarchy of sciences was that a science could not prove its own subject matter, which therefore had to be proved by another, higher, science, and the connection between the various sciences was a result of this principle. All the sciences had their respective places clearly defined in this hierarchy, and metaphysics stood at the top of the hierarchy. In medieval philosophy, sacred theology towered over all the philosophical disciplines and the sciences. This means that some metaphysical and spiritual concepts straddle the various disciplines and are found in ancient and medieval physics, such as the concept of form and particularly substantial form. We also find in ancient and medieval philosophy a strong teleological approach, which highlights the role of the final cause. The preeminence of metaphysics begins to wane in the modern period, once the empirical sciences start to become independent.

Conclusion to Spirit and the History of Philosophy

Student: We have delved into the history of philosophy in search of the meaning of spirit. How can we sum up the outcome of our research? How do we understand spirit based on the history of philosophy?

Teacher: We saw that both theology and philosophy tend to see spirit as something immaterial, unextended, possibly infinite, that is apprehended by the intellect or the mind and not the senses. Therefore, it is related to the mind and not the senses. In theological terms, spirit is opposed to the body or the flesh. We also saw that spirituality is central to several religions. In Christianity not only is God spiritual, which is to say that he belongs in the spiritual domain, but he is himself spirit, and he is spirit as a person, as the third person of the Trinity. As we have mentioned, Christianity was to become a major influence in Western philosophy from late Antiquity. Jewish and Islamic philosophy also view God as spiritual since he is not material and does not have physical or anthropomorphic characteristics that would limit him. The theological aspects come to the fore in medieval philosophy, but spirit is not absent from ancient philosophy either.

Spirit is contrasted with nature, already in ancient philosophy, but more explicitly in Hegel. Spirit is related to intellect and the rules of logic for the Presocratics. Spirit is akin to knowledge and to intellect, which employs the rules of logic. Spirit is also related to reality or being. Some Presocratic philosophers hold that knowledge is obtained by the intellect while others emphasize knowledge obtained by the senses. We could view this opposition as the forerunner of the later distinction between rationalists and empiricists.

It is clear that spirit at this stage is related to purpose and the meaning of life, and is opposed to randomness and haphazard events. Materialist philosophers such as Democritus and Epicurus after him believe that matter constitutes all reality. They do not accept that providence rules the world, but hold that the atoms move and come together in a haphazard way. According to other Presocratic philosophers there is an intellect, or a spirit, which governs the world according to a good purpose, and Anaxagoras would be counted among those defending this view. So from the start of philosophical thinking there were important spiritual elements, related to knowledge, which by itself is not physical, and to intellect and logic. The term "philosophy," as you know, is reported to have been coined by Pythagoras, who claimed that he searched for knowledge in general and was not a specialist in any particular subject. Generally speaking, philosophical thinking in its historical origin is seen as a departure from religious thinking, but we observe that the birth of philosophy does not mean a relinquishing of questions relating to spirit.

Socrates marks a watershed in the history of philosophy. With regard to his thought we only have indirect accounts by various contemporaries, rather than his own writings. However, Cicero recounts that he brought down philosophy from heaven to earth, in the sense that, unlike his predecessors, he devoted himself to the relationships between human beings and was not concerned with what happened in the sky, that is to say, with natural phenomena. Socrates introduces ethical questions, but they have a metaphysical underpinning and justification. If we read Socrates as a philosopher, as he is portrayed by Plato in his dialogues, we see that he was acutely interested in the question of spirit, which had epistemological as well as metaphysical and ethical overtones for him. Spirit for Socrates is related to the truth and the good. If the world is ruled by spirit, as he believes, the good and the truth also reign in it and are ultimately attained by those human beings who search for them in earnest.

In Plato, the various themes related to spirit become more explicit. He associates what we understand as spirit especially with the forms, which give meaning and being to all existents. We saw that the forms are the ultimate reality. Nothing exists unless it participates in the forms, and equally, nothing is known unless it participates in the forms. Those forms are recognized by the intellect. The intellect which perceives the forms is akin to those forms and the nature of reality is intelligible by way of these forms, which structure reality. Plato also opposes the forms to the material. They are invisible, everlasting, unchangeable, immaterial, in contrast to the material objects that surround us. He also opposes the soul and the body, the soul being akin to the spiritual—especially the rational part of the soul—and the body being akin to the material things that are never the same and come to be and pass away. Clearly, for Plato all that is ethical and pertains to the good comes from the intellect and the forms, such as the sense of purpose and the virtues, indicating a close link between metaphysics and epistemology. One can only be good by being wise and contemplating the forms, although for Socrates anyone can potentially reach this level. This means that Socrates is not selective or elitist in his attempts to bring out knowledge of the forms in his interlocutors through recollection—he dialogues with anyone who is willing to meet with him. In Plato, therefore, the spiritual is present in his theory of forms and well as his epistemology and his ethics. This latter discipline is grounded in the form or idea of the good, and this good is a purpose to be contemplated and to be attained. The spiritual dominates in Plato's philosophy, since reality is spiritual rather than material, even though he does not deny the existence of matter or the body. The guiding principles of reality are the forms and the ideas.

Student: Given Plato's emphasis on ideas, can he be considered an idealist?

Teacher: Plato has been regarded by some scholars as an idealist, but his idealism cannot be termed subjective idealism, since reality itself (and not just the human subject) is ideal and spiritual. The ideas are not merely subjective but real; they exist outside the mind. Although this aspect of Plato's theory of forms has been criticized, not least by his pupil Aristotle, the principle that there are independent free-standing forms out there in a separate realm means that Plato is not advocating any kind of solipsism or subjectivism. As we have seen, there are different kinds of idealism, and Plato's philosophy could only be described as objective idealism.

Student: If Aristotle criticizes the theory of forms it must indicate that he is definitely not an idealist. And therefore, perhaps he does not emphasize spiritual reality as much as Plato does?

Teacher: It would be difficult to consider Aristotle an idealist, but the differences between his and Plato's philosophy are not as great as they may seem. Neither Plato nor Aristotle denies the existence of forms or of matter, and both stress the primacy of form over matter.

Student: Where can we find the concept of spirit in Aristotle's philosophy?

Teacher: For Aristotle, as for Plato, spirit is related to knowledge, and knowledge is knowledge of the causes, more specifically the four causes. The causes are responsible for the existence of something, namely their effects, and they also explain their existence. In ancient Greek, the word used by Aristotle for "cause" ('aitia') also means "explanation." Therefore in Aristotle, the causes are productive of being or existence, and they are productive of knowledge. They allow things to exist and to be known. There is naturally a hierarchy of causes. Later Hegel too would say that philosophy is the science of causes, which means that it is a general science. It is, in fact, the most general science, and it is therefore the highest science or branch of knowledge for Hegel.

In Aristotle the concept of spirit is more complex than in Plato because his philosophy is more systematic, in the sense that it seeks to cover all the fields of knowledge and all the disciplines, individually and as a whole. Aristotle is credited with the foundation of the various branches of knowledge which led to the philosophical and scientific disciplines as we know them today. Averroes, in particular, praises Aristotle for founding the disciplines of logic, physics, and metaphysics, which were the three main philosophical disciplines, under which the remaining philosophical disciplines were classified.

Student: Can we say that these are the same sciences as we know them today?

Teacher: Ancient and medieval science was dominated by Aristotle and his views concerning the four causes. Since the modern period, science has been conducted in a very different way, with different methods, and as we have seen, with mathematics playing a much greater role. However, the general subject matter of the sciences, and the questions these are concerned with, are basically the same as they were defined by Aristotle. Logic studies the rules of valid (and invalid) arguments, physics studies phenomena like motion and forces, and metaphysics studies the question of being. On the other hand, modern science appears to be closer to Presocratic science when it comes to the question of the components or nature of matter. The view that matter is composed of atoms was revived by modern science, which now views atoms not as indivisible but as made up of particles. Modern science clearly departs from Aristotle, as we have seen, but the themes studied by science have remained fundamentally the same.

Returning to Aristotle, we find the predominance of spirit in the various disciplines. In this way many aspects of logic with its categories, rules, and principles are part of spirit.

Student: In what sense can we say that the principles of logic evince the influence or presence of spirit?

Teacher: The principles of logic concern the structure of thought and language, but also of reality. These principles are not just descriptive, but also causative. Logic is not simply a description of language, which in turn describes reality, but it structures reality. The logically impossible is contradictory but also unreal. Logical principles are used in language and knowledge but they are not purely mental categories, since they describe real substances, phenomena, and situations. They are applied in knowledge and in the various branches of knowledge but they are real, almost like the Platonic forms.

And there is causality present in logic. We saw how Aristotle, like Plato, strongly defends the theory of causality or causation which links an effect to its cause. This implies that the effect issues from its cause or causes in a determinate way and would not have existed, or would not have existed in that way, without its causes. We find causality in logic in the way that in a syllogism the premises are the causes of the conclusion, which could not have existed without its premises. The rules of logic can be considered to be the domain of spirit, in the way they unite knowledge, intellect, and reality.

Student: How is spirit present in the other disciplines as described by Aristotle?

Teacher: Aristotle's theory of knowledge—which goes hand in hand with his psychology, since both consider the faculties of the soul, and particularly the intellect—describes aspects of spirit, such as intellect, idea, and reality, and idea as reality. For Aristotle, the faculties of the soul are clearly defined and demarcated functions of the soul. Knowledge for Aristotle can be said to be spiritual because it is knowledge of the universal, which does not contain any material or particular aspects. This knowledge is complex in the sense that it involves many intellectual aspects and categories. We know something if we know its causes, which explain substances and phenomena. In the process of cognition we use the rules of logic and grammar, and the categories. All these intellectual or spiritual aspects both describe and structure reality. Knowledge is also knowledge of the forms, including the substantial forms. As we have seen, form in Aristotle is a cause.

Student: Aristotle's theory of the four causes clearly plays a central role in his metaphysics, physics, and epistemology. Does Aristotle favor one of the four causes over the other three?

Teacher: He clearly does not privilege matter and we have seen that he groups the other three causes, formal, final, and efficient, together. With regard to spirit, it is particularly evident in the formal and the final cause, and it may be that Aristotle privileged these two causes since they have far-reaching consequences, more than the material and even the efficient cause.

Returning to Aristotle's epistemology and the question of spirit, knowledge for him is also of accidents, which inhere in particular subjects, but are in themselves universal. The collection of his works later titled the *Organon* comprises his works on logic and on the theory of knowledge. It begins with the analysis of language and the categories and proceeds to the description of the rules of logic, and finally scientific, or demonstrative, knowledge in a way that is coordinated with metaphysical knowledge. Aristotle is keen on stressing the universal nature of knowledge by describing the process of cognition as proceeding from the particular to the universal, which is the goal of knowledge. In terms of the acquisition of knowledge by an individual, the process goes from the particular to the universal and it is known as induction. The reverse process implies the passage from universal to particular, in a process known as demonstration. This process is an essential aspect of scientific knowledge since it allows us to reach conclusions on the basis of particular or universal premises. Aristotle includes such universal principles as definition in this conception of scientific knowledge. Spiritual in this context means universal and not particular or material. As we have seen, Aristotle does not deny the existence of matter; rather, he assumes its existence, but knowledge itself is completely spiritual, or universal and nonmaterial.

Student: Does this emphasis on the spiritual nature of knowledge lead to an idealist position?

Teacher: Aristotle is considered a realist in the sense that the immediate objects of knowledge are external to the mind, and these objects are primarily individual things. Knowledge refers to individual material things, although knowledge itself is universal and not particular. For instance, there is no definition of a particular thing; definitions are always of general concepts.

Student: Naturally, Aristotle's metaphysics brings together all these formal or spiritual aspects?

Teacher: His metaphysics, like his logic and epistemology, is also spiritual, since matter plays only a supportive and mysterious role in explaining the nature of reality. For Aristotle metaphysics overlaps with and grounds the other disciplines of knowing, as we have seen. Causality is discussed in physics and in metaphysics, and Aristotle introduces some basic principles of logic in his *Metaphysics*, namely the laws of thought. The spiritual in Aristotle is present in his metaphysics, in his logic, and in his theory of knowledge. Given that his views on causality, with its emphasis on form, straddle his physics as well as his metaphysics, his conception of reality ultimately rests on a spiritual foundation. His view of reality includes form and matter, but form leads the way and is the truly active and explanatory element. In logic, the rules of reasoning are rules of thought and they are applicable to reality. His theory of knowledge, encapsulated in his psychology or theory of the soul, studies the intellect. All the dominant elements in Aristotle's philosophy are spiritual, even if he cannot be called an idealist.

Student: We have also looked at spiritual elements in the schools which developed after Plato and Aristotle.

Teacher: After Plato and Aristotle, the new schools which emerged, Stoicism and Epicureanism, were more concerned with practical matters and the question of seeking happiness by living the good life. However, the Stoics, who in some ways can be considered to be materialists, since for them only individual material objects exist, hold that there is a universal reason governing the universe, and that we should live according to nature by recognizing that universal reason. Nothing escapes the dictates of the universal reason.

The last great school of ancient philosophy, Neoplatonism, explains the origin of the universe as an emanation from the One, which produces an intellect and a soul. Being starts only with the intellect and is identified with the intellect. Matter is the last effect of emanation, and pure matter is equivalent to non-being. Naturally, there is a spiritual principle at the heart of this philosophy, which explains the universal through the intellect, which in turn proceeds from the absolute One.

In the medieval period many aspects of Aristotle's and Plotinus' philosophy are maintained, such as the categories, the emanation from the One, the gradation of being, Aristotle's rules of logic, and his metaphysical and physical considerations, with the prevalence of form over matter, as well as their views on the human and the divine intellects.

Student: We saw that there is a focus on God in medieval philosophy given the influence of religion.

Teacher: Yes, the distinctive character of medieval philosophy is the focus on God, who is seen as spirit par excellence, and who concentrates all aspects of spirit. The theory of God as spirit or intellect is observable in Islamic and in Jewish philosophy and not just in the Christian tradition, where this view is most explicit given that the third person of the Trinity is properly called "Spirit." Naturally, the theological considerations are of paramount significance. There is a rich medieval theological literature explaining the nature of the Holy Spirit. The gifts of the Holy Spirit are spiritual gifts, such as counsel, knowledge, understanding, and wisdom, and naturally the fruits of the Holy Spirit are also spiritual.

Student: We have touched on ethics with reference to Plato and we have found that virtue ethics dominates ancient philosophy. How does ethical theory develop in medieval philosophy?

Teacher: In the field of ethics, Aristotle's theory of virtues is kept in medieval philosophy, but in Christian philosophy new virtues are added, under the influence of theology. These are the theological Christian virtues of faith, hope, and charity. They are supernatural virtues because they are infused by God and are not innate in human beings; they point to the afterlife instead of basically assisting in the regulation of ethical life among human beings in human societies.

Student: We have also seen other disciplines emerge in the Middle Ages in addition to the ancient philosophical disciplines.

Teacher: Yes, the Aristotelian disciplines are maintained and developed, but in Christianity a new discipline of sacred doctrine or theology emerges to integrate the scriptural texts about God and creation. Sacred doctrine is independent from philosophy and it is considered to surpass philosophy, but Aristotelian logic and concepts are used to analyze scripture and to formulate or clarify Christian dogma.

In medieval philosophy we find a harmonization of Neoplatonic and Aristotelian philosophy both in the Christian and in the Islamic tradition, as well as in Jewish philosophy. Following the spirit of scripture, reality is seen as twofold, God and creation. God concentrates all aspects of spirit, being himself fully spirit and infinite spirit. Creation issues by decree from his intellect and his ideas. Within creation there are intellectual beings, such as the angels and humans, and non-rational beings like animals, plants, and minerals. Spirit pervades creation through ideas, and given the spiritual origin of the universe, based on the fact that God creates by his intellect, medieval philosophers stress the spiritual aspects even of non-rational elements of creation. Plants and animals grow and act in an orderly way and according to a purpose. Creation displays a spiritual order and meaning, whether explicitly or implicitly.

In medieval philosophy knowledge involves the forms and the other causes along the Aristotelian model. The subjects of knowledge are the various intellects, angelic and human, which intelligize those forms and understand the causes of things. These forms are to be found not just in intellects but also in individual natural beings. Matter is considered to be part of reality, but it is subordinated to form, and metaphysics ranks above all the philosophical disciplines, including physics and ethics.

Some medieval philosophers place limits on the powers of human reason and intellect, but the universe is ruled by an infinite divine intellect who is also provident. The universe is made up of the celestial world and terrestrial world, and the human soul bridges the two worlds. This is because the human soul controls the body, which is material, but in addition it intelligizes the eternal forms and contemplates God. As we have seen, in the medieval period, Neoplatonic and Aristotelian philosophy is understood in the light of scripture, producing a synthesis which would lead up to the following period in the history of philosophy, modern philosophy. For the medieval philosophers, reality is essentially spiritual.

Student: In the medieval period both religion and philosophy are purely spiritual, are they not? Perhaps we could phrase it differently and state that the influence of religion reinforced the spiritual nature of philosophy in the Middle Ages?

Teacher: Yes, the influence of religion served to reinforce the spiritual element in philosophy. While the ancient philosophers were certainly preoccupied with the question of God, there were many different approaches to religion, and religion certainly influenced philosophy. There is no doubt that ancient philosophers were expected to follow the traditional religion of their societies (the charges leveled in Athens against Anaxagoras, Socrates, and Aristotle certainly bring this reality home, although there were political reasons for the accusations too). In the Middles Ages, religion becomes even more influential for philosophy, and, with some exceptions, religion and theology become part of a dialogue with philosophy such that they become practically inseparable, particularly in the Christian world. In the Islamic world, the interaction between Islamic philosophy and the Islamic sciences is more subtle or implicit, hence the clash between philosophers and some Sunni Islamic theologians, who resisted the encroachment of Aristotelian philosophy and science on religion.

Student: The modern period does not ignore the question of spirit, but it takes on a different form.

Teacher: In the modern period, with new scientific discoveries being made, there is an emphasis on the human spirit, especially the human intellect and the conditions and limits of knowledge. Epistemology is at the heart of the concerns of modern philosophers, in its connections with metaphysics and science. Skepticism has a role to play, arguably more so than in ancient philosophy, as it seems to influence the main schools of philosophy in the modern period. The father of modern philosophy, Descartes, was greatly influenced by skepticism, as his *Meditations on First Philosophy* show, and his successors had to take this philosophical challenge into account. The methods for obtaining knowledge, whether through sense perception or reason alone, are examined, and the extent of human reason is debated, culminating in Kant's affirmation to the effect that reason cannot discern the kernel of reality, the thing in itself. The question of God is still present but it is not as central as before. Different philosophers offer different perspectives on God, and some of these clearly depart from scripture, for instance Spinoza. However, an examination of the human mind implies a study of spirit, and not just the human spirit.

Student: We have looked into the role of spirit in ancient and in medieval philosophy. Aristotle's realism appears to dominate the various approaches to the theory of knowledge in those periods of the history of philosophy. We only find idealism as a position which is explicitly stated in modern philosophy, once the human subject of knowing becomes the center of attention.

Teacher: In the modern period, there is certainly a connection between the emphasis on the human subject and the development of idealism, which states that all is spirit or that matter is subsumed under spirit. We observe a kind of idealism in Berkeley, who denies the existence of matter, and therefore describes his position as immaterialism. This philosophical trajectory culminates in German idealism.

Student: And it culminates in Hegel.

Teacher: Hegel systematizes all views on spirit. In fact, he thinks of his philosophy as the culmination of the previous philosophical systems. In this sense we could apply his theory of spirit to the various kinds of spirit to be found in the history of philosophy, such as subjective and objective spirit, as well as absolute spirit. In later works, Hegel identifies objective spirit with collective spirit, or collective forms of spirit in human societies, but it is possible to consider objective spirit simply as spiritual forms that are the object of subjective spirit. Therefore, if we think of human spirit or intellect as subjective spirit, it became the special interest of modern philosophy. Ancient philosophy considers especially reality in itself and knowledge of reality. We could view this period as a study of objective spirit, with the rules of logic, the question about forms, and universals taking center stage. And medieval philosophy considers absolute spirit in the figure of God. These three senses of spirit, subjective, objective, and absolute, can be seen to exhaust the meaning of spirit in theory of knowledge, since any kind of epistemological conception of spirit will fall within these categories.

Student: Does this mean that we can summarize all the aspects of spirit and explain them for our own purposes by having recourse to this threefold classification of spirit?

Teacher: We can sum up the result of our findings by using these categories and say that there is finite subjective spirit, which is identified with human spirit, in all its forms. It is identified with the faculty of knowing and the process of cognition, or rather the special activity or forms of knowing. This may be identified with consciousness, self-consciousness, intuition, imagination, memory, and higher forms of intellection, such as understanding and reason. Sensation is a lower kind of consciousness and it also belongs to the subject. Subjective spirit comprehends the different faculties such as understanding, will, and judgment. It also includes anything related to the thinking subject, namely the soul, the "I," the self, and the acts of the faculties of the soul. It includes the passions, and matters relating to assent and withholding assent, such as certainty, doubt, belief, and faith. Other acts of the subject include intention and attention, intention being the more specific of the two. All these are subsumed under finite subjective spirit. Aspects related to practical philosophy also come under finite subjective spirit, such as the virtues, which issue from the mind or the soul, and also the speculative virtues. Under subjective spirit we understand the faculties and the acts of spirit. Subjective spirit is spirit understood in the guise of the subject, that is, in so far as it is a subject.

Student: And there is no subjective spirit without objective spirit?

Teacher: Subjective spirit necessarily implies objective spirit, which is identified, for instance, with general concepts, the rules of logic, and the categories of science. Objective spirit is present anywhere we find spirit objectively outside the human mind. However, objective spirit is related to the human mind and it is understood by it.

Anything that is understood by the mind can be seen to belong to objective spirit. Consequently, objective spirit constitutes the object of consciousness, self-consciousness, intuition, imagination, memory, and higher forms of intellection, such as understanding and reason. A philosopher like Berkeley even considers sensation as a spiritual experience. In other words, if we follow Berkeley we can even say that sense perception is a spiritual apprehension of reality. Matter cannot be perceived in any way, so the object of sensation can be classed as objective spirit if we consider this experience as part of the process of cognition. As part of objective spirit we can include Plato's ideas or Aristotle's universals, and generally speaking, any universal concepts, or indeed any concepts. Opinions would also be classed as part of objective spirit. The different sciences, and the theories which constitute those sciences, should be considered integral to objective spirit. Subjective and objective spirit mutually imply each other.

Student: You also mentioned absolute spirit, in addition to subjective and objective spirit.

Teacher: We can consider a third form of spirit, which is absolute or supreme spirit, as the ultimate form of spirit. In absolute spirit, the contents of objective spirit are present in themselves and they exist in so far as they are present for subjective spirit. Therefore nothing spiritual escapes absolute spirit, which however, is not just the sum of finite subjective spirit and objective spirit but rises above them as something transcendent. Since knowledge surpasses opinion, absolute spirit does not require opinion, nor is doubt or uncertainty a part of it, and it contains the contents of finite subjective spirit.

Student: Is absolute spirit also subjective and objective spirit?

Teacher: Absolute spirit is infinite subjective spirit, and it contains all of objective spirit, in other words, all there is to know. Consequently, all the sciences in their perfection belong to absolute spirit. This absolute spirit corresponds to the idea of God, because only an infinite spirit can contain the objects of subjective spirit and all the elements of objective spirit, and rise above them.

Student: How does absolute spirit further relate to subjective and objective spirit?

Teacher: Subjective and objective spirit are contained in absolute spirit as their cause such that absolute spirit is the cause and origin of finite subjective and objective spirit. This means that absolute spirit is the cause of ideas, for instance, and it is also the cause of other spirits, which are all finite, since there is only one infinite spirit. We can discuss further details pertaining to these kinds of spirit as we proceed with our investigation.

Student: What is the relation between the three types of spirit?

Teacher: There is a certain identity, or rather correspondence, between subjective and objective spirit, in the sense that finite subjective spirit recognizes and knows elements of objective spirit but not objective spirit in its entirety. There are contents which only exist for absolute spirit, and escape the notice of subjective spirit, given that subjective spirit itself is finite. In other words, although absolute spirit is also subjective spirit, given that it thinks, subjective spirit, considered in itself, and not as identical with absolute spirit, is finite. Therefore, there is a difference between finite subjective spirit and infinite subjective spirit. Only the latter can be identified with absolute spirit. Equally, objective spirit is the same for the two kinds of subjective spirit, but because finite subjective spirit does not apprehend all of objective spirit, the entirety of objective spirit is only fully apprehended by absolute spirit.

Student: In this instance we are not following Hegel's definition of subjective spirit in its relation to absolute spirit?

Teacher: No, because for Hegel all spirit is ultimately one. We choose to keep the distinction between the different kinds of spirit in all their variety and specificity. Absolute spirit surpasses not only subjective spirit but also objective spirit in its nature, which means that absolute spirit rises above finite subjective spirit and it comprehends all of objective spirit. On the other hand, since there are no boundaries between spiritual things, there is continuity between the various kinds of spirit, and they are of the same nature, but absolute spirit is infinite and transcends the two other kinds of spirit.

Student: How can we justify the existence of an absolute spirit? Naturally, if we know, we know something, and therefore we are certain of the subject and of the object of knowledge, of ourselves and of what we apprehend. But what about another kind of spirit or mind which knows everything? How can we as finite spirits, who are limited in our apprehension of objective spirit, be certain of the existence of an absolute spirit?

Teacher: We keep discovering new things every day, individually, as individual subjects of cognition, and collectively, for instance when new findings are discovered by scientists and shared with the entire scientific community and with the public. The fact that we keep learning means that we do not have absolute knowledge because there is no end to the process of cognition. However, while we discover only parts of reality and not absolute reality, we have the notion of complete or absolute knowledge and this confirms the concept, and the existence, of an absolute spirit who apprehends all reality and possesses absolute knowledge. Nevertheless, to learn more about the connection between finite and infinite knowledge we have to study the connection between spirit and matter, as other philosophers have done.

Student: In Hegel and in the sciences there is a belief in the progress of knowledge, and even in a linear progress, which implies that there is no regress. I wonder whether there is also knowledge that is lost?

Teacher: Naturally, there is knowledge lost, as is clear from the many things that our ancestors could produce and we no longer can produce, at least not in the same way. We could mention as an example of this the Pyramids in Egypt, or ancient Greek art. This loss affects both practical and theoretical knowledge, the arts and the crafts. When it comes to theoretical knowledge, many books from the ancient world were lost and without doubt they contained much information and wisdom which we no longer possess. Clearly the ancients knew many things that we are no longer aware of now. This reality casts a shadow on the belief in progress which states that there is constant progress in human knowledge towards ever more positive developments. When it comes to knowledge, some aspects improve while others decline. Each epoch has its advantages and disadvantages.

Student: As you have stressed, Hegel writes more profusely on spirit, from a philosophical perspective, than any other philosopher. Spirit is an absolutely central concept in his works. Another important aspect of his philosophy is his dialectic, which he adopts from ancient philosophy, and in particular Plato. Hegel's dialectic aims at reconciling opposites and this applies also to spirit, for instance in the attempt to reconcile finite or human spirit and infinite or divine spirit. Will we include Hegel's dialectic in our understanding of spirit?

Teacher: Hegel's dialectic is an essential aspect of his thought. For instance, in the *Phenomenology of Spirit* he introduces a central concept in his philosophy, which is the concept of life and organism. He seeks to apply it to his own philosophy, especially in the way progress and development occur in the process of cognition as described in this work. Dialectic is the process whereby the process of cognition evolves in a seamless way and takes on different shapes, culminating in absolute knowing. The basic principle of his dialectic is the reconciliation between two opposite theses or concepts in a harmonious synthesis. Therefore, the central idea of his dialectical logic is the reconciliation of opposites or extremes. Moreover, in his dialectic he seeks to fill a gap in the syllogistic logic which was still in force in his time. He states, correctly, that modern logic was essentially based on Aristotelian logic, which was adopted and developed during the ancient and medieval period through to the modern period. Hegel seeks to develop a new kind of logic which would allow for the meeting of opposites. Some scholars have argued that Hegel seeks to abolish the principles of Aristotle's logic, including the principle of non-contradiction, but Hegel does accept them at a certain level. However, his philosophy is averse to any kind of dualism. Consequently, he seeks to reconcile extremes such finite and infinite, subjective and objective, material and spiritual, human and divine. While Hegel himself sought to harmonize opposites, his successors tended to stress one of the opposites, which explains some of the differences between the various schools of thought which issued from Hegel's philosophy. Left Hegelians, for instance, stressed the human and the finite in his philosophy, and Right Hegelians stressed the infinite and the divine. Hegel aimed at uniting these extremes so that the difference would cease to exist, but his readers would emphasize one of the two aspects.

Student: With regard to the question of spirit, we have already decided that it would be better to keep the distinction between finite and infinite spirit.

Teacher: The problem with the use of dialectical logic when it comes to the relation between the different kinds of spirit is that if they are truly all one, the differences ultimately cease to exist. This means that it is the same spirit which exists in the beginning as subjective spirit. The latter is a finite kind of spirit which stands in relation to objective spirit. Then this subjective spirit develops into objective spirit, and finally it becomes absolute spirit. The same spirit is first simply subjective spirit which develops into objective spirit, and later, it discovers that it is absolute spirit. This means that there is nothing truly transcendent for subjective spirit, and the three kinds of spirit are all one and the same. It is difficult to see how there is a true distinction between subjective and objective spirit, and especially between finite subjective and infinite or absolute spirit, since they all turn out to be one and the same spirit. On the one hand, this accounts for a certain coherence in the concept of spirit, but the due distinction between the various kinds of spirit is not maintained. It is also not clear at which point the different kinds of spirit become one and why they are seemingly separated at the start. Even in the *Phenomenology of Spirit* it is not clear how and when human spirit becomes united to absolute spirit to become absolute knowing. The final section of the *Phenomenology of Spirit*, on absolute knowing, is a short chapter and the details are lacking.

For our part, we prefer to maintain the differences between the various kinds of spirit. Subjective spirit truly knows its object when it knows the contents of objective spirit, but the infinite contents of objective spirit never cease to be learned and apprehended by finite subjective spirit. In this way, subjective spirit grows in the sense that it gradually learns, acquiring progressively more contents of objective spirit, although it never exhausts those contents. In addition, finite subjective spirit does not exhaust the contents of absolute spirit (standing as objective spirit for finite subjective spirit), since the latter is transcendent. Consequently, it is important to keep the boundaries between the different kinds of spirit, although they are similar in nature. Absolute spirit is infinite and human spirit is finite, although it can develop. Also, Hegel appeared to assume that absolute knowledge had been attained, through philosophy, by finite subjective spirit, as it merges with objective and finally with absolute spirit. However, we keep making new discoveries by the day, for instance in the natural sciences, so we cannot say that complete knowledge has been obtained or that it will ever be fully obtained. The dialectic model used by Hegel will not avail us in our purpose of describing the nature of spirit and the different kinds of spirit. Spirit is said in many ways, and these ways cannot all be reduced to just one thing or one thinking substance. It is better to maintain the differences between the different kinds of spirit, in order to ensure the true or independent existence of an absolute spirit, which is like a first principle and the cornerstone of the other kinds of spirit.

Therefore, we will not use Hegel's dialectic to show the complete identity between the three kinds of spirit. The fact that we keep learning and knowledge seems endless shows both the possibilities and the limitations of our knowledge, and it points to an absolute knowledge which we do not possess but is possessed by an absolute spirit.

Student: From our study of the history of philosophy I understand the nature of spirit and how it is contrasted with matter and with nature, surpassing both in its reach and power.

Teacher: We have seen that the vast majority of philosophers have defended the view that spirit is superior to matter and nature and that it determines their action. We have also looked at spirit as a leading category explaining reality and knowledge in various philosophers, regardless of whether the term was used explicitly or not.

Part II

Spirit and the Philosophical Disciplines

Student: Now that we have studied the concept of spirit in the history of philosophy, how are we to proceed?

Teacher: Based on our findings from the history of philosophy, we will look into the different philosophical disciplines—such as theory of knowledge and metaphysics, or ethics—to ascertain the presence of spirit in them.

Student: With which discipline shall we start?

Teacher: With regard to spirit in the different philosophical disciplines, it is best to start with the theory of knowledge.

Student: Why not start with metaphysics, since it is the most fundamental discipline in philosophy, dealing as it does with reality itself?

Teacher: We must first examine what we can know and then speak of the reality that we know. As we will see, the two disciplines are inextricably bound together, since reality is what we know, or at any rate what can be known or is known by some mind. There is no knowledge without reality, and some philosophers would say that there is no reality that is not perceived or known.

Student: Is there nothing beyond what we know? Perhaps we are starting from an idealist position? Or should we assume the existence of a thing in itself that is unknown to us?

Teacher: The kind of position to be taken with regard to the debate between idealism and realism will have to be determined as we proceed with our investigation. Realism states that we know the objects as they are and that they exist without our knowing them, since they are independent of our knowledge. Therefore realism states on the one hand that we can know the truth as it is, but on the other hand that the object may exist even if we do not perceive it. Reality is greater than knowledge, as it were, whereas an idealist would say that everything is known or perceived according to the prism of the knowing subject.

Student: Starting with the theory of knowledge could mean reverting to certain questions that preoccupied modern philosophers concerning the nature of knowledge, and taking some kind of idealist position such as saying that we cannot know reality in itself or that there is nothing beyond our knowledge of reality. If theory of knowledge is our starting point we could be assuming an idealist position without justifying it first.

Teacher: It is true that starting with the theory of knowledge could create a bias. However, we can begin with the theory of knowledge and consciousness and then ascertain if there is anything beyond it. We will have to determine whether there is anything beyond what can be known, by us or by another mind. It is safe to start from that which we know, and see if there is something that we do not know or do not currently know. At any rate, this investigation must start from the reality that is accessible to us. Since Hegel devotes his *Phenomenology of Spirit* explicitly to the question of spirit, it is good to follow his principle of analyzing human consciousness and cognition, from the point of view of the human subject. When we speak of subject we are necessarily talking of a theory of knowledge. Moreover, if we follow Hegel's conclusions in this work, and also the principles of medieval philosophy, we will then have to assume the existence of an absolute spirit.

Student: I understand that in studying the subject we should not restrict ourselves to the human subject. However, I should like to know why Hegel and medieval philosophers, from within the domain of theory of knowledge, assume the existence of an absolute spirit.

Teacher: They assume the existence of an absolute spirit for different but related reasons. Medieval philosophers and Hegel believe that there is an all-knowing spirit which explains all reality and all knowledge. According to Aquinas, without revelation or scripture it would be very difficult to know the truth and reality, because of the weakness of our minds. For Hegel, absolute spirit constitutes the completion of subjective and objective spirit and justifies them, but for Aquinas and most medieval philosophers the divine spirit is ultimately transcendent, whereas for Hegel absolute spirit finds and knows itself in human spirit. In this way, it is important to start from the question of knowledge.

Student: Why not start from the question of being?

Teacher: The question of being has to be addressed since it is central to metaphysics, but we must take into account the fact that the concept of being is very broad and should probably be addressed in connection with other questions. That is to say, being must always be qualified in order to have a concrete meaning. Naturally, the question of being has always been very significant and perhaps the pivotal question in philosophy and not just in metaphysics. Being is equated with existence and reality, and also with that which can be known. There are variations on being and in the medieval period this is particularly important, given the distinction between God and all other beings. Already in Plotinus and the emanation schema he presents, there is a gradation of being. We have also seen that being is one, and indeed the first, of the chief transcendentals in the medieval tradition, and the most general one, preceding as it does oneness, truth and goodness.

However, although many philosophers have held that this was the central question in philosophy, namely to ask about being and existence, we have seen that Hegel holds that being is the poorest category. We can say that whatever we speak about, and is in our mind, has a certain kind of existence: physical or spiritual, possible or necessary, or simply mental. Being is an abstraction which can be discussed in philosophy but when it comes to further details, something else has to be added, and being does not stand alone. It can also be considered the most difficult question in philosophy, given its abstraction. Therefore we will consider being in conjunction with the question of knowledge and begin with the question of knowledge.

Student: I accept that starting with the question of knowledge does not necessarily lead to an idealist position that cannot be proved. However, if we start with knowledge instead of being, are we not privileging theory of knowledge over metaphysics? And does this not constitute a danger in the sense of possibly falling into the same trap as modern philosophers did, culminating in the decline and rejection of metaphysics? Initially, their position seemed to strengthen the powers of the human subject, but it ultimately ended in Kant's misgivings about the abilities of reason.

Teacher: We will discuss the theory of knowledge in order to reach a metaphysical position, and then it will be seen that the two main philosophical disciplines go hand in hand. The validity of this starting point, if there should be any doubt, is Descartes' position in the beginning of the *Meditations on First Philosophy*. According to this work, the first claims that can be taken for certain are: if I doubt, I exist, and if I think, I exist. These certainties cannot be doubted. This means that we must needs begin with the question of knowledge, and the first philosophical claims concern the nature of spirit. We must necessarily start from the assumption of spirit, and also from the assumption that spirit, generally speaking, exists. We are initially certain of the finite subjective spirit and then become certain also of an absolute spirit, God. In the process we will also reach certainty regarding objective spirit. We will speak of the different kinds of spirit first from an epistemological perspective and then from a metaphysical perspective.

Chapter 5
Theory of Knowledge

Student: What does theory of knowledge treat of?

Teacher: Theory of knowledge looks at the content of our knowledge and whether it is true or false, whether we can know reality or only appearances. It also studies the question whether human reason or mind follows the structure of reality and reproduces it, somehow imitating or resembling it, and it treats of certainty or the lack thereof, which results in skepticism. Logic, in contrast, studies the formal aspects of our knowledge and the validity of arguments and not the content of knowledge. Moreover, theory of knowledge concerns the process of learning and whether we start from the universal or the particular. As we have seen, Plato considers that we first have the forms in our minds and then particular objects help us to recollect them, while Aristotle believes that we start from particular objects and, through induction, which implies proceeding from the particular to the universal, obtain universal concepts in our minds.

Student: You mentioned logic as a separate discipline in relation to theory of knowledge, in the sense that logic concerns itself with the forms of thought while theory of knowledge studies the content of knowledge and thought.

Teacher: Yes, that is correct, generally speaking. However, logic and epistemology can overlap. Truth is a concept which is discussed in theory of knowledge and in logic, since the truth of propositions is an important element in logic. Truth can be identified with reality and the question of whether our knowledge corresponds to reality. Truth in language is based on the validity of an argument, and therefore it is about knowledge, reality, and the way in which we express that reality though language. Truth can mean the correspondence between our knowledge and reality. It is in this sense that an empiricist would argue that there is nothing in the mind which was not previously in the senses, meaning that knowledge corresponds to reality in the way that what is in the mind should reflect what is outside it. However, truth can also be about logical or conceptual coherence. For instance, Hegel states that truth is the correspondence between the object which is being considered and its concept or idea, or, in other words, the correspondence between the thing and its concept. Truth is also the ultimate reality, God or absolute spirit. Aquinas would say that truth is not in the things but in the intellect, pointing to its links with knowledge and language. We have seen that some philosophical themes, such as truth, are treated by more than one discipline.

Student: If we start with theory of knowledge, how are we to proceed with regard to metaphysics?

Teacher: Classical metaphysics has not been disproved. Perhaps a metaphysics of the substance in Aristotle and the Aristotelian tradition has been abandoned in the modern period, but an attempt to discard all consideration of being and the nature of reality cannot be successfully undertaken. The abandonment of metaphysics was a consequence of the limits imposed on reason, but this is not a justification for abandoning metaphysics. Medieval philosophers also believed in the limits of reason and the fact that the human mind was prone to error, but they accepted the validity of metaphysical investigations. Although modern and contemporary science is much more complex than Aristotelian science, we should not refrain from metaphysical considerations simply because the main scientific presuppositions of Aristotle's philosophy have been abandoned.

Furthermore, the metaphysical consideration of being cannot constitute a purely materialistic approach, stating that all being is material, or that the material is the starting point and that any spiritual reality, if it exists, is the result of matter. Descartes' main point in the *Meditations on First Philosophy* shows that reality is first spiritual, which was indeed what he was trying to prove. There have been philosophers after Hegel who assume these materialistic principles, but in reality we can never abstract from the knowing subject. The knowing subject must accompany and precede all acts of knowledge and hence the spiritual principle prevails.

Student: Should we consider contemporary philosophy as leaning towards materialism?

Teacher: Many schools of philosophy today assume a materialist principle without proving it, including analytic and continental perspectives which are based on an empiricist or a materialist presupposition. Empiricism need not necessarily imply materialism, but it does sometimes go hand in hand with a materialist position. Curiously, many of these positions arose from a reaction to Hegel's philosophy, on which most schools of philosophy commented, especially in the 19th century, but also in the 20th. Much continental philosophy follows a materialist reading of Hegel, based on

Marx's interpretation, which is rather truncated or selective, to say the least. Some modern readings of Hegel even refuse to accept Hegel's affirmation of God's existence, as it is laid out, for instance, in the *Phenomenology of Spirit*. This implies disregarding a good part of Hegel's writings and also a fundamental part of his system.

Student: Does skepticism still pose a significant threat to knowledge generally speaking, and to metaphysics?

Teacher: Descartes already proved conclusively that complete skepticism is unwarranted because we are certain of the acts of our mind and we can therefore proceed to the task of seeking knowledge on a firm footing. Berkeley develops his immaterialist theory in opposition to skeptics, since he links materialism and skepticism, but Descartes' solution to the problem seems satisfactory as a starting point.

Student: Since we are starting with theory of knowledge, what can we say are the first stages of knowledge?

Teacher: It is natural to assume that our knowledge goes from the particular to the universal, as we saw both in Aristotle and in Hegel, as well as other philosophers. The universal is based on the particular and is a generalization of the particular. We may also safely assume that knowledge starts with sense perception, since this is the first kind of contact we have with the world. This happens individually as human beings grow up and also in scientific experiments. In the latter case, the experiments serve to test a general theory or hypothesis, in order to confirm or to disprove it, but in any case the contact with particulars is essential. Finally there is no question that with sense perception we are dealing with particulars, which are the first object of the senses and also the mind, before any generalization can take place. When we speak of sense perception, we mean the five senses: seeing, hearing, smelling, touching, and tasting. The traditional view among philosophers is that the senses have both a cognitive function and a corporal one, telling the body what is useful for it and what can be harmful. The senses are the source of sensation. Perception is a more general term than sense perception, which naturally means perceiving by the senses. Sensation can be related to quality or quantity, or both, such as when we think of a color or a sound with a certain form or proportion. Our starting point with regard to theory of knowledge is therefore consciousness, which is a form of spirit, and which includes sensation.

Student: After the senses, which faculties help us in the process of cognition?

Teacher: It is important to notice that there is a continuity between the different faculties. In relation to sense perception we find feeling, which can point to external perception or internal perception, within the body. Sensation is also akin to feeling but it is more obviously about something external and physical than is feeling, which has a more complex meaning and is closer to the universal or the idea and notion than is sensation. Among the various feelings are hope, fear, joy, pain, anguish, and others. Sense perception, feeling, and sensation are all related to the particular. They all presuppose the presence of the object at hand when they are active. With regard to the five senses, seeing and hearing tend to be more general and encompassing, and the other three senses are more particular and material, more closely connected with matter, for they are in contact with the object while seeing and hearing work at a distance. Saint Augustine developed important views concerning the senses, making a distinction between common sensibles, or objects of sense perception, which can be sensed by more than one sense, like shape, which can be both seen and touched, and proper sensibles, which can be sensed only by one sense, such as color, which is perceived by sight. We tend to think of the senses as passive and the intellect as active, but the intellect, as we shall see, can be illuminated and the senses can be actively directed by the will or by the intention of the knowing subject. This means that in certain cases the senses can be active and the intellect can be passive.

Student: We use sense perception when the objects are actually present to the senses. What happens when they are absent?

Teacher: Once the object is absent, we can still retain sense data in the memory, although this is a general faculty since it can relate to sense data but also to universals. In other words, there can be memory of particulars or of universals. Memory can be rather active, as for instance productive memory, but it can also be rather passive, such as retentive, reproductive, or mechanical memory. Recollection is the act of memory in recalling things or events from the past. In addition there is imagination, which reproduces sense data in the absence of sense objects, and productive imagination, which combines them at will. Therefore we make a distinction between two kinds of imagination, one which we can call reproductive imagination and one that can be called creative or productive imagination.

Student: What else do we know about imagination? Does it work in coordination with other faculties besides the senses?

Teacher: Imagination stands in between sense perception and sensation on the one hand, and reason and understanding on the other. Imagination already takes a step back in relation to the data furnished by the senses. Imagination is related to image, which means that a connection with the senses, primarily sight, is generally assumed. Representation is related to imagination because it implies having an internal image, which is recollected.

Student: Which faculty comes after imagination in the process of knowing?

Teacher: We have an immediate kind of knowing, which is intuition, but intuition can use the data of the senses and also work with imagination or reason. Moving further from the particular and towards the universal we have understanding and reason. Judgment, which is applied to particular cases, is more specific than understanding or reason but works with or bases itself on both. Intuition can be closer to the senses or to the imagination, or to reason, because one can speak of an intellectual intuition or a rational intuition as much as an empirical intuition.

Student: What is the distinction between reason and understanding? I understand that they are the highest faculties of human cognition.

Teacher: We can follow the medieval model, which takes into account the etymology of these terms, and say that reason is discursive and understanding or intellect is a direct knowing of the object but presupposes the various stages attained by reason. Understanding or intelligizing means to grasp something in general; reasoning means to go through several propositions to reach a conclusion. It involves judgment. We can also think of reason as natural reason in opposition to faith or revelation.

Student: How does this relate to the classification used by Kant and Hegel?

Teacher: Kant held that the understanding, which operated in connection with empirical data, was reliable in furnishing knowledge and could be used in science. Therefore the understanding served in the process of knowing the sensible world, but reason had to do with universal principles, the knowledge of the thing in itself or immaterial objects. And Kant placed severe limits on reason. Hegel accepts the distinction between understanding and reason made by Kant, but he thinks of human reason as practically unlimited and thus capable of knowing reality itself. In fact, in Kant we find a reversal of the traditional order between the two kinds of thinking, reason and intellect, which goes back to Plato and is taken up by Aristotle. While Kant thinks of reason as going over and above the intellect, medieval philosophers thought of the intellect as the higher faculty of the two. Moreover, in medieval philosophy, the distinction between reason and intellect is basically a distinction between discursive and immediate knowing. Discursive thought is termed *dianoia* by Plato and immediate thought is termed *nous*, which is intellect or understanding, and the highest human faculty, as we have seen. This terminology is also used by Aristotle. Kant takes "reason" to mean intellect as the highest faculty of knowing, and "understanding" to mean a lower faculty, as we have seen. Regardless of the terminology, it is important to keep the distinction between discursive and non-discursive thinking. Therefore we prefer to use the ancient and medieval terminology, which keeps this distinction, instead of Kant's.

Student: With regard to the powers of reason, should we follow Kant in limiting them or should we adhere to Hegel's belief in unlimited rational powers?

Teacher: It is important to keep all options open for the intellect (Kant's reason) and not assume that it cannot know the thing in itself, because then we would be tied only to empirical data and we would not be able to say anything about the purely spiritual. This could lead to agnosticism, and to the denial that we can know metaphysical or spiritual truths. On the other hand Hegel believes in the unlimited powers of human reason. In this regard, a middle position between Kant and Hegel, perhaps represented by Aquinas, would be the golden mean regarding this question, given that human reason or intellect is limited but that this does not mean that it cannot know spiritual truths. In placing these limits, Kant is being influenced simultaneously by skepticism and empiricism, in a combination which limits the rightful scope of reason or the intellect.

Student: How may we distinguish the rational and the intellectual kinds of thinking today?

Teacher: It is quite clear that when we approach a problem from a philosophical perspective we may use an intuitive kind of thinking which is intellectual, but we can also use discursive reasoning, particularly if we employ logical reasoning. Mathematics, for instance, always requires a proof, and so implies discursive reasoning. Mathematics then is used in the sciences, while intuitive thinking could be more prevalent in the humanities and the arts. However, this does not mean that in the same art or science the two kinds of thinking cannot overlap. For instance, in thinking of a hypothesis or theory in science we are using intuitive thinking, and even in the humanities we use logic, which implies reasoning. When employing logic, which is a powerful tool in philosophy, we are using discursive reasoning, although philosophical thinking can be intuitive too. This was already clear to Aristotle and the medieval philosophers, as we have seen.

Student: Is one kind of thinking superior to the other?

Teacher: They complement each other. It is important to have intuition but it is also important to substantiate our claims with solid reasoning.

Student: Therefore knowledge is the object of the intellect?

Teacher: Yes, and in saying "knowledge" or "cognition" we mean the objects of knowledge. We could make a distinction between the process of cognition and the actual objects of knowledge but we can also understand these as interrelated concepts.

Student: What are the general characteristics of knowledge?

Teacher: Knowledge is generally opposed to opinion, which is an unfounded view or position, as we shall see. Knowledge must have theoretical or empirical confirmation, or both. Knowledge means certain knowledge. When we say that we know something, that something must be true or it must be the case. Knowing does not always imply or require empirical verification, as the empiricists or the verificationists (for instance in the Vienna Circle) would have it, but also there can be knowledge and certainty of intellectual and spiritual truths. In this case, logical and coherent reasoning provides the proof. It is important to stress that experience need not always be tied to the senses, but there is also intuitive or spiritual experience.

For Hegel, however, intuition lies in between sense perception and representation, which means that it is not related to reason. For him, images are more universal than is intuition.

Student: There is also a distinction between theoretical and practical knowledge, is there not?

Teacher: Knowledge can be practical but we usually think of knowledge as primarily theoretical, as involving concepts and ideas and theories. Ancient philosophers made practical knowledge or wisdom depend on theoretical knowledge; and it is right to make this assumption, for practice that is not grounded in theory could be misdirected or without a purpose or aim.

Student: Theoretical and practical knowledge are also respectively related to the intellect and the will, are they not?

Teacher: Knowledge is in principle related to the intellect in a general way, which means that both theoretical and practical knowledge depend on the intellect. However, practical knowledge also involves the action of the will. The will implies putting in practice the decisions of the intellect. This means that the will is like an associate of the intellect and works in conjunction with the intellect. We have also seen that according to Aquinas the truth is the proper object of the intellect, while the good is the proper object of the will. Therefore the intellect and the will work closely together. We can say that the will implements the decisions of the intellect, and that the intellect only becomes truly practical intellect through the will. So the will is also an essential part of the intellect or the intellective power.

Student: What is the relation between wisdom and knowledge? I assume that wisdom also includes a theoretical and a practical aspect, like the intellect?

Teacher: Wisdom is complete knowledge, and knowledge of the first principles, as it was clearly seen by Aquinas. It is knowledge of the spiritual and deepest truths but it is also a practical knowledge. It is therefore a knowledge that leads to a coherent and good practical life and thus includes both theoretical and practical knowledge. In a certain sense, wisdom is even above knowledge. Wisdom therefore is essential for the attainment of happiness in this life, because achieving this aim has a practical as well as a theoretical component.

Student: Could we add counsel to the aspects of subjective spirit and its acts?

Teacher: Counsel is the ability to put knowledge and wisdom into practice, in specific situations, so it is also important, and it allows us to distinguish right from wrong in concrete situations. It is important to mention that wisdom, understanding, counsel, and knowledge count in Christian theology among the gifts of the Holy Spirit, in addition to fortitude, piety, and fear of the Lord. The first four gifts direct the intellect towards God while the latter three direct the will towards God. Being gifts of the Holy Spirit means that they are prompted by the Holy Spirit.

Student: What about thinking and consciousness?

Teacher: Consciousness is an awareness of the object which is potentiality an object of knowing, therefore it accompanies all the actions of the faculties and all the acts of the mind. It accompanies feeling, sense perception, imagination, recollection, reason, and understanding. Consciousness is a general term indicating the activity of the mind. One might say that someone is conscious if their brain is working, so perhaps even in the sleeping state there is some conscious activity.

Student: Does this apply also to self-consciousness; is there self-consciousness every time we are conscious of something?

Teacher: When consciousness turns to itself and makes itself its own object, it is self-consciousness, it is aware of the "I," of the thinking subject. Therefore self-consciousness is more specific than consciousness. Whenever there is self-consciousness there is consciousness but not necessarily the other way around. According to Bradley, self-consciousness is the experience of both subject and object in one self.

Student: The concept of knowledge, and also spirit, has many associated terms and concepts. What do we say that thought is?

Teacher: Thought is more specific than consciousness because it is a reflective mode. This means that it is not simply sense perception or feeling, but something more specific and not directly related to matter. Thought does not imply the immediate presence of an object of the senses, but perhaps we can say that thought is already present at the level of memory, representation, and recollection. Thought can be related to images or it can be more abstract. Naturally, thought applies to reason and understanding. It is important to stress that the various activities of the mind are not strictly separate but they can work at the same time and towards the same end. They can be juxtaposed or combined, depending on the object being contemplated. A particular object can evoke a general concept or a universal, which means that we may sense and feel at the same time and we can even reason while we sense and feel something.

Student: Thought appears to be similar to consciousness. Perhaps consciousness is a form of thought, or thought implies consciousness?

Teacher: Thought implies consciousness but it is more abstract or less related to matter than is consciousness. Therefore, thought is more specific than consciousness. There can be consciousness without thought, especially in the case of sensation, which involves consciousness but not thought. And thought pertains to the general more than to the particular, given that the latter is more closely connected with the physical or material. Understanding and intelligizing go hand in hand and are modes of thought, and thought includes imagination in addition to reasoning and understanding. Thinking is the activity of thought, or active reason.

Student: It occurs to me that language is also an essential aspect of knowledge and thought.

Teacher: That is correct, and in fact in ancient Greek the term "logos" refers to reason and to language. When Aristotle says that a human being is a rational animal, this means also an animal which uses language.

Student: In what sense are reason and language related?

Teacher: There is clearly a close connection between language and the universal which is apparent in the way languages evolve and in the way they are used. Several philosophers connect the birth of language to the appearance of reason or abstract and universal concepts. While gestures, which may have been an early form of communication, can indicate single particulars, when we use verbal language we use terms that refer to many particulars, and therefore denote universals. We can use these general terms to describe single events or particular things, but those same terms can be rearranged to signify other events or particular things. Therefore, the main characteristic of language and its components (verbs, nouns, pronouns, adverbs, and so forth) is its universality. And the universal is, as we have seen, a product of reason and the intellect. Therefore language is closely tied to reason. Moreover, language is also related to thought. There are questions surrounding the relation between thought and language, or thought and the use of words. Some philosophers hold that it is not possible to think except through words. This may be the case if we conceive of thinking as something abstract. If we link thinking to the imagination, then surely it is possible to think by means of images, and in this case it is possible to think without words.

Student: Naturally, intelligence is related to thought and also to spirit?

Teacher: Yes, intelligence is the activity of reasoning or the content of thought. It can also mean the capacity for thinking or knowing, as well as the actual knowledge acquired by a thinking subject. Therefore it has at least three distinct meanings: the process of thinking, the ability to think and know, and the actual knowledge acquired through that process.

Student: I see how under the theory of knowledge we have described all the mental activities that lead to the acquisition of knowledge. How do all these activities of the mind relate to spirit?

Teacher: All these activities or operations of the mind are spiritual because they ultimately lead to knowledge, potentially at least, and knowledge implies the activity of the intellect, which is purely spiritual. It is true that activities such as sensation or feeling may have direct contact with matter, but ultimately the purpose of that contact is to lead to knowledge.

Student: Even the use of the senses always leads to knowledge?

Teacher: Philosophers have traditionally ascribed a twofold purpose to the senses: on the one hand, they help sentient beings to detect any potential harm or to seek a potential benefit with respect to their bodies. For instance, with the sense of taste we distinguish good food from food that has gone off or food which is not appropriate for human consumption. On the other hand, the senses ultimately lead to knowledge, as we have seen; but even the most basic use of the senses, which concerns the preservation of the body, leads to knowledge since that knowledge protects the body and human life. Therefore, all the operations of the mind which we have mentioned are spiritual in some way or other.

Student: Yes, and we have mentioned the main operations of the mind, but there are other acts of the mind which are related to the main operations or faculties which we have discussed. For instance, what is the role of attention and intention in the process of cognition?

Teacher: Attention is when our mind is focused on a particular object or a particular set of objects and other considerations recede into the background. Intention is the specific focus of attention, so it is more specific even than attention. Intention is a particular focus of our attention. We may be looking at a picture and in that sense our attention is focused on the picture. However, our focus is on a particular part or aspect of the picture and that is the intention of our focus on, or attention to, the picture, in this particular case.

Student: Intention also has a practical dimension, does it not?

Teacher: Yes, intention can be theoretical or practical. Theoretical intention relates to knowledge and the focus on an object of knowledge, while practical intention is an idea or goal which the subject wishes to put into practice. In its practical dimension, intention refers to the will. We can say that the intention is moved by the will. In its theoretical aspect, intention is the specific focus of the intellect. In its practical aspect, intention is the focus of the will. Moreover, in its practical aspect, intention is a final cause or purpose of action.

Intention also plays an important role when it comes to language. Verbal language is a very complex phenomenon. While its main purpose is to convey a message or information, there are many aspects that inform and specify this message. These aspects or circumstances are for instance context, such as the way of conveying it— for instance, the tone of voice, and the connotations of what is said through the choice of words used, and naturally, the intention of what is said. Therefore not all language is direct or literal, but there is much in language that is indirect and subliminal.

Student: When we speak of the mind it is difficult not to think about the soul, which was such an important theme from ancient to modern philosophy. Indeed what we call the operations of the mind were identified with the faculties of the soul. How does the soul fit into our conception of the theory and acquisition of knowledge?

Teacher: Indeed the human soul cannot be disregarded when we speak of the mind, in the sense that there is a clear connection between the two. Many current discussions about mind mirror or correspond to ancient, medieval, and modern discussions about the soul. In other words, to speak of mind today evokes previous discussions about the soul. Sometimes mind refers to the intellectual part of the soul, as we have seen, which means that "soul" is the broader concept of the two. Clearly the soul performs different operations and is related to the body while it has also a clear intellectual aspect. For our purposes, it is important to highlight what is specific to the soul, especially regarding the process of knowledge, and its relation to spirit, without delving into the various ancient and medieval discussions surrounding the faculties of the soul. We have seen that the soul is mind when we consider it from the perspective of the process of cognition. The soul displays other spiritual and religious aspects which it is important to mention.

Student: What are the specific spiritual and religious aspects of the soul?

Teacher: The concept of soul is fundamental in understanding human and individual personality. In this sense, soul is related to the self, the "I" as well as the knowing subject. The question of personality has religious significance. Moreover, with respect to the religious connotations, the soul can be defined in such a way as to favor a belief in its immortality, from a religious perspective and supported by logical arguments. The concept of soul should also embrace the concept of life, given that many philosophers have associated soul with life. The soul should be considered also in relation to the subject of all branches of psychology, and, from a philosophical perspective, it should be understood as a principle of knowledge. Finally, what ancient and medieval philosophers have said about the soul remains valid today, since the soul cannot be reduced to other principles. For instance, it cannot be reduced to a purely physical reality. In addition, it combines various aspects, such as personality, personal identity, and intelligence.

Student: Speaking of the soul in its cognitive function, there are acts of the mind which we could further discuss, such as belief and faith.

Teacher: Belief is a kind of thinking and it has a cognitive content. Faith is belief applied to supernatural truths. Faith can mean assent to a proposition, but also trust in a person or an authority, and especially trust with regard to religious truths. Faith is the foundational aspect or act of religion. Moreover, religion also has a cognitive content, which is especially explicit in theology, which consists in the explanation and articulation of dogmas in any given religion.

Student: If we mention the concept of belief, surely we must also speak about certainty?

Teacher: Certainty is closely connected with judgment, namely, it is a result of judgment and implies reaching a conclusion.

Student: How should we summarize the result of our findings concerning theory of knowledge?

Teacher: We cannot exclude the role of sense perception in obtaining knowledge and that means the role of the senses. This implies also that the object of learning is external to the mind, and thus the existence of matter must be assumed. Animals share with us the use of the senses, and in some cases have sharper senses than we have. It is clear that the senses help them to survive and to learn. The senses and their findings, what they perceive, point to the existence of matter.

Student: Yet we have seen that Berkeley holds that all impressions are created by God and are not caused by material objects which come in contact with the body and the senses.

Teacher: Berkeley was concerned with the spread of materialism, which he believed would lead to atheism, hence his efforts in denying the existence of matter. However, there is nothing intrinsically bad or negative about matter, and we can think of it as resulting from spirit, as being created in conjunction with form or forms or some kind of spiritual principle. It is more difficult to deny matter than to accept its existence in principle, not just when it comes to the theory of knowledge but also in the sciences. Taking away the existence of matter, and explaining its existence as a created impression on the part of God, leads to a very roundabout way of explaining reality. In other words, Berkeley defends the idea that the concept of matter is not necessary for the sciences, but it is not clear that it is possible to speak about the natural sciences and scientific theories and their findings without presupposing the existence of matter. Moreover, matter can be described in different ways as composed of particles, and mass can be associated with energy. There can be many ways of talking about matter. The important thing to keep in mind in considering matter is that it comes after spirit and must be subordinate to it. If we follow this principle there is no danger of materialism as Berkeley feared. Therefore we can conclude, regarding the theory of knowledge, that the nature of knowledge is spiritual since it is based on mental acts, discussed by us, which are spiritual to a greater or lesser degree. We can think of different types of knowledge, either more particular, such as a piece of information or a particular fact, or more general, such as the laws of physics. Philosophers tend to prefer universal knowledge, since it covers more particulars or cases than more specific knowledge. And this universal knowledge is purely spiritual, given that it is far removed from the senses and matter.

Student: You mentioned the fact that animals also possess and make use of the senses. Does this mean that they reach abstract knowledge?

Teacher: Biology has made great strides in its efforts to understand animal life and animal psychology. Animals are much more complex sentient beings than we used to think. Some develop a kind of language, and some make use of tools. Animals are probably capable of general thinking, given that, for instance, they recognize members of their own species. However, they are not capable of the same kind of abstract thinking as human beings, as we know.

Now that we have treated theory of knowledge with regard to the concept and role of spirit, we may turn to metaphysics and the presence of spirit in this discipline.

Metaphysics

Student: You mentioned that from our theory of knowledge we may deduce the existence of matter?

Teacher: Yes, in the sense that accepting the existence of matter makes more sense in connection with the sciences, which means that taking away matter makes scientific explanation much more difficult and complicated, if not impossible. In fact, the natural sciences deal with the material world, although scientific theories themselves are not material but spiritual. It also makes sense to accept the existence of matter in the context of the theory of knowledge, as we have seen. Otherwise it is difficult to explain the difference between the senses and imagination, for instance. Therefore it is natural to assume the existence of matter also in metaphysics. Then we have to articulate the existence of matter with spirit, which has also been proved by the theory of knowledge. Returning to the question of matter, we have seen that philosophers such as Aquinas and Hegel did not deny the existence of matter. A certain rejection or abhorrence of the material led to a kind of dualism with regard to reality. We do not find a dualism in Berkeley because he explains what many philosophers consider to be material, or to be linked to the material, in a spiritual way. We have seen how he holds that any kind of perception, including sense perception, is a spiritual experience. In addition, he does not accept the existence of abstract ideas, although he accepts general ideas, which are not so far removed from sense perception. Moreover, he cancels the difference between sensation and thought and thinks of any kind of perception as spiritual, and he thinks of the objects of perception as ideas. All that exists are ideas or minds, which is to say, active or passive spirit. For Berkeley, everything is purely spiritual, and therefore there is no dualism between matter and spirit. If we do not wish to deny the existence of matter, we can avoid this kind of dualism by taking one of these realities as dominant or prevalent. We consider the prevalent reality to be spirit.

Student: You mentioned a certain kind of dualism which is associated with the repugnance of matter?

Teacher: This dualism was to be found in Antiquity and in the Middle Ages, often in connection with religion or a radical interpretation of it. Certain strands of Gnosticism advocate a way of salvation through knowledge, and by avoiding the material world. We saw that Manicheism, a religion which claimed to proceed from Christianity and to follow Christianity, also held a dualistic worldview in which the material was acknowledged but repudiated; this implied, in addition, a disdain of the body and of bodily functions. They did not deny the existence of a material principle, which they considered inferior to the spiritual principle. However, the material and the spiritual did not coexist harmoniously but they were ever fighting each other, and it was not clear how they were related or how they interacted with each other. There were other versions of these dualistic philosophies during the Middle Ages, namely those proposed by the Albigensians and the Cathars. These positions were rejected by the Church because they assumed that creation was bad, especially material creation, in contrast to the scriptural message to the effect that all of creation was good.

Therefore the rejection of matter in this way is not helpful and does not explain natural phenomena or even reality as whole.

Student: We have mentioned some materialistic philosophies.

Teacher: There are also materialistic philosophies but these are unable adequately to explain the emergence of the spiritual. We will also see that a purely materialistic approach cannot account for the spiritual in itself or for the ethical, which is one of the main aspects of the meaning of spirit. The ethical meaning of spirit is apparent, as we have seen, in Socrates and in Plato in connection with the question of the purpose and the final cause. We can only think of morality and the ethical in connection with a purpose which is good. We are no longer looking at the mechanical and efficient causes but the goal and the purpose of an action, and in ethics the question of intention is extremely important, as we have seen.

Student: How should we consider matter if we wish to have greater detail? Where does the study of matter belong?

Teacher: In Aristotle, the study of matter, given that it does not exist by itself but actually exists in nature through form, is part of metaphysics. Today, it should be studied by philosophy of physics. Following modern philosophical considerations, it is generally thought that matter is solid, extended, and divisible. In a certain sense, contemporary science looks at matter in a way that could be compared to that of the Presocratics, in the sense that it involves an assumption of the existence of matter, sometimes leading to materialism (which is a philosophical position), based on an empirical observation of reality. According to modern science, matter is composed of atoms, which are divisible and made up of several further components. These components become more and more complex and diversified. The scientific method is still in force, since the birth of modern science, and the proof of those theories relies on empirical testing of scientific theories, which is to say that scientific theories are only confirmed through experimentation.

Student: There have been different views on matter among ancient and medieval philosophers, which leads us to think that matter is a complex concept that keeps changing.

Teacher: Yes, and not least in contemporary science, since new elements are regularly being discovered. We can leave this discussion until later, when we study the philosophy of science. At the level of metaphysics, it is important to assume that matter exists, since this is in line with the principles of the sciences. We have seen that to try to explain natural and physical phenomena without having recourse to the concept of matter is more complicated than to assume matter, and this shows that matter truly exists.

Student: You have stated that metaphysics also explains the articulation between matter and spirit. How does matter relate to spirit?

Teacher: As we have seen, we cannot abstract from the thinking subject or the conditions of knowledge. This means that the spiritual element must always be taken into account, even when we are talking about matter and about natural phenomena. In studying reality and in the cognition of reality we must take into account the subject and the circumstances in which it finds itself. This does not detract from the testimony of the senses or even from common sense. We know that other animals perceive the world surrounding them in different ways from ours, hence the need to take the circumstances of the subject into account. Naturally, we can also take account of the characteristics of the subject, but in our case it is clearly always the human subject who is carrying out the investigation.

Student: Taking into account the human subject implies the prevalence of the spiritual, does it not?

Teacher: That is right. Knowledge is about theories, and scientific knowledge is about theories. One can also have knowledge of particular facts, but we only truly understand a general fact if we can explain it as part of a theory, whether we speak of the natural or the social sciences. Knowledge is about theories. Therefore the spiritual element must prevail.

Matter can be seen as something solid, extended, and perceived by the senses, or, if we follow contemporary scientific theories, as being composed of different elements, but in metaphysics matter must be seen as coming after spirit. In reality we find both material and spiritual things or substances, and the spiritual cannot be disregarded. Spiritual and material are integrated in reality, but in our approach to the world, the intellectual and spiritual prevail, even if many scientific theories are based on sense perception and the assumption of the basic reality of matter.

Student: What can we say more specifically about the spiritual aspect of reality in metaphysics?

Teacher: While theory of knowledge deals with subjective spirit, metaphysics and logic deal with objective spirit. The rules of logic constitute or inform objective spirit. We have seen that objective spirit is the object or the objects of subjective spirit, the subject matter of subjective spirit or the knowing subject.

Student: If objective spirit is the subject matter of metaphysics, what are the elements of objective spirit?

Teacher: The objects of objective spirit are, for instance, ideas, theories, concepts, rules of logic, or the laws of nature.

Student: How can we define ideas?

Teacher: An idea is a general term to designate the object of thought and it can apply to several aspects of objective spirit. We can take "idea" in a broader sense than Plato's ideas, which applied to concepts, qualities, accidents, and were considered to be eternal.

Student: In that case, what is the general meaning of idea?

Teacher: An idea can, for instance, mean a solution to a present problem. Moreover, ideas do not always apply to single concepts but can include a set of concepts. In this sense, there are simple and complex ideas. Ideas can be definitions, theories, theorems, and so an idea can be a combination of concepts. They are no longer directly related to sense perception and can represent a synthesis of several concepts. In a certain sense they can be the picture of something we have seen or perceived, which is closer to the original Greek meaning of the word, as "image." In Greek, the word "idea" is related to the verb "to see." Idea is, moreover, related to intention and plan.

Therefore idea usually relates to the intellect rather than to the imagination, but for some philosophers it can mean also something that is imagined. For our purposes we prefer the more rationalist meaning. Idea is also rather active than passive.

Student: Is an idea always active? And what does it mean to say that it is active?

Teacher: An idea is active in the sense that it describes a certain reality and it can lead to action. It is also active given its close connection with action, as the product of the activity of thinking. Therefore, an idea is active insofar as it can be productive and as the result of reflection. However, sometimes we have the impression of an idea imposing itself on us like evidence, suggesting that it is passive, or rather that we are passive in the face of an idea that imposes itself. Idea is also related to ideal, which is a more complex idea involving several concepts. An idea can be a paradigm or a pattern, too.

Student: Among the objects of the intellect are concepts.

Teacher: Like ideas, concepts are devised by the mind—for a concept is something conceived by the mind—but they are usually more specific than ideas. An idea can comprise several concepts. Concepts usually refer to single terms, and they generally go hand in hand with definitions, although definitions tend to be more precisely formulated than concepts. A definition involves different terms while concepts may be translated into an equivalent term.

Student: What do we say about theories?

Teacher: A theory is a set of concepts about something, with the aim of explaining a phenomenon or a set of phenomena. Theories can be found in any domain, such as science or the humanities and the social sciences.

The rules of logic are also part of objective spirit, as we have seen. To sum up, the contents of objective spirit constitute the object of subjective spirit and they structure subjective spirit.

In this way we can say that subjective and objective spirit are the same insofar as they are interrelated and mutually imply each other. There is no subjective spirit without a content, without objective spirit. The contents of objective spirit are what they are in themselves as they are for subjective spirit, which means that objective spirit inheres in subjective spirit and subjective spirit exists in objective spirit. We can think of the intellect as at rest or nearly at rest considered in itself, as a self-contained reality, but in principle subjective and objective spirit imply each other.

Student: If subjective and objective spirit are so closely related, how else can we distinguish them?

Teacher: Subjective spirit is always somehow active, as long as there is consciousness, and even if the intellectual part is not active. In turn, objective spirit does not exist independently of a spirit, which is to say, independently of a subject. These ideas or concepts exist in a divine mind even if they do not exist in the human mind. We can also think of subjective spirit as active in thinking ideas, and objective spirit as passive when it is thought of. Even if in receiving ideas subjective spirit can be seen as passive, it is actively receiving them. In a metaphorical way objective spirit is active in the sense that it can be a paradigm for action. The divine mind is also subjective spirit, obviously, because it is active and thinks itself and it thinks objective spirit, and it creates objective and finite subjective spirit.

Student: What is the object of the intellect? Is it the same as the object of subjective spirit?

Teacher: The object of the intellect is specifically the truth, according to the medieval philosophers, following in the footsteps of Aristotle. Equally, the good is the object of the will, but in a certain way, we could say that the goal of the intellect is the truth and its object is anything it thinks about. Aquinas holds that the object of the intellect is simpler and more absolute than the object of the will. However, the objects of the will and the intellect are shared, for the true is good, and the good is true. The objects of the will and the intellect include beliefs and opinions, and not just proven truths.

Student: We have spoken about the difference between knowledge and opinion. What is an opinion, exactly speaking?

Teacher: It is important to distinguish opinion from knowledge, as we have seen. Knowledge entails a proof, more so even than certainty. It is possible to invoke certainty without having knowledge, which means that certainty is a personal conviction. However, when we use the term "certain" properly it means that that which is certain is verified. An opinion ranks below knowledge in terms of proof, or rather because of the lack of it, but an opinion may lead to knowledge, hence its significance. An opinion is an unfounded idea, but in science it can constitute a hypothesis, and therefore opinions are very important in the process leading up to knowledge.

Student: We have explained the presence of spirit in metaphysics as subjective and objective spirit, as well as absolute spirit. These aspects of spirit are also part of theory of knowledge. I wonder what is specifically metaphysical regarding spirit?

Teacher: We say that metaphysics studies reality. How do we describe reality? It is spirit. As Hegel said, the real is the rational and the rational is real. We have seen that matter should not be denied but its origin is from spirit, especially if we think of creation according to a plan and a design. We approached the question of knowledge from a spiritual perspective because knowledge and perception are spiritual. Spiritual here, in epistemology, means that it originates from the subject, from the "I," which construes knowledge even if it is originally based on sense perception.

We have seen that matter is also part of reality. The study of matter in general can be undertaken in physics or philosophy of physics, or philosophy of nature, which is a more general consideration about nature and the natural sciences. The study of matter is not out of place in metaphysics, nor is the question of causality, which as we have seen is both a physical and a metaphysical question for Aristotle. In addition to matter, metaphysics studies being and spirit. Being is an abstract category, as we have seen, which does not stand alone. In order to avoid any kind of dualism, such as a dualism between spirit and matter as irreducible to each other, or between the mind and the body, one principle must prevail over the other. Consequently, spirit is seen to prevail over matter, and matter is seen to be reducible to spirit, especially in knowledge, which is the level at which we communicate and act and operate. To conclude, metaphysics studies spirit and matter, or spiritual and material being.

Student: What is the difference between being and existence?

Teacher: The two terms overlap, but "existence" is arguably more specific, dealing with concrete being, while "being" is more general. Existence could almost be identified with sensible existence but that is not always the case, as, for instance, when we talk about the proofs of God's existence. Therefore existence is concrete being or autonomous being or subsistent being. Being, as we have seen, is a very broad concept. When we try to conceive being we cannot go any further without adding some qualification, and naturally, we think primarily of material or spiritual being, or both.

Student: Do we say that all spiritual being is mental?

Teacher: We have seen that spiritual being is mental, but reality itself is spirit, which means that spirit surpasses the confines of a finite mind although it does not go beyond the reality of absolute spirit, which encompasses all spirit and all reality. More specifically, we can say that objective spirit is mental, which is to say that the object of the subjective spirit is mental; it exists in the mind. Spirit always exists for a subject and in that sense the spiritual is the mental. If we said that the content or contents of the mind subsisted by themselves independently of a subject we would have to subscribe to Plato's theory of forms, which is supported by a narrative that does not have a place here. Where spiritual being subsists alone is in the case of absolute spirit, although we can say that it does not exist without being thought, since absolute spirit thinks itself and it thinks all spirit, subjective and objective. All objective spirit is thought by some subject, but not necessarily by the human subjective spirit.

Student: You have said that metaphysics deals primarily with objective spirit, while subjective spirit is the subject matter of theory of knowledge.

Teacher: Metaphysics deals primarily with objective spirit—in addition to matter—which is all reality there is, spirit and matter. Matter, as we have seen, is reducible to spirit, although we must not deny its existence. It must be reduced to spirit because it is for us, and for a subject, in so far as it is perceived or thought. Matter comes after spirit and results from it, as we have seen. Subjective spirit, in the sense of human spirit, is primarily the domain of theory of knowledge. Absolute spirit is also a subject, but it is an absolute subject which thinks the object absolutely, from all angles. Therefore, metaphysics deals primarily with objective spirit and with absolute spirit. We could also say that philosophy of religion or theology deals with absolute spirit, but as we have seen, metaphysics has a stake in every philosophical discipline since it thinks about the principles of every discipline.

Student: How do the two disciplines, theology and metaphysics, relate in dealing with absolute spirit?

Teacher: Philosophy can speak of absolute spirit in a general way, as infinite spirit, as both subjective (and active) spirit, and as objective spirit (as capable of being known). However, scripture gives us more detail about this absolute spirit, and therefore we should not disregard these data furnished by scripture and analyzed by religious or scriptural theology (or sacred doctrine). This means that for a complete picture of spirit, especially absolute spirit, theology complements philosophy. In this and in other matters, philosophy does not replace scripture or religion.

Student: While philosophy and theology (as sacred doctrine rather than philosophical theology) are two clearly separate disciplines, philosophy of religion combines
the two perspectives, the philosophical and the religious, does it not?
Teacher: Naturally, philosophy of religion combines the two disciplines, religion and
philosophy, but theology is independent of philosophy, while philosophy of religion
is a discipline within philosophy. Because religion is based on scripture, philosophy
of religion does not disregard scripture. In addition, theology constitutes a rational
understanding of religion and an analysis of scripture in rational terms, hence theology and philosophy of religion overlap in many senses. They have their own specifici-
ties, naturally; in some cases, philosophy of religion seems to be an analysis that is
external to religious belief, and not an internal perspective on religion, from the point
of view of the faithful. While philosophy of religion builds a bridge between religion
or theology and philosophy, sometimes it sides with philosophy rather than with religion.
Student: At any rate, you said that philosophy and theology complement each other.
Teacher: We can say that they complement each other, since philosophy offers a
rational perspective on spirit, and theology or religion gives us an insight into the
nature of God as spirit, and into creation.

Philosophy was particularly influenced by religion and theology in the Middle
Ages, but in ancient Greece a religious influence on philosophy was also present. In
the modern period the religious considerations are extremely important for philosophy and there is a debate on medieval categories of thought even in Leibniz and
Berkeley.

In addition, it can be said that both religion and philosophy share the same subject. All sciences treat of reality, but each from its own perspective. Philosophy and
religion look at all of reality, and at different kinds of being or intellect and spirit.
Even if much of philosophy has abandoned its ties with theology, the link between
the two disciplines has not disappeared.

For our purposes, however, we must focus on philosophy, since the subject of
our discussion is spirit in philosophy. This may mean using different terms to designate the same reality. We can say God or absolute spirit and mean the same reality by
the different appellations.

Student: What does philosophy, or specifically metaphysics, have to say about absolute spirit?

Teacher: We have seen that absolute spirit is subjective spirit because it is a knowing subject and it contains objective spirit. It is the cause of both finite subjective spirit and objective spirit. In religion, the fact that absolute spirit creates finite subjective spirit is expressed by saying that God creates the soul. The soul, as we know, is the seat of the intellect and of the other faculties. And God is the creator of life, which means that any kind of perception and imagination, and life in general, proceeds from absolute spirit, in the way that the finite comes from the infinite.

We must adhere to the principle which states there is nothing in the effect which is not in the cause, which goes back to ancient philosophy. We can observe this principle at different levels. We can speak about reality, physical or otherwise, and say that there is nothing in the effect which is not in the cause. In logic, for instance, we can say that there is nothing in the conclusion which is not in the premises, unless we have an invalid kind of reasoning or syllogism. Indeed, logical deduction is a kind of causality, and an example of causality. We have seen that the logical mirrors reality and vice versa, and this is another way of saying that the rational is real. The structure of reality is spiritual, otherwise we would not be able to understand it. This is how subjective spirit meets objective spirit.

Student: You have said that the subject matter of metaphysics is primarily objective spirit and absolute spirit. However, we have also seen that the three kinds of spirit are related to one another. How does subjective spirit relate to objective spirit from the perspective of metaphysics?

Teacher: Subjective spirit can only be understood in association with objective spirit, not only for the purpose of cognition but also for practical purposes. In this sense, subjective spirit is also the principle of activity and of freedom in general. The subject is that which actively knows and acts. Acting is based on willing and willing is based on knowing. It follows that God is subjective spirit, and it is infinite subjective spirit, unlike human beings, who constitute finite subjective spirit, or rather spirits, as we have seen. Absolute spirit naturally implies absolute knowledge and a perfect will, and perfect freedom, which is lacking in other subjects. Absolute spirit is omniscient and omnipotent, since action by absolute spirit is spiritual and commensurate with the level of an infinite intelligence. There is therefore no limit to God's knowledge, power and goodness. Absolute spirit is infinite spirit. Infinite here means complete and fulfilled, not infinite in the sense of incomplete and imperfect. God is also objective spirit, and in two ways. God is the object of knowledge by human beings and other intellects. God also contains all forms of objective spirit and is in this way an exemplar cause and formal cause, if we were to speak in Aristotelian terms. God contains and is the cause of all the perfection and forms of objective spirit, such as ideas, concepts, and theories. However, these are known by him not in stages and imperfectly as we do, but all at once. Infinitude means perfection and transcendence. Consequently absolute spirit means infinite subjective and infinite objective spirit, comprising them both as absolute spirit.

Student: How does absolute spirit relate to finite human spirit, since the former is infinite and the latter is finite?

Teacher: We have seen that in addition to creating or causing finite spirit, absolute spirit also causes the elements of objective spirit that exist in human minds and illuminates the subjective spirit. These are the three ways in which absolute spirit is active in subjective finite human spirit.

Student: And how does absolute spirit relate to reality?

Teacher: Since absolute spirit creates reality by his intellect, he is the cause of reality and all existing things, both material and spiritual. Absolute spirit is cause, and it is the absolute cause of objective spirit, too.

Student: Some philosophers have questioned the link between cause and effect, noticeably Hume, and within medieval Islamic thought, the theologian al-Ghazali.

Teacher: Yes, Hume questioned the link between cause and effect based on his conviction regarding the limits of the human understanding. Al-Ghazali questioned the principle of causality on theological grounds. Al-Ghazali did not wish to exclude the possibility of miracles and therefore determined that all causation is divine. For him, there was no cause other than God, such as human or natural causes. In this way, he denied secondary causality, as for him there was only primary or divine causation or causality. However, both al-Ghazali and Hume admitted the link between cause and effect as something that can be expected, since it is habitually observed. This means that the link between cause and effect comes from the habit of seeing the effect succeed the cause. Hume approached the question from an epistemological point of view, while al-Ghazali approached it from a theological or metaphysical perspective.

Hume, who was an empiricist, held that when we see a succession of events, we do not necessarily see a relation of cause and effect. What we see is the succession between what we consider to be a cause and what we believe to be its effect. His objection had something to do with his belief that causation was a metaphysical assumption and therefore not compatible with his empiricist assumptions.

Student: How can we be certain that a succession between two things constitutes an example of causality, in which an effect is produced by a cause?

Teacher: We must assume causality as the production of certain things by others. How do we know that we are not merely observing a succession of events but a relaying of the cause to the effect? We see that the effect, if it exists before the cause, comes to possess characteristics which belong to the cause and which the effect did not initially have. To illustrate my meaning, a hot object can cause heat in a different object, and the heat is passed on from the cause to the effect. If we speak of events, this can also be observed as a transmission of forces, for instance if someone sets a ball rolling. A stronger example of causality is when the effect does not exist without or before its cause, for instance in the case of the child and its parents.

Student: We have seen that the law of causality applies in different philosophical disciplines.

Teacher: That is correct, and where the theory of causality is most obvious is in metaphysics and in theory of knowledge, but also in logic, as we have seen. We saw that causality is discussed by Aristotle in his *Physics* and in his *Metaphysics*. Causality is observable in physical and in natural reality, and also in metaphysical reality, or reality in an absolute sense. Within logic, causality is observable in the relation between premises and conclusion, as the premises are the cause of the conclusion. In logical deduction the principles are seen to be the cause of the conclusion. What does cause mean? It means that one thing comes from another such that it could not have come from other than that cause. Therefore the link between cause and effect is not casual but necessary. If it is casual, there is no causality, or there is no way to prove the link between cause and effect. Consequently, there is a necessary connection between cause and effect. The cause determines the coming into being of the effect absolutely or in a certain way, that is, it determines that it has certain qualities. Causation can moreover apply to events or substances, things.

Student: What kind of causality should we consider?

Teacher: We can roughly distinguish between two kinds of causality, material and spiritual or intellectual. If we seek to expand on this twofold causality on the basis of Aristotle's theory of causality, we can say that the material cause corresponds to material causality, in the sense of matter coming from matter (although not without the assistance of the other types of cause), and the other three causes (the efficient, the formal, and the final cause) illustrate spiritual causality. The efficient cause can use matter or not, and so be considered in alliance with the material cause, as when a material object or artifact is produced. The formal and the final causes by themselves appear to be most truly spiritual. The final cause or goal or purpose can also be called an ideal, that which is to be achieved or aimed at. The formal cause means that some quality or concept is causative. Formal cause strongly indicates spiritual causality, although one could add that according to the medieval philosophers, the forms (whatever kind of universals they represent) are not causative by themselves except through God, who applies those forms for creation. God is cause of material things and is in them in a formal way by his power. He is in everything by his essence, power and presence.

Student: How do the two main aspects of causality, material and spiritual, interact?

Teacher: Given the predominance of the spiritual aspect, material causality goes hand in hand with and is subsumed under spiritual causality, in the form of universal concepts or the laws of nature. Even if we cannot always determine the exact causes of a particular natural phenomenon, that phenomenon is due to and explainable by some law or principle or theory. The laws of nature do not simply explain natural phenomena, they actually govern them. Therefore the material cause and effect come under a theory or principle which is the governing spiritual law. This is how we should consider the philosophy of nature. Naturally, when operating within their domain, the particular natural sciences should assume the existence of matter and need not constantly concern themselves about the philosophical aspects of the theories (this is a task for philosophy of science and the philosophies of the particular sciences). However, the intellectual principles are evident.

Student: Is it possible to think of a predominance of the spiritual with regard to the material without presupposing an absolute spirit?

Teacher: Absolute spirit is also infinite subjective spirit and infinite objective spirit, as we have seen. If we rely solely on finite subjective spirit and objective spirit, it is clear that objective spirit and material reality are always greater than finite subjective spirit. This would correspond to some kind of qualified realist position, in the sense that reality is greater than what we know and it is greater than what can be known. This means that something is left unexplained and unaccounted for, that a gap remains between finite subjective spirit and objective spirit, and objective spirit is always beyond the ken of finite subjective spirit. This limited realist position could potentially lead to skepticism or relativism. Paradoxically, also, a limited realist position is not entirely dissimilar to a kind of limited or subjective idealism, since in both cases reality or some part of it remains beyond the ken of the knowing subject, which in this case is finite subjective spirit. The only way to guarantee a link between subjective and objective spirit is through the assumption of an absolute spirit who is infinite subjective spirit and infinite objective spirit. This infinite spirit links subjective and objective spirit in an absolute way, on the one hand, since it encompasses them both, and it also ensures the connection between finite subjective spirit and objective spirit; it is the guarantor of the possibility of knowledge. To sum up, absolute spirit explains the correspondence between subjective spirit and objective spirit and encompasses both, as we have seen.

Student: I can see that the assumption of an absolute spirit as you have described it also ensures the prevalence of the spiritual as the absolute category and the absolute reality. With an absolute spirit we have an absolute spiritual principle of reality and knowledge. However, I wonder whether we have completely disproved a materialist position. If we wanted to take a materialist position, could we not say that our knowledge simply mirrors reality, which is material, and derives from that material reality, and that knowledge and the mind can be also understood in a materialistic way as having a complete physical expression in the brain?

Teacher: In principle one might defend that position, but we have seen that we cannot abstract from the knowing subject and therefore from spirit as our starting point. One could argue that this is a chronological order and not the order of reality, and that once we know it becomes clear that reality is material, but I believe that in the process of cognition the spiritual foundation of the subject always accompanies the process of knowledge, which means that spiritual reality always precedes material reality. This holds both for finite subjective spirit and for the absolute spirit, which is purely spiritual but is also, in its spiritual capacity, cause of the material reality.

Student: How does the principle of the primacy of the subject revert to a spiritualist position?

Teacher: In our case, as finite subjective spirits, we must include in our findings the fact that we know, as subjects, and what we know. In the case of absolute spirit, God enjoys an absolute point of view and so he knows everything. We are limited and finite and that has to be taken into account in the process of knowing and in our findings. This does not mean that we cannot know or that our knowledge is not true, which is a contradiction in terms, but that we must take those limitations into account and not assume an absolute point of view on our part. However, we must assume it in the case of absolute spirit. Absolute spirit represents absolute reality and absolute knowing. Generally speaking, knowledge is not without a subject and that subject is always spiritual.

Student: With regard to the question of knowledge, how does the absolute spirit relate to the finite subjective spirit?

Teacher: We do not have an absolute point of view, but we must assume the existence of an absolute point of view; otherwise our findings, in spite of any progress made, will not be closer to complete knowing. In this way, our knowledge is ensured by that absolute spirit and by the assumption of an absolute spirit and an absolute knowing.

Student: It is clearly difficult completely to separate metaphysics from theory of knowledge if we accept the import of spirit, but what can we say about the prevalence of spirit in metaphysics?

Teacher: Yes, the link between the theory of knowledge and metaphysics is very close indeed, but in metaphysics we can say that the rational is real and the real is rational, following Hegel's motto. Moreover, without the notion of reality as rational, and as reverting to one infinite being which is absolute reason, knowledge would be impossible.

Student: If we assume the prevalence of the spiritual in metaphysics and in theory of knowledge, this principle must extend to the other disciplines, too.

Teacher: Yes, the acknowledgment of the spiritual as an absolute principle must be generally assumed, but it is also important to stress the autonomy of the various disciplines. Philosophy thinks freely about the principles of reality and of knowledge. However, each discipline has its domain and naturally the different disciplines contribute to each other and enrich each other. On the other hand, they must have freedom to operate according to their principles, which in the sciences is related to experimentation and observation. In addition, the natural sciences deal with material reality. The theories about nature are themselves intellectual constructs, but those constructs concern the nature of material reality.

Student: I understand that a limited kind of realism, which separates the subject from the object of knowledge, is not unrelated to subjective idealism. Similarly, objective or absolute idealism can become a kind of absolute realism, where reality can be known in its totality by some mind and equally exists for some mind. However, an idealist position can be criticized for its effects on the finite subjective spirit. One of the accusations that can be leveled at idealism, for instance, is that is promotes laziness when it comes to cognition, since we can never go beyond our thoughts.

Teacher: That criticism could only apply to subjective idealism. With absolute idealism, it is quite the opposite, since we know at the same time the limitations of our knowledge but also the capacity to progress, as well as the existence of an absolute spirit. Therefore, we will always be seeking further knowledge. And knowing that there is an absolute spirit that is omniscient and from whose knowledge we benefit will also prompt us to further our aims and goals and our efforts to obtain knowledge. Idealism is not a denial of reality or that reality can be known. It is the affirmation that reality is rational or spiritual and it can be known wholly or in part. Our knowledge can certainly progress since there is an absolute mind which knows everything and shares its knowledge with us. There are other kinds of idealism, stating that the thing in itself cannot be known. But this is idealism mingled with skepticism.

Idealism does not deny the existence of things or the reality of creation. We know that spirit exists, and this alone would safeguard the existence of reality. In addition, we do say that matter exists and is perceived and is part of reality.

Student: How can we summarize our views on spirit in metaphysics?

Teacher: To sum up, spirit is ultimate reality. There is one spirit, absolute spirit or God, to which other spirits are related. Metaphysics contains the doctrine of being and reality, and also the doctrine of spirit in the sense that spirit is real and reality is spiritual. This is why metaphysics and theory of knowledge go hand in hand, and they cannot be separated. This principle extends to the sciences, which first formulate a hypothesis that is then confirmed by experience. The spiritual is the first element in science too. Moreover, recent research in science appears to favor idealism in the sense of stressing the knowing subject.

Student: If we say that science is close to a materialist or at least an empiricist position, how can we include idealism in this picture of the natural sciences?

Teacher: Contemporary science does not talk about absolute space and time, which was such an important part of the structure of modern science and philosophical reflection about modern science; rather, it discusses relative time and space. In quantum physics also the perspective of observation is not without its effects, and one cannot separate the knowing subject from the object observed. Therefore the subject must be taken into account in its observations, its hypotheses, and its theories. After dealing with spirit within theory of knowledge and metaphysics we turn to another important subject, namely ethics.

Ethics

Student: Ethics is a pivotal philosophical discipline, and its significance remains central within philosophy today. You have mentioned how the survival of any ethics, and even morality, comes down to the role of spirit, indeed the primacy of spirit, in ethics.

Teacher: Yes, ethics remains a central part of philosophy and a fundamental element in human society, and spirit plays a fundamental role in ethics. This is the case in modern ethics, and also in virtue ethics, which is characteristic of the ancient and the medieval period although there has been a revival of virtue ethics in contemporary philosophy. Obviously, ethics is one of the domains where the spiritual is most obvious. It is not possible to defend a materialistic ethics; or rather we can say that a materialistic ethics is a contradiction in terms. Ethics is a complex discipline within philosophy and its various aspects are related to spirit rather than matter.

Student: How can we explain the presence of the spiritual in ethics?

Teacher: If we revert to the famous passage towards the end of the *Phaedo* where Socrates offers his assessment of Anaxagoras' philosophy, it is clear that ethics, which studies relations between human beings and the concepts of right and wrong, of goodness and virtue, is guided by the notion of the good as a purpose. Ethics describes not what is the case but what ought to be the case. In this passage Socrates stresses the final cause or the goal, which is what is to be sought, and that goal is the good. In ethics we do not look for the efficient cause of action but for the final cause, which in this case is the intention. Socrates states that he is in prison not because his muscles brought him there but because he thought it was right and good to be there and to accept the verdict of the Athenians, unfair as it was. Naturally, action that is guided by the final cause or the purpose, under the aspect of the good, reveals the prevalence of spirit, which is that which recognizes the truth and the good. Having recognized that the object of the intellect is the truth, the implementation of the good results from the recognition of the good as real and as achievable.

In the *Phaedo*, Socrates evokes the final cause and the goal, in contradistinction to the efficient cause. In human action, which is typically intentional, a good must be achieved. Ethical action and moral action are means to attain a certain good, for ourselves or others, and this good must be spiritual and must take the whole into account. Good guides action and this is, as we have seen, a general and a spiritual principle. The good is one of the transcendentals which surpass even the most general categories as conceived by Aristotle. Ethics focuses on the will and the choice of good as opposed to evil. We have seen that it depends on the intellect since we can only choose or judge that which we know or we think we know, in other words, that which we perceive.

Student: How does the final cause, which you said is an eminently spiritual cause, relate to the other causes in ethics?

Teacher: The final cause is the most important one in ethics. It is the goal of the action, the intention to do something. The formal cause is central in the sense that it constitutes the idea or goal which is to be achieved; in other words, it is the form or the idea which is to be implemented. This shows a very close link between the formal and the final cause. Sometimes, the final cause is the intention to implement an idea, which is the formal cause. The final cause is also important as managing or informing the efficient cause. The efficient cause is preceded by an intention and in this way it is preceded by the final cause. Some medieval philosophers, for instance Avicenna, stated that the final cause is the efficient cause of the efficient cause. For instance, if someone wishes to carry out an action, the purpose will set the action in motion, and thus it effects the efficient cause or begins the process to be undertaken by the effi-

cient cause. Let us say that there are many actions one can carry out; it is the intention which selects which of the possibilities will come true.

Student: Is it correct to say that the material cause also has a role to play in ethical
action?

Teacher: The material cause can also be important. In the *Phaedo*, Socrates says that
he cannot be in prison unless he has muscles to carry him there, so that the material
cause is an instrumental cause. The material cause is a necessary cause in some cases,
and the action cannot be carried out without it, but it is not a sufficient cause, as it
does not by itself determine the action.

Student: I understand that the final cause is the central cause in ethical theory. I
wonder about the connection between the final and the other causes in determining
human action.

Teacher: In ethics the determining cause is the final cause or intention, as we have
seen. However, the formal cause is also essential in this process, although it is associated with cognition and theory of knowledge. In carrying out an action, one first
forms an idea and then the intention to carry it out is put into practice, as we have
seen. First comes the idea, which is the formal cause, followed by the intention or
plan to carry it out, which consists in the intention. We first find the action of the
intellect and then the will, informed by the intellect; they produce respectively the
knowledge and the intention. First the intellect and then the will determine action,
and these correspond respectively to the formal and the final cause or purpose. This
order mirrors the traditional connection between the theoretical and the practical
order, the former being followed by the latter. Then the efficient cause and the material causes are subordinate to the formal and the final cause, and they concern the
material execution. To sum up this process, the intellect moves the will, which is
helped by and employs the efficient and the material causes. The material cause in
ethical action is instrumental and it is a subordinate cause because it is at the service
of the efficient cause. Ethical action relies on the final cause, which is especially
spiritual. The material aspect plays a supporting role, and ethics cannot be based on a
materialist perspective, because matter only concerns what is, and not what ought to
be. Ethical action concerns what ought to be the case and the attainment of the good,
and this relates to the formal, the final, and the efficient causes rather than the material cause.

Student: You also mentioned that, according to Aristotle, the formal, the final, and the efficient causes are closely related to each other, while the material cause stands apart and cannot be reduced to the other three.

Teacher: Yes, and the specificity of the material cause is very important for Aristotle, and for Plato before him. Returning again to the *Phaedo*, when Socrates becomes disillusioned with Anaxagoras because the latter does not truly take into account the final cause, he is rejecting the primacy of the efficient cause, but also the material cause, which in the passage in question is subsumed under the efficient cause. The final cause explains action at the individual human level but also at a broader level. Denying the final cause and following only the efficient and the material causes means that events in the world happen for no purpose. Although the idea of providence becomes truly explicit only later with Hellenistic philosophy, it is implicit in this passage of the *Phaedo*, in which Socrates upholds his belief that the world and what happens are governed by the idea of the good. This means that the idea of providence relies on the notion of good and also on the notion of a final cause and purpose. If one follows only the efficient cause and the material cause, that would mean that there is no purpose governing events and everything happens only on the basis of the nature of matter, and not according to an apparent good which is ultimately achieved.

Student: I understand the discrepancy between the material and the final causes, and the need to uphold the latter in the field of ethics. What other aspects prevent us from basing ethical action on material premises?

Teacher: The material cause is subordinate to the efficient cause, and the latter must also be seen as subordinate to the final cause; otherwise we do not have ethical action, because the intention of an action is indicated by the final cause. The efficient cause determines and immediately precedes the action or event, in the sense that if we only consider the efficient cause we obtain a mechanical action. Therefore, in modern and contemporary science, the most important cause (in addition to matter) is the efficient cause. Matter is not considered a cause as such in the Aristotelian sense, unless it is conflated with the efficient cause.

Student: Ethics, however, privileges the final cause, as you said.

Teacher: Given the significance of the question of intention and the fact that it involves the final cause, the efficient cause is subordinate in ethical action. In science we speak of efficient causes and see how the effect follows from the cause necessarily; in ethics, the agent must have a final cause and be judged according to that final cause. For instance, if someone gives to charity because of external constraints, the efficient cause is present and clear, but there is no freedom or an intention to practice the good, and in that sense there is no ethical action.

Student: How does the preeminence of the final cause evince the presence of spirit in ethics?

Teacher: This is clear from the inspirational passage from the *Phaedo* in which Socrates mentions the role of intellect in human agency and as governing earthly events. The final cause or the purpose is considered to be extraneous to scientific explanation. However, ethical action is guided by intentions, and intention is related to the intellect, which in turn is one of the aspects of spirit. In other words, to be guided by intention implies the use of the intellect, and therefore the use and the agency of spirit.

Student: What determines ethical action, other than the final cause or intention?

Teacher: The significance of the final cause and the focus on intention cannot be understood without explaining the question of free will which is central in ethics, whether secular or theological ethics. One is judged by one's action and intentions and not by any material causes involved. The cause of the action must be the agent's mind and free decision, without coercion. In religious or theological ethics, the intention and autonomy of the agent is important because otherwise the agent cannot be made responsible for her or his actions, and this would invalidate the idea of any reward or punishment. God cannot reward or punish someone who does not act freely, because in that case clearly other causes are responsible for the action, and not the immediate human agent. Even in secular ethics this is important, because generally speaking the action must be seen to start in the agent and not come from some other agent, human or natural.

Student: The question of responsibility for one's actions is clearly at the heart of ethics, and it is very much part of religion too. In philosophy, Kant also explained the difference between the natural and the ethical order, in connection with the issue of free will.

Teacher: Yes, Kant defended the importance of free will in his third antinomy of pure reason, which centers precisely on the question of free will versus determinism, as we have seen. In nature, it is important to regard everything as necessarily determined by its causes. This ensures the efficacy of scientific explanation and also predictability. However, in ethical action the human agent must be the free initiator of action; otherwise the action cannot be truly ascribed to her or him. If we are seen to be completely constrained by natural factors in our dealings with others, then we do not act freely and cannot be considered responsible for our actions. Therefore, Kant sees a need to separate natural causation, which is necessary, from human causation, which is free. This reverts to our former distinction between science, with its focus on the efficient cause, and ethics, with a focus on the final cause, which is a pivotal distinction between the two fields.

Student: I understand the centrality of free will for ethics, but is there an explicit link between free will and the spirit?

Teacher: When we speak of will in connection with human beings, we can speak in principle of free will and of a will which is not free. However, as a matter of fact, the will is, properly speaking, free will. A will which is not free is a conditioned will and consequently it relies on external factors. The will, strictly speaking, is in human beings free will. We saw how the will in turn relies on the intellect and how the intellect is an aspect of spirit.

The spirituality present in ethics is clear to be seen, coming as it does from the human subject and the human mind, and it cannot be reduced to any material causes or any other efficient cause. Ethical action is a strong and definite proof of spirituality and cannot be dissociated from it.

Student: You have mentioned the significance of the purpose or goal in ethics. Surely this is a multifaceted aspect in ethics?

Teacher: Yes. For instance, the question of the end is also clear in Kant's formulation of the categorical imperative to the effect that human beings are to be treated as an end and not as a means. The end and the intention in ethics are crucial, and the material aspect is subordinate and never a main point in ethics. Materialism, which states that reality is primarily or purely material to the detriment of a spiritual reality, cannot support ethics because matter does not give us any sense of purpose or of what is morally right or wrong.

Hedonism, namely the theory that pleasure (usually understood as physical pleasure) is the ultimate good, also cannot sustain an ethical theory because the sense of right and wrong are lacking. The very notions of right and wrong have a strong spiritual dimension, while they have no meaning in the material world.

To sum up, the question of purpose, or the end and the final cause, is decisive in ethics. In human action the end takes the shape of intention, and we have seen that the final cause is a spiritual and not a material cause.

Student: How does ethics relate to other fields of philosophy with regard to the question of spirit? I mean, how does the question of spirit establish links between ethics and the other philosophical disciplines?

Teacher: In the history of philosophy, especially in the modern period when epistemology becomes the dominant philosophical discipline, we find an influence of epistemological theories on the basic questions of ethics. In the modern period, rationalists would say that the idea of good, the goal and subject matter of ethics, is an innate idea, or at least an a priori idea that we find within ourselves. In contrast, empiricists, who deny innate ideas, would say that we know the idea of good from experience.

Student: If we have knowledge of the good, whether from reason or by experience, what about knowledge of evil?

Teacher: As the philosophers in the Aristotelian tradition stressed, knowledge of a certain principle implies also knowledge of its opposite, which means that by knowing the good, we also know what evil is. Returning to the difference between rationalism and empiricism, ethics revolved around the knowledge of good and evil, and the different ways in which that knowledge was obtained.

Student: With regard to ethics, knowledge of good and evil, which is knowledge of moral good and evil, is significant in its relation to good deeds and evil deeds.

Teacher: Yes, and the moral quality of these deeds is in turn related to the virtues, which can be theoretical or practical, but in any case they involve practice and experience on the part of the human subject. To act in a good moral way is to act virtuously. Therefore, a discussion of ethics must consider the nature of virtue.

Student: Plato and Aristotle portray the virtues differently, for according to the former they are ideas, but in Aristotle the practical aspect of the virtues is emphasized.

Teacher: That is right. The virtues are frequently mentioned in Plato's dialogues, and in many cases they are the very subject matter of the dialogue, virtues such as justice, courage, friendship, and piety. It is clear that for Plato, knowledge and ethics are related, because the various virtues, which allow us to be good and virtuous, are forms or ideas. The implication is that we can only be virtuous and good if we discover within ourselves the idea of the good and of the other virtues. First we have the knowledge of those virtues, and having that knowledge, we can practice the virtues and become good. For Aristotle, virtue is primarily a question of habit and experience. We become virtuous by practicing virtue, although there is naturally also an epistemological side to virtue ethics generally speaking.

Student: Ethics has connections with metaphysics, too.

Teacher: Yes, and ethics takes into account the main metaphysical theories and the conception of the human being in any given period of history. In ancient philosophy the place of human beings is related to the cosmos and the function of human beings within the cosmos. In the medieval period, the emphasis is on the relation between humans and God and between a human being and other human beings. In the modern period, the emphasis is on human reason and what is best for human beings and society. Accordingly, the rules of ethics and the notion of good can be seen to come from human reason or from God through revelation, or from both, depending on the connections established between philosophy and the other disciplines. In this sense, the very notions of good and evil can be seen to issue from human reason or from God.

Student: How do we relate good and evil to God?

Teacher: God is absolutely good, according to the philosophical tradition. As for our knowledge of the good in connection with God, the concepts of good and evil can be considered to be objective or subjective, in the sense that good is an absolute and objective value recognized by God and by us, or it is established by God as an absolute subject and then recognized as good. In other words, good is good objectively, or it is good because it is commanded by God.

Student: The term "ethics" is also linked with customs, which is not unrelated to the role of the virtues.

Teacher: Yes, ethics is related to customs and the way we treat other human beings, other animals, and other living beings in general. In this case, we are not focusing on the question of natural good and evil, or the principles and laws that rule nature, or metaphysical realities, but the relations between human beings and other living beings. Moreover, the question of the virtues is essential, because it is something theoretical in the sense that they can be defined and issue from the intellect; however, virtue is also something which is practical and needs to be practiced. With regard to the virtues, some philosophers stress the theoretical aspect, such as Plato, others the practical aspect, like Aristotle.

Aquinas synthesizes all these different aspects pertaining to the good and the virtues. He treats the good as a transcendental, and in this sense it is a theoretical principle. He believes that God is infinitely good and his commands are good, and that ethical principles derive from the Bible, but he also admires Aristotle's ethics and examines action and the virtues from an Aristotelian and practical perspective.

Student: Can it therefore be said that three main parts can be discerned within the discipline of ethics: the question of good and evil, theological ethics, and the question of virtue? How do these principles relate to spirit?

Teacher: Yes, those are the main aspects, and they are the ones we have emphasized. It is obvious that ethics firmly rests on philosophical and also religious foundations, and on a spiritual principle. In relation to philosophy, we saw that the will is subordinate to the intellect; and the intellect and what it knows, its object, is spiritual. With regard to religion, ethical and moral rules issue from a higher, spiritual principle, God, and hence they have a spiritual origin. The question of freedom is also very important because an ethical action, or an action considered good or bad, must be done voluntarily and according to a goal which is good or a particular good. Freedom is closely linked to spirit and to truth. There is no ethical action without the will and the intellect, as we have seen, and freedom is based on these two faculties or principles of action.

Student: We have seen how important is the affirmation of free will in ethics, and the consequent rejection of determinism.

Teacher: The difference between freedom and determinism, as respectively guiding the human sphere and the natural sphere, has been tentatively formulated by Kant as an antinomy of pure reason, as we have seen. These two domains should be considered as having two different chains of causality. If everything is subordinate to the material and the efficient cause there is no place for ethics. The ethical domain, by definition, and regardless of the material circumstances of an action, must exclude matter as a decisive factor. Matter can only be the means and not the end of explaining an ethical action.

Student: We have seen that the distinction between the natural and the physical order was already established by Plato, and it is explicitly affirmed by Kant. In Aristotle too there appears to be a distinction between the natural order and the idea of the universe as governed by the good.

Teacher: Yes, Aristotle makes a distinction between the constraints imposed by matter on natural beings and final causality as governing nature and indeed the universe. Aristotle often uses the expression "the necessity of matter" to indicate that which determines the life and death of a living being in nature and the limitations imposed by matter on natural beings, which he considers to be by nature corruptible. This expression also indicates a lack of purpose and an aspect of inevitability. It is an aspect which pertains to biology or physics. However, in the ethical domain freedom must be assumed, more specifically freedom of the will and freedom of choice. This issue goes back to Aristotle and his ethics, and the idea of the good as the object of the will. The example of the *Phaedo* is illustrative. Socrates states that he is in prison after being convicted of impiety and corrupting the Athenian youth. He thinks it is right and good for him to do so—to accept the verdict of the Athenian jury—which is the final cause, and not because his muscles had brought him there, which is the efficient cause and under which the material cause is subsumed, as we have seen. Ethical action follows a goal and an intention which is good or bad.

Student: Would it not still be possible to defend ethics from a materialistic or hedonistic point of view, as promoting the good of the individual?

Teacher: These positions, materialism and hedonism, are highly problematic from a metaphysical and an epistemological point of view, but they are downright objectionable from an ethical point of view. In addition, it is not science, that is, the natural sciences, which study the material aspects of reality, that can pronounce themselves on good and evil, for science simply studies reality as it is. The questions pertaining to good and evil must be addressed by ethics or theology because these disciplines are by nature concerned with good and evil and what is morally right and wrong. Moreover, ethics concerns the good of all individuals and not that of one to the exclusion of others. We live in society, which means that we have to consider the common good as well as the good of the individual.

Student: I can see how ethics is related to the intellect and therefore issues from a spiritual principle. Are there other aspects of ethics which relate to spirit?

Teacher: We have analyzed ethics from the point of view of its subject matter and in particular the question of the will and its objects, good or evil. There are different kinds of ethics or ethical theories, but in the medieval period there is a focus not just on virtue, which was the emphasis of ancient ethics, but also on the idea of good and evil generally speaking and on divine commands as ethical norms that are to be followed. This tendency continues, to a certain extent, in modern philosophy; in any case the intellectualist approach dominates the philosophical tradition, whether we think of modern ethics or ancient and medieval virtue ethics. The norms prescribed by God are spiritual and they tend towards a spiritual good, the fulfillment of goodness. Even if we dispense with divine command theory, and the goal of ethics is simply to fulfill one's duty, on the basis of the human autonomous decision regarding what constitutes good and evil, the guiding principles of ethics in both cases are rational and hence spiritual, and the goals are also spiritual.

Student: The question of the goal of ethics is also central to this discipline.

Teacher: Yes, this is a central theme in ethics. The end of ethics is the good, but that good can be considered under the guise of happiness. Then a discussion follows on what constitutes ultimate happiness. We could say that the end goal, happiness, consists in the contemplation of the truth or God, and so in any case the goal of ethics is the spiritual and the intellectual fulfillment of human beings as human beings. In defense of this goal we can state that other goals are not permanent or not truly satisfying, or both.

Student: How is this reflection on the goal of ethics present in the history of philosophy?

Teacher: Ancient ethics considers happiness to be the goal of human life, and this goal is tied in with the definition of human nature and its fulfillment. This means that ethics concerns the fulfillment of human nature. In Aristotle it is clear that the fulfillment of a potentiality, the actualization of a potentiality, within a species will inevitably happen, to most if not all members of that species. In Plato too, the virtue of a human being is to be and to act fully as a human being in accordance with human nature, and for both philosophers being human entailed rationality as an essential characteristic. For both Plato and Aristotle the virtues play a vital role in ethics. There are different kinds of virtues, as we have seen, but they are tied to human rationality. Therefore the virtues are something belonging to the spiritual life of human beings. Even though not all virtues are intellectual virtues, even the moral virtues issue from wisdom, which is an intellectual virtue. Some philosophers accepted that the aim of ethics is human happiness but considered happiness to be pleasure, such as Epicurus, or at least the absence of pain. However, he is criticized by ancient and modern philosophers alike and it is not clear how such a position could ground an ethical theory.

Student: In what sense could a principle of pleasure possibly ground ethics?

Teacher: Only if we link that principle to happiness, such that happiness consists in physical rather than spiritual pleasure. The Epicureans would defend the idea that it consists in physical pleasure. In that case, happiness would have to be confined to this life, because the body is corruptible. Epicurus does not defend the notion that the gods care for us or look after human affairs, or the idea of an afterlife. This conception of happiness and of pleasure is, however, very narrow. We can retain the notion of pleasure as leading to happiness if we focus on spiritual pleasure, which would involve the activity of the intellect and not the pleasures of the senses, as defended by Epicurus. One would say that the principle of pleasure is an alternative way of grounding ethics, and pleasure in this sense would not be physical but spiritual. All this belongs to the notion of happiness.

With regard to this question, it is important to note that the majority of philosophers in Antiquity, such as Plato and Aristotle, consider the goal of human life to be the contemplation of the truth.

Student: And with regard to the modern period, what is the goal of ethics?

Teacher: In the modern period, the goal of ethics is also related to human nature, and to the rational part of the soul. The goal of ethics is to do what is right and good, and this is decided by reason alone. Ethics consists in fulfilling one's duty. Kant is the foremost representative of this position.

Student: Concerning these two conceptions of the essence of ethics, one focusing on the practice of virtue and the other on the fulfillment of one's duty, how do medieval philosophers position themselves?

Teacher: Medieval philosophers actually offer a middle term, as a golden mean between these two positions. On the one hand, as in modern ethics we find the view that human beings should follow the divine commandments. These are good because they are ordained by God. With regard to the question of values, as we have seen, some theologians hold that something is good because it was commanded by God, others believe that God naturally and logically commands us to do what is good in itself, and that goodness is naturally known by human reason too. The distinction between good and evil, according to medieval philosophers, does not issue simply from human reason; rather, human reason knows how to recognize the good in God's commands, in creation, and within itself. Virtue ethics is another important part of medieval philosophical ethics, given the strong Aristotelian influence. In addition to the moral and the intellectual virtues, as we have seen, medieval philosophers and theologians introduce the theological virtues. These virtues, when practiced regularly, complete and accomplish human perfection in accordance with human nature. In other words, they lead to the fulfillment of human nature. Therefore medieval ethics preserves the spirit of virtue ethics while advancing a kind of normative or duty ethics.

Student: You mentioned that the notion of good comes from God's commandments but that it is also present in human reason.

Teacher: Within normative or divine command ethics there are two aspects: the external commandments given by God, but also the ability to understand the good by ourselves. In both aspects, the spiritual element prevails. Virtue theory is vastly developed in the Middle Ages. We have the same virtues as in ancient philosophy, namely the intellectual and the moral or cardinal virtues, and also the theological virtues as we have seen. From the ancient period, the cardinal virtues are taken up; Cicero lists them as justice, fortitude, prudence, and temperance.

Student: What is the meaning of the cardinal virtues?

Teacher: Two of these virtues concern our relation to others. Justice is to give others what they are due. Fortitude is to show courage or bravery in the face of adversity. Prudence is the complement of fortitude, as it tempers fortitude; by prudence one avoids being foolhardy. Temperance implies one's relation to oneself and avoiding any excesses with connection to our use of the body and the needs of the body. These virtues are adopted by Augustine and by Scholastic philosophers. In addition, we have the intellectual virtues, of which wisdom is the foremost virtue. For medieval philosophers, the virtues acquire a theological dimension, as we have seen. In the case of the intellectual virtues, there is an overlap with the gifts of the Holy Spirit, as in the case of wisdom. The virtues thus acquire a theological grounding. This means that we are not just talking about ethics in a human sense but also with regard to our relationship with God. In particular, the theological virtues, faith, hope, and charity, describe our relation to God, faith being predominantly intellectual, as is hope, while charity has a more volitive character. The intellectual and the cardinal or moral virtues are purely human, while the theological virtues are supernatural since they are infused by God.

Student: Could you please explain again the connection between these virtues and spirit?

Teacher: We see that the virtues issue from the intellect or the will. They are related to that which is typically human, the intellect and the will, which are purely spiritual. The virtues involve the action of the body naturally, in particular the moral or cardinal virtues. Temperance means, for instance, not to overindulge in food. Regardless of whether the virtues have as their object God, or other human beings, or other living beings, they come from the soul or the spiritual part of human beings. Therefore they are related to knowledge and volition, as we have seen. The nature of ethics is also informed by religious considerations, in particular the question of divine commands.

We can analyze the various aspects of ethics in terms of the three kinds of spirit we have specified, subjective, objective, and absolute. In virtue ethics, finite subjective spirit is realized and fulfilled and comes to accord with objective spirit, which are the principles leading to the fulfillment of human nature. In other words, in virtue ethics, the subject of the action, in acting virtuously, realizes its own nature and purpose. On the other hand, if we think of divine command ethics, the rules, the principle, and the purpose of actions are furnished by absolute spirit, and they are part of objective spirit, which are the actions commanded, leading also to the fulfillment of human nature. If we follow rational normative or duty ethics, the finite subjective spirit prevails but follows objective principles which it discovers as elements of objective spirit. We have seen that medieval philosophers offer the combination of ancient and modern ethics, by developing the former and anticipating the latter, and fusing them.

Student: The good is also a determining aspect in ethics, as we have seen.

Teacher: Yes, and it is worth looking into the question of the good, since it is a central question in ethics, and a complex one. Do we naturally or innately recognize the good, or do we come to learn it from others or from God? According to Plato, we recognize the good within ourselves, as a form which is recollected by the soul. The soul is akin to the forms, and the supreme form is the form of the Good. Plato compares it with the sun, in the *Republic*, as illuminating everything, and in this way allowing everything to be seen or to be known, given the analogy between sight and knowledge. We saw how the verb "to know" in Greek comes from a root which means "to see." Therefore in Plato the virtues and morality in general have strong intellectual underpinnings. This resembles a rationalist approach, as we have seen. Other philosophers claim that we can recognize or learn the nature of the good. This position has its roots in the analysis of human nature, as it becomes clear in the medieval period.

Student: How so?

Teacher: We recognize the good if we have it within ourselves, that is, if we are good ourselves. In Manicheism, a religion that the young Augustine embraced, there is a dualism between good and evil, as we have seen. The spiritual was good and the corporeal and the material was evil. Consequently, human beings were good and bad at the same time. Manicheans held that the spiritual part of man, namely the soul, was good, and the material part, the body, was bad. There was a duality in human beings themselves, and the principles were not reducible to each other or reconcilable. The good did not prevail entirely over the evil although it was greater than evil. In Christianity, the whole human being is good and the good is recognized by an individual within himself or herself. In this way, human beings can recognize the good in itself and in themselves, practice it, and therefore be good themselves or fulfill that goodness within themselves and towards others.

Student: Saint Augustine also mentions the effects of original sin on human beings. Does it not imply that human nature is essentially flawed and sinful?

Teacher: Human nature becomes flawed after the Fall, and humanity inherits original sin, but before the Fall human nature is naturally good, just like the rest of creation. And this goodness can be restored, particularly through the sacraments. There is a recognition of the goodness of human nature in Christianity and in the other religious traditions. We can only be good if we apprehend that good within ourselves. It cannot be completely alien to us; whether it is present in our soul or we come to learn about it, it has to be something akin to us. This is clear from a philosophical perspective if we look once more at the medieval theory of the transcendentals, such as being, one, truth, and good. The last two are the object of the intellect and the will respectively, as we have seen. Being, as well as the one, is intelligized by the intellect, and the will specifically aims at the good, rendering it akin to the intellect and the soul. The transcendentals are to some extent interchangeable.

Student: In what sense are the transcendentals—being, one, truth, good—interchangeable?

Teacher: Being can only be recognized in connection with the one, for instance when we are talking about composite objects. We know "pen" on account of the oneness of the concept of pen and the oneness of the object "pen," which means that the aspect of unity allows us to know it and allows it also to be or to exist. Equally, truth is said of propositions that describe reality, or being. Truth is specific to propositions which are intelligized by the intellect. Those true propositions—for truth is a predicate of propositions, not of reality itself—correspond to real facts, so that the truth refers to reality, and the intellect can see the correspondence between reality or being and truth. Finally, being is good, as well as one and true. We have seen that truth and good are predicable of each other. One cannot find categories that are more spiritual than the transcendentals, and they are at the origin of the virtues.

Student: Are there not other kinds of theories of ethical action which rely less on the role of the intellect and more on the will, or consider other, less rationalist, goals?

Teacher: Even if ethical action is considered with respect to other principles or goals, the intellectual principle prevails. Hegel defends the idea that thought determines itself into will, in the sense that the will issues from thought.

Student: Is this not a position that is found in philosophy up to the modern period and then reversed in the modern period? You mentioned that Descartes and Rousseau hold that the will is greater than the intellect or the judgment.

Teacher: In the *Meditations on First Philosophy* Descartes attributes human error to the difference between the intellect, which is finite, and the will and judgment, which are infinite. Obviously, the question of error is central to Descartes' concerns, since true knowledge by definition cannot contain error. He starts from a skeptical position in order to avoid error. Skeptics suspend judgment in order to avoid error because error consists in assenting to something which is not true. Descartes defines intellectual error as the result of a judgment which is not based totally on the intellect; that is to say, sometimes we assent to an opinion or a position without confirmation or proof; and then we may err because the will goes further than the intellect and finds no solid basis in the intellect. Consequently, the intellect still holds pride of place in relation to the will. However, to say that the human will is infinite in contrast to the human intellect is not really in line with medieval conceptions about the human will and intellect, which are considered by most medieval philosophers to be both finite and prone to error.

Student: Does not Rousseau privilege the will in relation to the intellect?

Teacher: Rousseau departs from the philosophical tradition in many respects. We have seen that ethics is strongly dependent on a philosophical anthropology, that is, the idea of a human nature, and the definition and understanding of human nature. In other words, it depends on what it means to be human. Rousseau subverts the classical and medieval ideas about human nature, by saying, in the *Discourse on the Origin of Inequality*, that the essential characteristics of human beings in the state of nature, which is the original state, are free will and perfectibility, or the ability to develop and adapt to surrounding circumstances. He holds that reason only develops later. Whether we wish to interpret this as a historical affirmation or an essentialist affirmation about human nature (given his explicit affirmation to the effect that he is not discussing facts when trying to portray the state of nature or the original state of human beings, before the development of civilization), it is an important step and a departure from previous conceptions about human nature. According to his interpretation, reason is not constitutive of human nature originally; it is something that develops and is acquired in connection with civilization and in particular through contact with other human beings in society. Rousseau famously depicts his "savage man" as someone who does not live in community but is happy by himself without any human company or society whatsoever. In this way, Rousseau strongly emphasizes the will (understood as free will) in human beings. He does not state that we are just like animals in the state of nature; he does think of human nature as distinct from animal nature, but what distinguishes us from animals is the will, or rather free will and the capacity to choose from among different option or choices, rather than reason. Reason develops later, with language and the need to communicate with other human beings once they are led to or forced by natural circumstances to live together.

Student: I understand that Rousseau does not view man as an essentially rational animal. Does this position not undermine the view that ethics is based primarily on the intellect and therefore on an intellectual or spiritual base?

Teacher: No, in fact Rousseau's position confirms the link between morality and rationality, in spite of the fact that, according to him, human nature is not, initially, rational. Natural man, according to Rousseau, has no morality, or duties towards other people, since he lives by himself and seldom has contact with other human beings, although he has a natural sense of goodness, so to speak, given the principle of pity which is common to all animals. Pity, which is acutely felt by both humans and animals, means that human beings and animals will not harm any other sentient beings needlessly. It is only when society develops that morality and ethics develop. This proves our point, namely, that morality and ethics are grounded on rationality and on the intellect. Even Rousseau acknowledges that.

Student: Rousseau's position on human nature also excludes sociability, which goes hand in hand with the view that morality results from the formation of human societies.

Teacher: We have seen that ethics and morality pertain to human customs and the way we deal with other human beings. There is no need for ethics or morality when we are by ourselves, unless we include our relationship with God under the purview of ethics. However, religion or society is not part of Rousseau's depiction of the life of original man, who in actual fact only has contact with nature and is thus perfectly happy and fulfilled. It is the relationship with other human beings which calls for ethical principles and action, and for morality. These latter are founded on reason and the operations of the intellect, something which is not denied by Rousseau; on the contrary, he ties morality (which for him is based on civilization and therefore not natural but artificial) to rationality and civilization, and the development of language.

At any rate, it is clear that any true ethics must rest on a spiritual principle.

Student: Perhaps there is another way of looking at the question: even if ethics relies on reason and the intellect, does it not involve other elements, such as feelings and emotions?

Teacher: Yes, but that is a different question regarding ethics. Although ethics rests on a rational basis, it may admit of emotions, but this does not contradict the position we have established concerning the prevalence of reason in ethics. We can give two examples of two different positions in this regard. The Stoics, as we have seen, famously ban emotions and feelings from the essential characteristics of the wise man, who is the ideal human being for Stoics. These feelings and emotions would somehow contaminate the unwavering principles and the moral strength of the Stoic wise man. Aquinas, on the contrary, following in an Aristotelian vein, holds that when we act virtuously, it is better for our virtuous acts to be accompanied by emotions rather than to abstain from them. Nature must accompany rationality since both emotions and rationality belong to human nature, even though rationality and the different virtues are that which should come first and guide action. This position relies on a well-rounded conception of human beings as possessing rationality but also sensibility. Rationality and sensibility complement each other, much in the same way as body and soul work together.

If we take a theological approach, freedom is an essential aspect of human nature. It shows that we are fully rational, which in turn is a condition of free will. Freedom here, in theological ethics, as in ethics generally speaking, means free will and freedom of choice. In addition, the theological sense of freedom is very significant because it goes hand in hand with the gifts of the Holy Spirit. It is a freedom which allows us to know God and choose what is right and good.

Student: I understand the theological roots of the question of free will, which is essentially an ethical question. Are there other significant consequences of the affirmation of free will in theological ethics?

Teacher: When it comes to judging moral action, it is necessary to ascertain whether that action was performed from one's free will. An action is only considered to be good or bad if it is freely carried out. If someone was forced to perform an action, this means that it did not depend on the agent's free will and so he or she cannot be held accountable for it, as we have seen, which means that he or she cannot be praised or blamed for it.

Student: The question of responsibility has a long history in the philosophical tradition.

Teacher: Yes, and in the Middle Ages the aim was to explain it in relation to divine action. In other words, if God is omnipotent and causes all actions, then human actions too must be caused by God, and therefore human beings cannot be praised or blamed for them. This outcome of the affirmation of God's omnipotence could be deemed irreconcilable with the idea of judgment and reward and punishment after death. If human actions are necessary because they are forced or carried out by necessity, then reward or punishment makes no sense in this life or the next. Heaven and hell would make no sense, either, and the attribute of God's justice, which consists in rewarding virtuous people and punishing evildoers, would be called into question. In the modern period, this question is also relevant but the emphasis is on the articulation with science. If the laws of nature explain every event and phenomenon, this would also detract from human beings' freedom in acting, and human beings could not be made responsible for their actions. Consequently it is necessary to think about human agency in a different way from natural causality. One has to think in terms of purpose and not in terms of the efficient cause, as we have seen.

Student: I see how important the role of spirit is in ethics.

Teacher: Ethics pertains to practical philosophy and as such is directed to action rather than theory. However, there is a link between theory and action, in the same way that the will and the intellect cannot be dissociated in their relation to action. The centrality of the final cause and the intention, in addition to the link between the will and the intellect, show the effects of spirit. The intellectual and spiritual aspect is also present in the question of good and evil, good being the object of the will but also a transcendental. We have seen that the material element in ethics can only be instrumental or secondary and cannot be a primary consideration.

Student: Politics is also a part of practical philosophy.

Teacher: Yes, already in ancient philosophy politics, alongside ethics, forms part of practical philosophy. Political philosophy looks at the organization of human communities, and here too the role of spirit is central. We do not look at the good from an individual perspective but from a more general perspective, including the common good of human societies. This discipline has the common good as its goal and there is much in common with ethics. The final cause is central as well as the notion of the good. Like ethics too, there is a strong link to philosophical anthropology, which discusses the nature or essence of being human.

Philosophy of Religion

Student: We spoke also about philosophy of religion.

Teacher: We have discussed the question of spirit in religion. While theology goes hand in hand with religion, philosophy of religion is a discipline within philosophy, as one of the branches of philosophy. It is a relatively new discipline, having developed as a result of the European Enlightenment, and it developed as a rational reflection on religion, which means that, unlike theology, it is not as closely based on scripture.

Student: The role of spirit in philosophy of religion has already been established.

Teacher: Philosophy of religion analyzes the rational structure of religion, and everything that pertains to religion, and spirit is very much a religious theme. We have seen that spirit plays an important role in several religions, as opposed to matter. Spirit has different meanings in philosophy and in religion, although they sometimes overlap. In religion spirit is identified with God and the spiritual guides the human relationship with God. Religion considers spiritual rather than material reality. Often, the meaning of spirit in philosophy and in religion overlaps, and the difference between them lies in the fact that philosophy takes reason as its starting point while religion takes into account the authority of religious texts.

Student: You mentioned that according to Hegel religion and philosophy are the highest forms of knowledge of reality. A similarity between philosophy and religion lies in the cognitive content of religion, does it not?

Teacher: We have seen that there are many similarities between philosophy and religion, and that both have a cognitive content. Both claim comprehensively to explain reality and the origin of things and living beings. One could say that religion overlaps with philosophy in this sense. It is usually considered that religion is the older of the two, but some religions, if not all, contain a philosophical aspect in the way that they describe reality. Initially, religion and philosophy were mixed before becoming specifically different, sometimes leading to clashes between the two. We see this clash first in ancient Greek philosophy. The Presocratics offered a kind of scientific rather than religious explanation for natural phenomena. Plato's works illustrate this issue abundantly well. Socrates is accused in the *Apology* of considering the moon and the sun to be purely material instead of gods. A process begins whereby a philosophical or scientific explanation replaces religious explanation, which is considered to be distinct. Nevertheless, a religious element is still clearly present in Plato's works but not as much in Aristotle, in the sense of resorting to a story that goes back a long time and explains the origin or natural processes of the universe. We saw that Presocratic philosophers, for all their experiments and naturalistic explanations, also had religious leanings and offered religious explanations for some natural phenomena. Religion was considered to rest on tradition and scripture or poetry while philosophy rested solely on human reason. This distinction still holds to this day, to some extent, and can serve to define the difference between philosophy and religion. The relation between philosophy and religion has served to define the various periods in the history of philosophy, and often philosophy also influenced religion, more specifically theology.

Student: Philosophy appears initially to have evolved out of religion.

Teacher: Ancient Greek philosophy shows links to ancient Greek religion, but also shows marked differences with regard to religion. Thinking, generally speaking, goes back to the birth of humanity and the birth of civilization, but it was first religious and subsequently philosophical, which means that philosophy had to emerge out of religion. In the Middle Ages, we find an endeavor to reconcile the two, although this meant, as we have seen, that in medieval Christian thought philosophy was seen as the handmaiden of theology. The language of philosophy was used, but scripture was not to be openly contradicted and remained the guiding light in matters of knowledge. Religion and philosophy meant the use of different faculties, mental acts, or virtues. In this way, philosophy employed reason, which was considered a faculty, and religion used faith, which is a mental act or a mental assent. Plato considered that belief—holding something as true without proof—was inferior to intellection. In the Middle Ages, however, the power of reason is seen to have limitations, while faith is exalted. Faith, which consists in believing without seeing, that is to say, without proof, is considered meritorious. Scripture dictates the rules, even if metaphorical reading of scripture is allowed. However, Catholic theology did include many aspects of Aristotle's philosophy, for example metaphysics and ethics.

Student: In modern philosophy there were changes in the relation between philosophy and religion.

Teacher: In the modern period the relation between philosophy and religion was set in different terms. Philosophy became more independent of religion and of scripture and the sciences emerged independently of religion. The sciences became more autonomous in relation to philosophy and they became more specialized. However, the question of religion was never too far from the philosophers' minds, as we have seen, because although the emphasis shifted to the theory of knowledge and the question of the human intellect, many questions from the medieval period remained, especially regarding the existence of God and the immortality of the soul. Hegel sums up the entire tradition since the time of ancient Greek philosophy and tries to reconcile all the different philosophical systems: we have seen how, in spite of his rationalism, he includes empiricism as part of his philosophical system, in particular in his philosophy of nature. With regard to the cognitive content of religion, he believes that both describe the same reality, God and creation, in different ways. Philosophy looks at reality in a conceptual way, and religion by using representation or imagination, and metaphors. According to him, philosophy centers on a universal language, and religion on a particular language which is closer to the imagination and the senses. Consequently, he interprets not just scripture but also certain principles of Christian dogma in a metaphorical way.

Student: This means that for Hegel philosophy went over and above religion in explaining reality.

Teacher: Yes, Hegel considers philosophy to surpass religion in the appropriateness of its depiction of reality, given that reason is superior to imagination and religion is based on the latter, while philosophy is based on reason. However, both the universal and the particular are important in understanding reality, and they complement each other, in the way that reason and imagination complement each other.

Whichever way we look at religion and philosophy, and at the philosophy of religion, which analyzes the religious phenomenon in all its different aspects, we are talking about ways of analyzing reality and knowing reality.

Student: You mentioned the links between philosophy of religion and theology.

Teacher: Theology looks at the tenets of particular religions and is more or less rationalistic in its attempts to explain those tenets. It does this based on scripture, naturally, and the issues addressed come from scripture. Philosophy of religion is a broader discipline in that it considers not just the creed but also different ways of practicing religion and even perspectives from outside each religion. Philosophy of religion overlaps in some ways with theology (and we have seen that there are different kinds of theology, one which is closer to philosophy and another which is closer to scripture). In some cases, philosophy of religion treats of issues that are outside the remit of theology, for instance anthropological or psychological aspects of religion.

Student: I understand the strong links between philosophy and religion, and how spirit is a central theme in both. More specifically, how can we relate these disciplines to spirit?

Teacher: We could say that philosophy and religion are two ways of speaking of spirit, different ways of understanding spirituality. Religion's approach to the spiritual need not always be purely rational, while philosophy naturally stresses the rational and universal element in the spiritual, by means of the use of logic, for instance. We have seen this rational emphasis in Hegel and in some medieval philosophers, not least in Islamic and Jewish philosophers and especially those working in the Aristotelian tradition. Religion presents spirituality also in a mystical way which stresses intuition over reason or intellect. In this way, spirituality can be associated with reason or, instead, with intuition, and thus with philosophy or with religion (or mysticism) respectively. Religion is closer to metaphor and an attention to the particular, while philosophy operates within the confines of the rational and conceptual or universal. And it is philosophy of religion which studies the links and the differences between philosophy and religion.

Student: Is there a middle term between these two views of spirituality, philosophical and religious?

Teacher: Yes, and there are different ways of seeing the link between philosophy and religion. In the medieval period the symbiosis between philosophy and religion was especially sought. The attempt to fuse them is particularly visible in the Neoplatonic tradition, which has a strong religious as well as a philosophical element. This is seen in some aspects of Islamic philosophy and also in medieval Christian philosophy (for instance, in Saint Bonaventure) and in Jewish philosophy. Another way of formulating the articulation between philosophy and religion (or theology) for those in the Aristotelian tradition, like Saint Thomas Aquinas, was to use Aristotelian language to speak of religious aspects, theoretical and practical, while upholding the primacy of scripture and sacred doctrine, or regarding scripture as a safe guide to the understanding and practice of religion.

To sum up, these are two different ways of looking at the spiritual, and in this regard also the two disciplines inform one another.

Student: Could we also see philosophy and religion as separate and autonomous disciplines?

Teacher: We must accept the autonomy of the sciences and of the different disciplines in general, as each has its specific domain. Religion is not reducible to philosophy. Religion and religious experience are something unique and they are not reducible to any other kind of experience. Philosophy has a theoretical aspect, and in its practical aspect it addresses the question of happiness, but religion too clearly has a dual epistemological and practical aspect, and its knowledge is always directed at the goal of salvation or ultimate happiness. Each of them is autonomous but, as we have seen, they inform each other. Religion can use logic and deductive reasoning and philosophy benefits from the insights of religion. And as we have seen they indicate different ways of seeking the spiritual.

Student: Can we find spiritual aspects in various religions?

Teacher: This is naturally possible, because religion represents an attempt to connect with God or the divine and transcendent. Cognition is very important in religion, although it can take the form of intuitive knowledge, and not an obvious kind of rational or logical thought. Many religions seek to attain a reality that is not material. In addition to knowledge, which constitutes its intellectual aspect, morality, in its practical aspect, is stressed in religion. The virtues are promoted and the practical relation with God is emphasized, as well as the relation with other human beings and with creation. There is certainly an attempt to rise above the material and seek a transcendent reality, and this is typically spiritual. As we have seen, the spiritual can be said in many different ways, and it can be intellectual in a logical or in an intuitive way.

Student: You have mentioned the significance of the practical side of religion.

Teacher: The experiential aspect in religion is significant. Ritual is important, as religious practice, in establishing the connection with the divine. The question of the nature and the immortality of the soul, as immaterial and incorruptible, although it was often analyzed by philosophers, appears in our days to be typically religious rather than philosophical.

Student: Yet many themes are common to philosophy and religion, among them spirit?

Teacher: Yes, spirit is common to religion and philosophy because spirit is associated with the immaterial and with God in both disciplines. Two other concepts which are central to religion and not just philosophy are the transcendent and the infinite, which are also associated with God and with spirit. Infinity is an important aspect in religion, for God is infinite in his attributes, in his existence, and the soul is infinite with regard to future time although it is limited in relation to God. And there are other spiritual beings mediating between the soul and human beings in general, and God. Religions, like many philosophical systems, seek to offer a comprehensive account of reality, but this is not a flaw, since the natural sciences also seek this aim, albeit from a different perspective.

Student: And philosophy of religion naturally studies all these aspects?

Teacher: Yes, as we have seen, it analyzes and studies all aspects of religion, and not just Christianity, or Christian theology. Like theology, it looks at rational aspects within religion but it does not concern just scripture in its theoretical aspects and in its practical directives; it also looks at the practice of religion generally speaking, as we have seen. It looks at some aspects in common with theology, such as God's attributes, and especially his main attributes of knowledge, power, and goodness, how these are interrelated, and how they relate to human beings and creation at large. In addition, contemporary philosophy of religion offers different approaches according as it is found in the analytic or the continental way. Analytic philosophy of religion often focuses on God as subject matter while continental philosophy treats of religion and the human subject, as worshipping God. Analytic philosophy of religion looks at particular problems, while continental philosophy of religion may analyze certain authors on philosophy of religion or study the cultural aspects of religion. Generally speaking, philosophy of religion also considers general aspects of religion, such as the relation between reason and faith, and the nature of religious belief, as well as the status of scripture and whether it should be read literally or metaphorically. Naturally, when we speak of spirit, religion cannot be disregarded, as we have seen. And given that religion treats of God, who is purely spiritual, philosophy of religion also considers spirit and the spiritual.

Student: What are other aspects of spirituality in religion?

Teacher: Faith is considered something spiritual because it means an assent to something, usually a proposition that describes a fact, without empirical evidence. The question of the acceptance of authority is central to understanding faith.

Student: What does authority mean in a religious context?

Teacher: It means to trust scripture and to trust those to whom scripture was revealed. Augustine says that there is nothing irrational about this, since we daily accept many things that we hear from people we trust and which we have not experienced personally. Moreover, there is something intellectual about faith, although Aquinas also states that faith comes from the will, in the sense that it is possible for us to will to have faith; and this is already a step towards receiving that theological virtue, which is infused in the human soul by God. Although faith means willing assent, it is not something that we choose to have but is produced by God in our souls. Modern accounts may stress the subjectivity of faith as a personal initiative of the human subject, but the medieval perspective is quite different, since faith is given by God. The relation between faith and reason is quite complex, and rationalist philosophers in the modern period would say that faith needs to be guided by reason, but others hold that faith is a surer guide to the truth than reason, because of the weakness of reason. It is a question of which (reason or faith) we choose to trust.

Student: I understand the spirituality present in religion because of its subject matter, God, who is spirit, and the subject's approach to God, which must also be spiritual. Consequently, philosophy of religion also deals with spirit as a central subject matter, and it cannot be understood without reference to spirit.

Student: Philosophy of religion treats of God, and other topics, but it also assumes the existence of a human subject, for instance when it discusses morality. What can we say about human nature, in connection with spirit?

Philosophical Anthropology

Teacher: We have seen how ethics is based on human nature although it can also be prescriptive, as in the case of normative ethics. We base our analysis of the behavior of human beings on our understanding of human nature. In ethics there is a distinction between what is the case and what ought to be the case, as we have seen. On the one hand, we study human nature, but there is also an ideal human behavior to which we should aspire in ethics and in philosophical anthropology. Human character admits of improvement, and virtue is something that is improved with experience and practice. Virtues constitute a golden mean since they contain a balance between two extremes. The virtues balance each other out, such as, for instance, the cardinal virtues of prudence and fortitude.

Student: What else can be said of human nature in connection with spirit?

Teacher: Spirit is a defining aspect of human nature, and therefore it should be mentioned in connection with philosophical anthropology. Philosophy goes to the heart of the questions, which means that philosophical anthropology is concerned with giving an account of the essence of human beings and how it is reflected in their specifically human activities. It is also important to take into account the specificity of philosophical anthropology in contrast to other kinds of anthropology, such as cultural anthropology. Philosophical anthropology looks at human beings as a whole and not at particular aspects, and it identifies what makes us specifically human. While we should not disregard what the sciences have to say about the human body or brain, philosophical anthropology looks at the essence of human beings, which is a metaphysical question, whereas science looks at phenomena or theories that can be empirically verified; and an essence cannot be empirically verified.

Student: How is human nature defined in philosophical anthropology?

Teacher: Ancient philosophers have a clear awareness of the specialness of being human, and they link this to rationality. Aristotle defines the human being as a rational animal, and this notion prevails until the modern period and beyond. Human beings are defined in opposition to other animals that are not rational. For the ancients, human beings stand in between animals and the gods, who are superior to human beings, midway between earth and heaven. They are linked to the earth by the body, and to heaven by the soul, which mediates between these two worlds. The two worlds were, for most ancient and medieval philosophers, quite distinct.

Student: Like animals, we have a soul, though not we do not share a rational soul with other animals, as stated in ancient and medieval psychology.

Teacher: Psychology is an important discipline for us because it deals with the human soul, which is an aspect of spirit. Initially psychology was the science of the soul, which according to Plato was eternal, incorruptible, immortal, and similar to the forms, although it was linked to the body. Later Aristotle develops his theory of the soul and in the Middle Ages philosophers expanded on these theories in conjunction with scriptural accounts of the soul. The question of the nature and immortality of the soul still preoccupy modern philosophers, but later in the nineteenth century psychology becomes a separate scientific discipline based on empirical experimentation and scientific rules.

Returning to human nature as studied by philosophical anthropology, rationality is linked with the will and free will, as we have seen. Human beings can choose to be moral or otherwise. Therefore, they are considered to be virtuous but also sinful, and the question of free will, which as we see arises from being rational, is pivotal. An intellect which allows us to understand the difference between good and evil and to choose between them indicates that we have free will. Human beings are seen as capable of doing what is good, but also evil. This is attributed to different factors by different traditions. In the ancient Greek tradition, we are inferior to the gods and prone to mistakes. For the Christian and medieval tradition, human beings carry the original sin of their first ancestors. As a result, reason as well as the body are considered to be frail and limited, and it is necessary to rely on a higher power. This view begins to be reversed in the modern period, in which we find an unlimited trust in reason, especially during the Enlightenment. There is also a redefinition of what it means to be human. We have seen that Rousseau favors the will over the intellect; nor does he define human nature as intrinsically or originally rational, but rather emphasizes free will. Later, in the nineteenth century, there were further redefinitions of human nature arising from the advances of biological research and Darwin's work on the evolution of species.

Student: Does not evolution place us in the animal world as just another animal species among the others, simply more developed as a product of evolution?

Teacher: Evolution, as a biological theory, looks at the material aspects of human identity. For instance, it speaks of the brain and not the soul. In philosophical anthropology, we must not look at human beings as purely the effect of evolution; otherwise we would simply be a different kind of animal, but not really different from the other kinds of animals. Ethical action is guided by the spiritual principles of the truth and the good, as we have seen, and to deny these aspects would lead to the forcible abandonment of ethics, in addition to denying the purely human, which is spiritual and metaphysical.

Student: Would it not be a fallacy to justify our views of human nature and its spirituality on the basis of a certain goal, worthy as it is, for instance to preserve ethics?

Teacher: We can look at it in a different way, and define the human, from a meta-physical or epistemological perspective, as rational, without looking at empirical evidence or the testimony of the sciences. For instance, Descartes' mental experiment in the *Meditations on First Philosophy* is not empirical, but epistemological and even metaphysical, and it also tells us about human nature. We have seen that the sciences by definition look at material aspects of nature. However, we can start with a meta-physical view of human nature, and derive free will and ethics from our metaphysical starting point.

The classical view is that human beings are rational animals. We clearly see the spirituality in philosophical anthropology because the spiritual sphere is so important in defining human beings. That definition is linked to the intellect and the will but also with the other faculties or actions of the soul, such as representation, imagina-tion, and one could say even sensation. And there are definite consequences for ethics if we include spirituality, as we have seen.

Student: The metaphysical and the scientific perspectives on human nature are then quite distinct?

Teacher: It is possible to distinguish a metaphysical approach from a scientific ap-proach, although as we have said the latter should not be completely disregarded. We have seen that science looks at human beings from an empirical perspective, and therefore for science a human being is simply a more complex animal. Science does not primarily look at what is spiritual in human beings, but what is natural, even though human achievements may be vastly superior to the achievements of other animals. For science, a human being is a complex animal. Consequently, we need to look at human beings from a philosophical and metaphysical perspective which is not limited to biology and evolutionary history. We need other domains such as meta-physics and ethics in our analysis of human being. Questions of morality and right and wrong belong to the domain of ethics. If we look at human beings from a purely scientific perspective we cannot justify the notions of justice or morality. These, and the virtues, are clearly spiritual aspects because they embrace all the spiritual aspects of ethics.

Moreover, we can study human nature from an individual or a collective per-spective. In other words, we can consider human associations and social behavior, or we can consider human beings individually, in spite of common characteristics. Some aspects of contemporary philosophy have emphasized the individuality of human beings with regard to their position in history and in society, in particular existentialism. We have seen that philosophical anthropology and ethics share common themes such as the study of the nature of human beings, for human nature explains what we can expect from human beings and their relation with others, including other human beings and God. The question of free will and choice is very important.

Student: You mentioned that for science we are simply animals like other animals, in contrast to philosophical anthropology.

Teacher: The contrast between human beings and other animals is very important, but the findings of biology regarding both humans and animals should not be disregarded. Animals have feelings and even some kind of understanding, as the medieval philosophers already recognized. For instance, Avicenna states that the sheep uses its estimative faculty when seeing the wolf, and in this way recognizes the danger it represents for itself. Animals can be tamed and trained, and they have degrees of intelligence. They even use some kind of language, although they do not use codified language as human beings do. We know that they can use tools and they even form societies, that is, societal structures where the hierarchy among the different members of the group is clearly understood by its members.

Student: What can we say is specific to human beings, and how does that relate to spirit?

Teacher: As a result of rationality, human beings developed civilization and writing, for instance, as well as the different cultures and forms of religion, the sciences, technology, and the arts. Animals belong to the domain of nature, but human beings surpass those natural aspects to build civilization and the different fields of knowledge, the arts, and technology. That does not mean that we have the right to mistreat animals; on the contrary, we have more duties towards nature and the animal kingdom. Therefore human beings are animals but they have a complex spirituality which is lacking in animals. We could say as scientists that human beings have a more complex brain than other animals, but from a truly human or spiritual perspective we can speak of the soul, and of the virtues and the knowledge that the soul possesses. The soul is not just intellect, but also the other faculties which we can say are at the service of intellect. In order to keep humans' specificity we must keep a certain hierarchy within the human soul and in nature. Some might argue that this human superiority only serves for the purposes of physical existence and the survival of human beings in nature, but this would not explain what is typically or even specifically human. Moreover the question of progress, rather than biological evolution, is specifically human, as Rousseau stated. Although animals can evolve in terms of their adaptation to the natural conditions, human beings evolve not just as a response to different environments and natural challenges, they evolve by themselves.

Other than free will and responsibility, we can also mention individuality as an important aspect of human life. Each human being is responsible for his or her actions, and this is a central aspect in philosophical anthropology. Rousseau also emphasized this aspect of human nature. In ethics, human beings are not judged for their collective actions, but for their actions individually. This is also quite clear in several religions, hence the need to preserve the notion of an individual human personality.

We have looked into a controversy surrounding Averroes' works because he defended, in his later works on the soul, the idea that the individual human intellect would become united to the active intellect, and this would involve a loss of individuality and personal accountability. These are very important aspects for ethics but also for our understanding of what it means to be human.

The question of personality is also very important, and a philosophical movement, personalism, developed around it from the nineteenth century, with ethical but also metaphysical questions.

Student: What are the main theses asserted by personalism?

Teacher: Personalism values the question of personhood in human beings, as well as subjectivity and self-consciousness; it also stresses will, freedom, and responsibility in human beings, and the uniqueness of each human person. These aspects are part of human experience, and they influence relations between human beings, and between them and God. Other important concepts are autonomy, reason, and creativity as defining human nature. Personalism strongly defends the dignity of the human person.

The question of personality applies to human beings, but it also applies to God, in particular in Christianity, in which God is understood as one God and three persons. Moreover, the question of personality in human beings has to do with dispensing personal attention, being a specific substance, and many other aspects of being human.

Student: And how should we understand human nature, generally speaking?

Teacher: We have seen that human beings are identified with the subjective spirit, specifically finite spirit. They are subjects of knowledge and producers of knowledge, and they conceptualize objective being. This latter can also be understood as collective forms of subjective activity in human societies, as we have seen in Hegel.

Human beings also produce culture and civilization; they are not simply passive subjects of knowledge, but there is a practical and active aspect to their agency. Culture and civilization are related to history because they flourish at particular times in history. However, even though human beings are limited and conditioned by the culture and times in which they live, they must also be considered contributors to culture and not just consumers and products of their times and culture. The voluntary aspect of human beings is extremely important; in this sense, we cannot be surprised by Rousseau for considering the will the main attribute of human beings. We can defend the idea that the will and the intellect are the main attributes of human nature, although some philosophers will prefer intellect to the will and others the will to the intellect. Rationalist philosophers will naturally favor the intellect over the will and render the will subordinate to the intellect.

Student: At any rate, the will, specifically free will, is an essential element in ethics and in philosophical anthropology.

Teacher: Yes, it is important to affirm the existence of free will in human beings, which makes them responsible for their actions. Each being is autonomous and derives his or her free will from himself or herself, or, in other words, free will is constitutive of what it means to be a human being. Free will is an essential aspect of human nature. This means that we are not exclusively determined by external circumstances, be they natural or social, but we have an autonomous principle of action within ourselves. Natural science looks for necessary external (that is to say, efficient) causes for every phenomenon. Therefore it is difficult for science, as we have seen, to justify free will, since science seeks to determine the exact natural, physical, or material causes of a substance or a phenomenon. If we used the scientific model to explain human action, there would be no room for free will. We have seen that Kant illustrates the difference between the ethical causal order and the natural causal order as the third antinomy of reason, in his *Critique of Pure Reason*.

Student: Is there something else in relation to the will which is significant in connection with human nature?

Teacher: The question of the human soul and human destiny has been traditionally central to philosophy, and this is not unrelated to the question of free will. Nowadays, philosophers who do not believe in the immortality of the soul would claim that all our responsibilities are towards other human beings or other sentient beings with which we have contact in this life, rather than towards any superior being; this means that we are only held accountable by other human beings and with regard to the actions we carry out in relation to other human beings, and also other sentient beings such as animals. There are some challenges to this position, which only considers the result of our actions in this life, even if one is not religious. This is because traditionally the denial of the immortality of the soul goes hand in hand with materialism regarding human nature. We have seen the dangers posed by materialism to any affirmation of ethics.

According to this naturalistic view of human beings, there would be no other existence beyond this existence on earth. However, medieval philosophers, and religious philosophers in general, hold that we are judged not just by other human beings but also, and more importantly and decisively, by God, with regard to human action. Naturally, questions about God's justice arise. God is just and would not punish those who are not responsible for their actions. Responsibility means having free will, which renders us accountable for what we do. At the same time, God determines everything that happens and knows the past, the present, and the future in an infinite now. Consequently, philosophers have sought to reconcile human free will with God's omnipotence and justice. Freedom and the soul are important aspects of human nature, for religious and non-religious philosophers. Only free will ensures accountability, in this life or the next. This is why the questions of individuality and personal accountability are so important. The individual is personally responsible for his or her own acts. This question is evidenced by a medieval debate regarding the human intellect and what happens to it in the afterlife. We have seen that after studying closely Aristotle's conception of the human intellect, Averroes concludes not only that the active intellect is a separate intellect which is always thinking, but also that the human material intellect is such that it joins the active intellect upon death, which means that every human intellect becomes united to this active intellect and loses its individuality. Aquinas and other Christian theologians were extremely critical of this view because it undermined personal and individual accountability and responsibility, and therefore God's judgment at the end of times. This shows how important the question of autonomy and responsibility is. With regard to human nature we can thus conclude that the will and the intellect, and intelligence and morality, are extremely important.

Student: What else can we say about human nature in connection with our main topic, which is spirit?

Teacher: The different faculties or actions of the mind or the soul are all part of what it means to be human. Being human implies the abilities and the actions which are characteristic of being human, such as work and play, action and contemplation. In addition, being human also includes theoretical and practical aspects, and among the practical or active aspects we could mention the emotions.

Student: The emotions are then an important aspect of human nature.

Teacher: The emotions or the passions of the soul were a central subject of studies in modern philosophy. This does not mean an endorsement of unbridled emotions; rather, they were considered something to be controlled. This is the view propounded by Spinoza, who showed Stoic leanings in this and other respects. The emotions were analyzed according to their active and positive or passive and negative aspects. The intellect was supposed to control the emotions, or the passions, as they were known.

Student: This theme is still studied today, not least in psychology.

Teacher: Today we see that intelligence, or the capacity to understand something and engage in specific reasoning, is related to the emotions. The emotions and directed attention are extremely important in our perception of reality; we see the central role of the intellect, of the emotions and of taking a personal interest, in attaining an intellectual objective. It is not just the question of realizing how one's mood can affect learning; in the learning process it is important to stress how the things we learn relate to us. Our personal experience influences the way we learn and remember things, and how we interpret them. Therefore the study of human personality is much more complex today, as we find the connections between these different aspects concerning the learning experience. We should not ignore what science has to say about these aspects of human nature and experience. This is not to say that previous philosophers, in the ancient and the medieval periods, did not seek to connect the various faculties, for they devised a very systematic way of linking them in a clear hierarchy. However, today they are understood as being even more connected, and the boundaries between them are more fluid. Nevertheless, it is important to see what is specifically human, and this means looking at ethics and metaphysics and not simply empirical phenomena.

When it comes to the universal and the particular with regard to human nature, we usually associate the theoretical or intellectual with the universal and the practical or active with the particular. However, this distinction does not always apply. The principles of politics or ethics are also universal, even though they were traditionally considered to belong to practical philosophy. And theory is often related to practice. If we think of contemplation, mystical or religious, as conceptual, we find that it is theoretical but also practical, or having practical rules or principles.

Student: We can then conclude that spirit is at the heart of philosophical anthropology?

Teacher: That is correct. And this can be observed from various perspectives. We see the connection between philosophical anthropology and the other philosophical disciplines, especially metaphysics, theory of knowledge, and ethics. Metaphysics affirms the existence of spirit, and allows us to perceive it in human beings, especially with respect to the faculties of the soul or the actions of the mind, and also in our relations with superior spirits, particularly God. The question of the human soul and intellect leads to the theory of knowledge, and in this case human knowledge. Theory of knowledge can treat of different kinds of knowledge, human, angelic, and divine, but it intersects with philosophical anthropology when it speaks of human knowledge, which, as we have seen, is spiritual since it does not make sense to for it to be purely material. The notion of material knowledge is a contradiction in terms.

Student: We saw that in our investigation of the meaning of spirit in the various philosophical disciplines, it makes sense to start from knowledge in our understanding of ourselves and of the world, as Descartes does in his *Metaphysical Meditations*. This reinforces our notion of human nature as essentially spiritual, and our knowledge is also spiritual. Knowledge is spiritual and reality turns out to be also spiritual.

Teacher: We cannot advance beyond our own perception and knowledge, which may include grounded opinions, even if we can recognize a superior knowledge in other beings. All knowledge is at bottom spiritual, as early as Plato and Aristotle. As a result, there is no such thing as sensible knowledge, unless we call sensation a kind of knowledge; but even sensation can be seen to revert to the domain of spirit. In ethics, spirit is also present, as we have seen. There is no ethics worthy of the name without the meaning of spirit and the sense of purpose and intention in action. Intention is the inner motive when an action is carried out according to a plan, which is to say in intentional actions. Ethics is something purely human, and it evinces the spiritual in human beings. Human beings are essentially spiritual in their actions and knowledge.

Student: Would it be possible to find spirituality in animals?

Teacher: That is a very good question. They are sentient beings, and if we include sensation as part of spirituality, they could qualify as spiritual, at least in part. Some species have a social life and form social communities, and some religions maintain that animals worship God. In that sense, one could speak of spirituality. Animals have perception, which is something more developed than mere sensation, and some of them dream in their sleep, which appears to indicate some kind of representation or imagination. They form strong bonds with human beings, and have complex feelings and even perhaps personal or at least individual traits. Still, they do not have such complex language or produce works of art as we do, and law does not consider them liable, which is perhaps the most striking difference between human beings and animals. We do not tend to make animals responsible for their actions in the way that we make humans responsible, which means that ethics remains something essentially pertaining to human action. However, there is some kind of limited spirituality also in animals.

Student: The link between human beings and spirit is significant?

Teacher: Absolutely, and we must stress the spiritual nature of human beings, otherwise we cannot speak of ethics or religion.

Student: In the same way that reality is also material, can we not say the same of human beings?

Teacher: The human being is not exclusively spiritual, and there is a material or corporeal aspect which must be contemplated as part of human personality. The connection between the spiritual and the corporeal is very important, and the two aspects should be articulated in the right way. Since spirit is superior to matter, the soul should control the body and the body serve the soul. This idea was already defended and illustrated by Plato in a moving and compelling way. The body should serve the soul as much as possible, although it has its own needs, such as sleeping and eating. We must not defend a dualistic philosophical anthropology but try to harmonize both aspects of human nature, body and soul.

To sum up, in philosophical anthropology, as in the other philosophical disciplines we have analyzed, the presence of spirit is abundantly clear. In philosophy of religion this spirituality is also observable, and again, we could argue that religion is restricted to human beings. Religion includes a theoretical and practical aspect, which we find respectively in dogma and worship. Religion means a connection with God, which moreover unites human beings in communities, and this is something typically human.

We will now see that disciplines such as aesthetics and philosophy of science also show the key presence of spirit in human activity and in reality.

Philosophy of Nature and Science

Student: If all knowledge is spiritual, scientific knowledge is also spiritual, and also the philosophy of science.

Teacher: Yes, other philosophical disciplines evince spiritual activity too. Philosophy of science shows that scientific theories are part of human beings' general knowledge and that they have a spiritual foundation. Spiritual contemplation and activity underlie aesthetics. These two latter disciplines point not just to spirituality but also to material aspects of reality. Science looks at the material universe, although it approaches it from a theoretical point of view. There is a practical aspect when technology is developed on the basis of scientific theories. In fact, the connection between science and technology shows the theory-dependent aspect of science and knowledge in general.

Student: How is that the case—I mean the primacy of theory in science?

Teacher: We see that, in the history of technology, often the scientific and theoretical basis of a technological advance precedes by a long time the actual technological development based on the implementation of a given scientific theory. In other words, theory develops before practice.

Student: We have discussed the interaction between philosophy and the sciences and nature in the ancient and up to the modern period.

Teacher: Yes, and it is important to mention that there is a distinction between philosophy of nature and philosophy of science. Philosophy of nature studies nature as a whole, as well as the concept of nature, while philosophy of science studies anything related to the natural sciences. Both disciplines issue from the discipline of natural philosophy, which included physics but also the natural sciences generally speaking. Philosophy of nature was developed especially in the modern period and particularly by the German idealists, not least Hegel, and also Schelling, in their efforts to reconcile spirit and nature. Schelling wrote on the relationship between spirit and nature, stating that nature is the product of spirit. More recently, with the development and the autonomization of the various natural sciences, the philosophy of science and of the particular sciences, such as mathematics, physics, and biology, came into being.

With regard to the development of the philosophical study of science, Aristotle's *Physics* considers various aspects related to nature and the natural sciences; it analyzes nature in itself but also the laws of physics and the essence of space and time. Aristotle considers nature to be the principle of rest and motion in substances, and this view is adopted by later philosophers who followed the Aristotelian tradition. In Aristotle, one finds both a philosophy of nature and a treatment of the various sciences. Later, philosophy of nature and the philosophy of particular sciences became separate disciplines. Physics was the science of nature, but for Aristotle it also embraced psychology because the human soul was in charge of the body and of physiological and bodily functions. There was a strict separation between the faculties of the soul according to the various philosophers. Psychology no longer considers the different acts of the mind as separate faculties, as we have seen.

After the Middle Ages, in which the Aristotelian conception of science dominated, the various sciences became gradually independent of philosophy and they became more empirically based, and more closely modeled on mathematics. The qualitative aspects in science were replaced by quantitative and measurable aspects. Therefore the forms and the substantial forms were banished, precisely because they were qualitative aspects, not quantifiable or empirically verifiable. Science also began to abandon metaphysical notions as well as its links with religion and philosophy.

Student: Did the Presocratics not advance some aspects of modern science?

Teacher: In a certain sense, there was a kind of empirical or materialistic science with the Presocratics, based on empirical observation, although there were also sweeping generalizations and recourse to qualities and mythical aspects. However, the empiricist or materialist trend was definitely reversed by Plato, who famously chose, in his dialogues, not least the *Phaedo*, to resort to the forms, which are qualities, in order to explain everything, including natural phenomena. He explains that someone becomes tall not by eating certain amounts of food but by participation or sharing in the form of tallness. Aristotle's views differ from Plato's in many respects. He did not believe in separate forms and he held that knowledge starts from the senses (hence the famous affirmation at the opening of his *Metaphysics* to the effect that human beings by nature like to know, which is proved by the fact that they are so attached to the senses). This means that for Aristotle cognition starts from the perception of individual material objects. In other ways he continued to resort to forms or qualities to explain natural phenomena. The form or definition of something was meant to explain its essential qualities. In science we have to include the material cause, as we have seen, and it explains the material characteristics of an object. Aristotle has a metaphysical way of looking at matter which is absent from the contemporary philosophy of science, by saying that it is passive and inert and only becomes active through form. In addition, the final cause is important for him in explaining natural phenomena. For instance, teeth are shaped in different ways according to their purposes, which explain their shape. In this way the prevalence of quality over quantity and number continued throughout the ancient and the medieval period until it was finally challenged in the modern period. This became apparent, as we have seen, in the abolishment of the substantial form. The medieval period follows Aristotle in its approach to science. This is not to say that there was no recourse to experimentation, but the qualitative and metaphysical element in science predominated.

On the other hand, we cannot say that modern science simply takes up where the Presocratics left off. Nevertheless, the return to empirical science and observation, and quantification, became very important.

Student: With regard to theory of knowledge, and including the knowledge of nature, the modern period presents a debate between rationalism and empiricism.

Teacher: Yes, and we have seen that later Hegel seeks to combine these various approaches to metaphysics and epistemology, contextualizing them in their disciplinary and historical context. Although his ultimate position is that of absolute or objective idealism, which means that he is more clearly aligned with the rationalists of the modern period, he accepts that empiricism is the natural approach of the natural sciences, in the sense that they accept sense data and they theorize based on the findings of sense data.

Student: In addition, we saw that in the modern period not only epistemological but also methodological questions are significant.

Teacher: In the modern period the question of scientific methodology is extremely important, given the development of the scientific method, which postulates the formulation of hypotheses which are then empirically tested. The development of scientific technology is also important in this period and it goes hand in hand with the development of the sciences; in fact, technology can lead to the development of new scientific approaches, although conversely new scientific theories can lead to the development of technology.

The two main epistemological approaches in modern philosophy, rationalism and empiricism, also apply to the philosophy of science or nature. In this way, the rationalists focus on the role of reason in the experimental process with an emphasis on scientific theories and also on the contribution of reason, independently of sense experience, to scientific knowledge. The empiricists in turn defend the idea that all knowledge comes from sense experience and the mind is a blank slate before the senses are used. Therefore, in their view the most important aspect in science and scientific knowledge, and indeed the origin of scientific knowledge, lies in experimentation.

On the one hand, these two views are present, to a certain extent, in Aristotle. Rationalism tends to be identified with Plato's philosophy (with its emphasis on the eternal ideas); and we have seen how Descartes likewise defends the notion of innate ideas that are inborn in the mind. Aristotle locates the origin of knowledge in sense perception, but he equally claims that all knowledge, albeit originating initially from sense perception, is actually purely universal. True knowledge is universal. In modern philosophy, Kant seeks to unite both aspects in distinguishing between the a priori and the a posteriori elements in knowledge, as well as between synthetic and analytic propositions. In this way, he seeks to highlight two aspects of cognition: that which comes from reason and the categories of perception on the one hand, and the sensory circumstances of scientific knowledge on the other. When it comes to the question of the scientific method, both reason and sense experience are interrelated and cannot be separated.

Student: How can we integrate the rational and the empirical aspects in scientific knowledge?

Teacher: A hypothesis is required before carrying out an experiment or a series of experiments, and there is a contextual framework in which scientific knowledge develops; equally, some ideas for hypotheses and scientific theories may originate from sense experience broadly construed.

Contemporary philosophy of science studies scientific phenomena, the laws of nature, and general philosophical questions applied to the sciences, such as the question of realism and anti-realism, causation and scientific explanation, and the unity of science. Philosophy of science is further divided into the different scientific disciplines considered by philosophy; in this way, there is a philosophy of mathematics, a philosophy of physics, and a philosophy of biology, for instance.

Student: Where can we find the spiritual element in the sciences, if the metaphysical outlook on the sciences was abandoned in the modern period?

Teacher: It is true that there has been an attempt to disregard any metaphysical aspects in the sciences, and also to remove any theological element from the sciences, although some philosophers may still attempt to see the connections between science and religion. Most of analytic philosophy of science is based on logical positivism or logical empiricism, the view that science concerns itself with and speaks only of what is empirically verifiable. This automatically excludes any metaphysical aspects, which are not perceived by the senses, and in that respect cannot be discussed in a meaningful and scientific way. Verificationism goes hand in hand with this position: only that which has empirical existence and can be empirically observed is meaningful in any way—in spite of the fact the science devises theories which are successful in predicting phenomena and are based on unobservable factors. In trying to exclude metaphysics, logical positivism paradoxically takes a metaphysical position, which is the assumption that only the material or logical is true to the exclusion of the spiritual. This position itself cannot be physically verified and is therefore a metaphysical theory.

Student: It appears that even in philosophy of science a metaphysical position cannot be avoided. I wonder if the distinction between empiricism and rationalism is discussed in philosophy of science today, and if there are other connections with episte-mology and metaphysics?

Teacher: In modern philosophy empiricism is usually associated with realism, and rationalism with idealism, for empiricism implies the acceptance of sense data, while rationalism is centered on ideas and theories with regard to science. However, there is also empiricist anti-realism with its distinction between observable and unobservable phenomena. Moreover, several theories can explain the same phenomenon, leading to an anti-realism in science which can be articulated with empiricism and even verifi-cationism.

Student: This means that the theories do not correspond exactly with facts or empiri-cal phenomena?

Teacher: Exactly, hence the difficulty of abandoning metaphysics, in spite of the fact that the practice of science itself has dispensed with metaphysics and religious influ-ence. We have seen that metaphysics is associated primarily with a certain Aristoteli-an or Neoplatonic perspective that unites all the different sciences under the same umbrella, which is first philosophy, or metaphysics. In the modern period, metaphys-ics included the belief in the existence of God and the immortality of the soul. The belief in God implied an associated belief in God's providence, but this was based on the defense of the idea of the final cause, which as we have seen was banished from modern science. The latter upheld the idea of a mechanical universe where the effi-cient cause was understood as the true cause. The final cause or the notion of purpose in nature was considered to be unscientific because it did not truly explain, let alone allow the prediction of, phenomena. Moreover, the spiritual element in nature, for instance the view that human beings have a spiritual, immortal soul, was abandoned, because this could not be quantified or empirically verified. Mathematics and the results of empirical testing became the guiding lines of science. In the early modern period the empirical and the metaphysical aspects went hand in hand, but the clash between them was becoming more and more apparent, and so the distinction between science and theology became evident.

Student: How does metaphysics remain present in contemporary philosophy of sci-ence?

Teacher: Although metaphysics was considered obsolete, the discipline of ontology remained active in contemporary philosophy, and even metaphysics as a whole is seen to be making a comeback. In our analysis of the spiritual in science we will therefore not limit ourselves to the explicitly metaphysical aspect, which would confine us to science up to and including the modern period, to the exclusion of the contemporary period.

In addition, we cannot judge the spiritual aspect merely by the metaphysical element, since the spiritual element is broader because it reaches other philosophical disciplines. Nevertheless, in other ways it can be identified with metaphysics because metaphysics looks at non-material, or pre-material, or pre-sensorial aspects of reality.

Student: Which spiritual elements can we find in science?

Teacher: In science we can discover several spiritual aspects which are part of the philosophy of science and which go hand in hand with the theory of knowledge. In science, there is a theoretical and a practical aspect. It is necessary to form a theory and then test it empirically. Clearly, the theoretical part is spiritual, because a theory has no material aspect in itself. Scientific methodology is based on theories. When the empirical test is carried out, it must fit with other theories and the initial hypothesis. Consequently we start with a theory and end up with a theory.

Student: The process of the development of science is then both theoretical and practical, but the theoretical aspect prevails?

Teacher: In the experimentation process, we use our senses and then rationalize the experiment and the outcome of the experiment. The instruments used are also important and serve as a filter between the subject (the scientist) and the object studied and experimented upon. Science, and scientific practice, involves concepts and ideas and theoretical constructs. We could call this the rational or conceptual aspect of science, and it truly falls within the remit of the spiritual, as it cannot be reduced to anything material or to anything that is not spiritual.

Student: Then the scientific method has a spiritual framework?

Teacher: An initial hypothesis is formulated which is related to other theories within science, and the experiment is conceived in relation to the theory. Finally, there follows the confirmation or negation of the hypothesis and the resulting adjustment in relation to the overall theory being tested. The theory constitutes the framework of the experiment or set of experiments. Naturally, spontaneous observations or impressions can lead to further hypotheses and theories, but again, science works essentially with theories and with universal knowledge. The central role of theory in the scientific process constitutes its spiritual framework.

Student: And what constitutes a scientific theory?

Teacher: There are criteria for scientific theories in the sense that they should be simple, comprehensive, consistent, and accurate, as defended by Kuhn. Any qualitative elements must be able to be translated quantitatively. The theory should offer predictive reliability. There are also creative and aesthetic aspects in science when a theory is chosen for its elegance or depth.

Student: It is obvious that the theoretical formulation and the experimental practice of science have an underlying spiritual element. Are there other spiritual aspects in science which can be formulated as part of philosophy of science?

Teacher: On the one hand, science itself, in its theory and practice, displays spiritual elements. We could think of philosophy of science as an added element which contributes to the spiritual in science. Even the question of idealism and realism, which originates in theory of knowledge, has a place in the philosophy of science.

Student: You have mentioned the presence of realism and idealism in philosophy of science. What is the meaning of realism or idealism in science?

Teacher: Realism and idealism apply here, naturally, to scientific theories. If the theory is seen to correspond exactly to reality, we have realism in science. In this case, the theory purports to show reality independently of our thoughts. If, on the other hand, theories and experiments do not correspond exactly to reality, then we have anti-realism or idealism in science. Realism derives from a general realist conception and the trust in the senses, and naturally also the assumption of an underlying material element. The idealist position is based on several aspects of scientific theory and practice. For instance, several theories can explain the same observation. And the fact that scientific experiments require complex instruments and technology also go some way towards supporting an idealist position in philosophy of science. This idealism claims that the theory corresponds to the experiment or the observation but not exactly or precisely. The instrument creates added problems and a veil between the subject and the object of the scientific investigation.

Student: Are there other basic epistemological positions influencing philosophy of science?

Teacher: There is also skepticism in science regarding some basic assumptions, for instance causality. These aspects can be observed in some contemporary theories in physics. In quantum physics, the causal link between cause and effect cannot always be exactly determined and an element of probability becomes fundamental in explaining phenomena.

Student: One would assume that realism and empiricism are the natural epistemological positions in science, but idealism appears to have an important presence in science too.

Teacher: There are other positions in the philosophy of science which go hand in hand with an idealist position or support an idealist position. This is, for instance, Thomas Kuhn's theory of scientific revolutions and paradigm shifts.

Student: What does Kuhn say regarding the development of science?

Teacher: He challenged several assumptions concerning scientific theory and scientific practice in philosophy of science. While science assumed the notion of a constant progress in science, Kuhn defended the idea of a succession of paradigms which are not necessarily related or commensurable. Science follows a certain paradigm or a general scientific theory or set of theories. During the period when a paradigm prevails there is normal science, in which scientists' work follows the prevailing scientific paradigm. Special scientific definitions belong to a certain period and may not be available before or after, or be compatible with previous definitions of the same subjects. When a paradigm ceases to explain phenomena a scientific revolution takes place and a new paradigm comes into place.

Student: What are examples of different paradigms?

Teacher: For instance, examples of two different paradigms are the Ptolemaic paradigm and the Copernican paradigm regarding astronomy and the place of the planet Earth in the universe. Kuhn is also innovative in taking into account the history of science in his theory of scientific theories, stressing the importance of historical factors, while science itself abstracts from these elements and seeks to isolate or eliminate them. On this view, science and the philosophy of science cannot be dissociated, and many developments of contemporary science prompt questions that pertain to the philosophy of science. The implicit idealism in this position boils down to science's dependence on theories. Scientific knowledge is based on theories which may not have an exact correspondence to reality. This approach could also be termed a constructivist account of science. It clashes with the previous tradition of logical positivism, which based science on empirical facts. Kuhn defended the view that the knowledge of fundamental laws by scientists within a certain paradigm was of an a priori character. In addition, observation was considered to be determined by theory.

Student: Is an idealist position in science inevitable, then?

Teacher: Certain objections, or at least exceptions, to an idealist position in science could be adduced by realists in philosophy of science. Realism is based on the idea of the reliability of the scientific method as a true description of reality; the predictability of scientific phenomena would confirm the accuracy of theories and their correlation to truth and reality. Naturally one's approach to the history of science is also important in this respect. We could see continuity or discontinuity. Kuhn stresses the discontinuity of paradigms, which according to him are self-contained moments in the history of science.

Student: How could the continuity or discontinuity of science be related to the question of realism or idealism?

Teacher: The question of continuity is quite complex. Some realists would claim that science follows certain rules. In particular they would claim that science uses the scientific method, which includes the setting of hypotheses and testing them, leading to a general theory which helps to predict further similar phenomena. According to this view, there is just one definition of science, and it came into being in the modern period. This view further states that ancient and medieval science was not truly science by modern standards, both in its theories and definitions and in its practice.

However, this rejection of certain periods of the history of science (prior to the modern period) in order to stress continuity is challenged by the fact that, if we use Kuhn's principles, there are different and successive paradigms in the modern period itself.

Student: So if modern science followed one single model, there would not be more than one paradigm in modern science.

Teacher: That is correct. In addition, it is now clear that some theories within the same period of science are not clearly related, or are downright incompatible. Therefore, this kind of realism within the history of science has been challenged. However, it seeks to present one clear definition of science in order to have a coherent general theory about science.

Student: Perhaps if we have a broader definition of science we can include ancient and medieval scientific discoveries as part of science in general.

Teacher: Yes, another way of looking at the history of science centers on continuity rather than on the breaks. Although the modern period clearly saw the rise of empirical science and the application of mathematics, which is a rationalist trait in modern science, some continuity in all history of science can be seen across the various scientific disciplines. For instance, the same general themes are present in science. Physics still talks about movement and force, as well as causation, space, and time, like Aristotelian physics. Moreover, we have seen that atoms feature in both ancient and contemporary science, although the ancient and the modern conceptions of atoms are very different. According to the ancients, an atom was not divisible into further parts, although both in ancient and in modern science they are the ultimate constituents of physical reality. Even modern quantum theory has something in common with ancient and medieval questions about science and changing phenomena.

Student: What is there in common between quantum theory and ancient and medieval science?

Teacher: Ancient and medieval science were preoccupied with the question of whether change from one substance to another and other such physical phenomena happened gradually or by leaps. In quantum theory this is applied to the place of the electron within the atom, whose movement occurs in leaps, rather than gradually. In biology, we still use the categories of species and genus which were conceived by Aristotle. Naturally, these are very different ways of considering the same scientific constructs, but the continuity can be seen. In addition, a new paradigm can be defined in relation and in contrast to its predecessor. It is also possible for us today to interpret ancient theories as corresponding to reality as perceived by the senses or by common sense.

Student: How can we understand the place of common sense in ancient science?

Teacher: For instance, the existence of the four elements is intuitive. The ancients saw how the earth was an important element and how it supported another element, water, which was essential for life. The air was considered to be placed above water, and it was followed by fire, which according to the ancients existed above the air given its tendency to travel upwards. Fire was thought to exist in the sky because of phenomena such as thunderstorms and lightening. In this way, the theory of the four elements, first devised by Empedocles, as we have seen, is an intuitive way of analyzing material reality. Ancient theories can still be seen to make sense in this way. When we think of the ancient philosophers of nature and their view of the four basic elements, we can see how they would make sense to them and to anyone using the naked eye to observe nature. These elements were seen as essential components of nature, like air and water, as well as the ground we tread. Their qualities correspond to sense perception; for instance, the fact that water is cold seems to correspond to our sense perception—it only becomes hot if heated.

Student: Today, however, common sense and the senses are not really considered a good guide to the perception of scientific reality.

Teacher: Today we have much more powerful technology which confirms existing theories and helps us to devise new ones. Nowadays, we have a much more complex view of all the elements of nature and each discipline is much more specialized, but ancient theories continue to have a meaning and an explanation. Even current relativity theory and quantum theory issue from an expansion of our horizons into the almost infinitely large and the almost infinitely small. Some scientific topics are more important than others in different periods of history. For instance, the nature of matter was very important in the ancient and the medieval period, and into the modern period, but it does not seem to be a focus of contemporary philosophy of science, and it is discussed by scientists more than by philosophers of science. Scientists now consider matter's relation to mass, or rather the relation between mass and energy, and they consider matter in terms of the different particles; the question of matter becomes even more complex with talk of dark or invisible matter.

Whether we believe in discontinuous paradigms or in continuity, what defines science is scientific theories, and they are spiritual. Naturally, it is easier to find the spiritual in an idealist position regarding science, but even the realists do not deny the centrality of theories for science.

Student: Should we prefer continuity to discontinuity or the reverse?

Teacher: Going back to Kuhn, it is possible to see different paradigms in different periods of history, but it is also the case that there can be continuity, and some scientists strive to maintain that continuity, even though history of science is very different from science itself. Science seeks the truth objectively, independently of the circumstances, historical or sociological, and therefore it avoids breaks, whereas the history of science looks at the historical and cultural context of scientific practice. Continuity would mean objectivity and coherence of theories across different periods in history. We know, for instance, that Einstein was concerned with the continuity of his relativity theory in relation to Newton's theories of gravity, and therefore he formulated the general relativity theory after conceiving special relativity theory. Perhaps there is some continuity and some discontinuity in the history of science. The most important thing for us is to state the role of theories in approaching science and nature itself, and in this way we stress the spirituality of science. As we have seen, the significance of theories links science not only with philosophy in its attempt to explain reality, but also with aesthetics, since some theories are chosen for their beauty and coherence, as well as their functionality and instrumentality.

Student: Are there other aspects of science which might be considered spiritual?

Teacher: Other aspects include that which sociology of science studies, in other words, the surrounding circumstances or conditions for science; namely, why certain topics are chosen in certain societies, and whether certain topics appeal more to women scientists or male scientists, or whether male scientists tend to study certain topics and women scientists others. This could include the question of whether a particular culture or religion tends to study certain topics. It often seems that science, in particular the pure sciences, are universal and do not depend on culture or circumstances, but the topics studied could vary from culture to culture. The application of science is also tied to cultural aspects. It is thought, for instance, that Islamic astronomy developed to a great degree in the Middle Ages because it was important to determine the phases of the moon, in order to know the precise dates of the start of Islamic festivals. In this sense, certain aspects of science could be developed according to cultural and religious needs. Many other examples could be adduced. The circumstances surrounding the practice and development of science could be analyzed in relation not just to groups of people and human societies, but also in connection with individual scientists; in other words, particular cases could be studied by psychology, in which case we would have a psychology of science. More generally speaking, some universal aspects of the sciences, including logic, may not be so universal after all. Hegel showed that there is a different kind of logic which does not apply to science as we know it today but applies to other fields of human culture and experience. In this sense the cultural aspects cannot be isolated from science and they must be studied in the philosophy of science. If science is completely objective and unchanging, it should not vary according to the culture in which it is practiced, but we sometimes see that a cultural influence is at work.

Student: Is there also a materialist perspective on science?

Teacher: Yes, and it takes on several forms. One way is to reduce all knowledge, such as epistemology, and philosophy itself, to an empirical science, and to say that all science and indeed all knowledge is empirical.

Student: We saw that empiricism need not be convertible with materialism.

Teacher: Empiricism and materialism are two different kinds of theories, since empiricism is an epistemological theory, that is to say, it concerns the nature of knowledge and the origin of knowledge. It states that knowledge comes from the senses and is based on sense perception. Empiricism means knowledge by experience, and experience can mean many different things. One could speak of a mystical experience, which is not sensory or perceptual; but usually by empiricism we mean sensory experience. And sensory experience relates to the result of sense perception, that is, sense data. Generally speaking, empiricism stresses knowledge by sense perception, and sense perception is of material things. Empiricism does not defend the knowledge of unobservable phenomena. Therefore empiricism usually means that our knowledge of reality is premised on the notion of material objects. A philosopher like Aristotle, who can be considered by some scholars to be an empiricist, in actual fact stresses that knowledge is spiritual, as we have seen. Moreover, a philosopher like Berkeley, who denies the existence of matter, can be called an empiricist, since he believes that all knowledge comes from sense perception, as Aristotle had claimed before. In fact, Berkeley claims that the senses receive the most vivid impressions, in relation to the intellect. However, as we have seen, he does not make a marked distinction between sensation and intellectual apprehension, so in some cases empiricism can go hand in hand with immaterialism, if we use Berkeley's own description of his philosophy. The senses perceive that which is material, unless we defend a theory of radical idealism as does Berkeley.

Materialism itself, on the other hand, is an assumption about reality rather than about our knowledge of reality, and it states that reality is material or is all based on material things. In the philosophy of science this has a different name, which is physicalism. Physicalism states that all reality, or all phenomena, are physical or composed of physical phenomena. However, physicalism itself is a theory, which means that it belongs to the realm of the spiritual. The theory itself proves that not all is material, and we could speak of a contradiction in terms in this case, or a self-defeating theory. Some philosophers of science, such as Arthur Fine, would hold that these theories about knowledge, such as realism, are metaphysical theories which cannot be confirmed or falsified by scientific experimentation and theories.

Student: Is there a particular science which is especially representative of the scientific method today?

Teacher: Physics holds pride of place among the natural or empirical sciences, because it looks at the fundamental aspects of material reality and the universe. Also, it has been successful in terms of predicting and explaining natural phenomena. Therefore, when we speak of reductionism within science or the unity of science we speak of applying the laws or principles of physics to the other sciences, even to sciences other than the natural sciences, for instance economics. However, mathematization cannot be applied equally in all the sciences, for instance in biology. We also see that in the hierarchy of sciences some low-level phenomena can explain higher-level ones, and vice versa, which means that the hierarchy of the sciences is not clearly defined.

Student: A theory of everything would explain all phenomena in the world?

Teacher: We can think of a united physics theory which would account for all physical phenomena at all levels and that would be a positive development. However, to say that a scientific theory of everything would replace other kinds of explanation, such as theological explanation, is reductive and a false approach. The natural sciences should have their autonomy and so should other branches of knowledge and aspects of human experience.

Aesthetics

Student: Speaking of different accounts of human existence, can we also think of aesthetics or philosophy of art in connection with the question of spirit?

Teacher: It is important to reflect on the disciplines related to art and to the understanding of the beautiful. Ancient philosophy considers beauty as a philosophical category. For Plato, the beautiful was naturally a form among the other eternal forms, and a beautiful thing was not to be explained through size or color, but through its participation in the eternal form. The principles applying to the other forms applied also to the beautiful, which was a purely spiritual principle. In Aristotle, the question was more about art and its function for the individual and society; in this way, Aristotle considers the art and the role of theatre and its function, which had practical purposes in addition to its theoretical principles. In the medieval period, art becomes mainly religious and this tendency remains in the modern period, only changing in the contemporary period. Even Hegel, in the *Phenomenology of Spirit*, considers art primarily as religious art. The link between art and religion is quite strong.

Returning to the beautiful, in medieval philosophy it is considered as an important concept and it was related to the transcendentals. The beautiful was in fact counted among the transcendentals for some of the medieval philosophers. In modern philosophy, the beautiful is considered to be spirit in nature; or, rather, beauty expresses what is spiritual in nature, and the fact that matter is subordinate to form, to order, and to an intelligence. We have seen how the classical tradition views the beautiful as something universal. For Plato, it was one of the universal and eternal ideas. For a modern philosopher like Kant, perception of the beautiful implies an agreement between the imagination and the intellect, and therefore a kind of intuitive thought.

Student: Naturally, there is a difference between aesthetics and philosophy of art?

Teacher: Aesthetics is derived from the Greek verb "to feel" and it has to do with perception and enjoyment. Moreover, aesthetics included knowledge and the science of the beautiful, which remains a pivotal concept in art. More recent considerations about art tend to be described as philosophy of art rather than aesthetics, since the beautiful is not always considered a central aspect in contemporary art. Aesthetics, a term coined in the modern period by Baumgarten in the 18th century, was related to perception and the beautiful, whereas today the focus is on the work of art itself. Aesthetics consisted in the study of the beautiful and how it affected our faculties. Nowadays there is a focus on the object of art itself, and how it is defined, for instance, as opposed to other artifacts and objects. In the modern period there was a debate concerning whether the notion of beauty was objective or subjective. The ancients believed that it was objective and was based on objective qualities such as proportion, order, and mathematical qualities. In the modern period it referred to the subject's apprehension of the work of art and therefore it depended on the eye of the beholder.

Student: I can see the link between the material and the spiritual in aesthetics or philosophy of art. More specifically, how do art and the object of art mediate between spirit and nature?

Teacher: That is certainly a valid way of looking at aesthetics and the philosophy of art. Art expresses itself in a material support and it affects the senses, especially sight and hearing, and in this way there is a material and a spiritual aspect to it. We admire art, for instance painting or music, with the senses.

Student: The spiritual starts with our intellectual appreciation of art, then?

Teacher: Yes. There are different conceptions about art, but it can be seen to start with the admiration of beauty in nature. Consequently, nature provides a model, and is itself a show of beauty. Art is something spiritual because it is not recognized by the senses but by the mind and the intellect, although it exists in a material support.

Student: Art is also spiritual in the sense that it is produced by human beings according to an intellectual plan?

Teacher: Naturally, art, or some kinds of art, can be seen to mimic nature and nature may stand at the origin of the work of art. However, art is something that is produced by human beings. In this sense, natural objects can be beautiful but are not considered to be art. Art is the product of human hands and human minds, and the material is a means to an end which is the project of the artist. Art relates to production, and to the reason or intellect of the artist, and art is enjoyed by reason.

Student: The plan or final cause is also an essential element in the production of the work of art?

Teacher: The final cause or the goal is central to the production of a work of art, because the artist works according to a plan. In addition, one might speak of the aesthetic enjoyment and well-being caused by the various forms and objects of art, and the social benefits of art, as a kind of goal or outcome of a work of art. This is a theme already present in Aristotle, when he speaks of the cathartic effects of theatre and in particular tragedy. He considered that theatre purged negative emotions and moral tendencies in theatre-goers, when they see the negative effects of certain negative emotions and false moral choices on the characters of the play. Others, however, stressed the final purpose of art as an end in itself; this was also a recurrent theme in aesthetics and philosophy of art. Kant stressed that the aesthetic experience was disinterested.

In art, the material aspect is elevated to the spiritual but both are present; nevertheless, the material cause is a subordinate cause. If we speak of matter and form in art, matter is subordinated to the form. Art also indicates the final cause, similarly to ethics. The centrality of the final cause is evident in the way that a work of art is executed according to the plan or the purpose of the artist, on the one hand. On the other hand art is an end in itself, and it serves no other purpose. One might say that it is educational or instructive, or that it produces aesthetic enjoyment, but those are not its main purpose or its specific characteristics.

To sum up, art relates to the universal, in showing the universal in the particular; it presents the idea in the form of sensible existence, as image. How does spirit appear in the arts? The artist has a conception of the work of art, according to the form and the goal, which is the intention of the work of art to be executed in some material support. Art is a combination of sensibility and spirituality. For we perceive art always with the senses but also with the intellect, and the artist likewise employs both intellect and the senses in the execution of the work of art. Moreover, the work of art seeks to maintain a balance between the form and the material which expresses the idea; indeed, this is an indication of a good or accomplished work of art.

Student: How does art relate to knowledge more particularly?

Teacher: The question of knowledge in art can be seen in different ways. On the one hand, art reveals knowledge; it reveals the knowledge of the artist, for instance in a historical novel, which implies a great deal of research. It is also knowledge of artistic techniques broadly speaking. Some of this knowledge might be implicit, for instance with regard to a certain period in history, which is conveyed implicitly by the artist living in that period and his or her work of art. We become aware of this implicit knowledge because it is often not the explicit purpose of the artist to convey an idea about a certain period in history, namely his or her historical period, but this is normally an intrinsic aspect of the work of art. This knowledge of the artist is conveyed to those who admire and contemplate it.

Student: In the Middle Ages, the arts had a broader meaning, did they not?

Teacher: The broader meaning of art includes the sciences, for instance when we speak of the liberal arts. These are disciplines that those with leisure studied in Antiquity and in the Middle Ages. It includes the rules and principles and theories of a science, like music or astronomy, grammar and rhetoric. This further shows the theoretical as well as the practical aspect of the arts.

Student: The creative side of the arts also shows the spiritual presence in art?

Teacher: Art is also spiritual because it implies a creation, and in this process we find the four causes in the Aristotelian sense. The artist thinks of an idea or project, which is the purpose and the final cause, and then puts it, as a form, into effect, in her or his capacity as efficient cause, through a material medium. The initial idea is the form or the formal cause that is finally brought to fruition. Therefore the spirit of the artist is the primary cause of the work of art. We see creativity in other fields of knowledge and even in science, but it is most evident in the arts. In addition, the intellect of the artist is involved in the creative process, but also the other faculties of the mind, such as the imagination, representation, and memory. The artist imposes a certain form on matter, and impresses the matter with form or an image. Although the main purpose of art is disputed, there is certainly an educational and moral aspect to it, therefore it leads to theoretical knowledge. This is very obvious, for instance, in religious art, which expresses religious theories and dogmas, but also in art in general.

Student: In this way, art has links to theory of knowledge and ethics.

Teacher: Some might argue that art has no moral purpose, but an educational purpose surely enriches art. In connection with knowledge, art also expresses the beliefs of the artist and his or her circumstances. And in addition art must be convincing. That is, if there is a narrative, for instance, and this is fictional, there has to be a resemblance with reality or a resemblance of truth, otherwise it is not considered good or compelling art. In its resemblance with truth, art employs all the faculties of the artist and the artwork is interpreted by using the same faculties on the part of the receiving subject. Art involves feelings and emotions on the part of the artist and of the observing subject but also the will and the intellect. Art can be representative or symbolic and thus it points to a certain reality beyond itself.

Student: The representation of truth in art comes under the concept of representationalism?

Teacher: The question of representationalism points to the cognitive content of art. If art seeks to portray reality there is a direct connection with reality and knowledge. In some cases this was not intentional but was an implicit assumption at a particular period of the history of art. For instance, most paintings until the modern period represented something real, such as real people or real landscapes. In the contemporary period this view was challenged, starting with impressionism, and the representationalist view of painting was called into question, whereas previously art was expected to portray nature. In some cases, realism is the name of the art movement itself, such as in literature or opera in the second half of the 19th century. The question of the relation between art and reality is an important one. However, even if art does not portray an external reality it can still be seen to convey information, about the artist and his or her surroundings, for instance. In this way we can say that we always learn from works of art, even if the main information pertains to the artist's circumstances.

Student: There is a strong link not just between art and knowledge but also between beauty and truth.

Teacher: Yes. There is an identification between beauty and truth, for instance in Shaftesbury; this is a link between beauty, a central property in art, such as it is found in form and shape, and knowledge. The symbolic in art also relates to the cognitive aspect in art, for the symbol, which is a convention, points to a certain concept or principle. However, Hegel, for instance, considers symbolic art as a primitive form of art in relation to later forms which are representational. Nevertheless, symbolic art appears to have made a comeback, in a different guise, after Hegel's time and particularly from the early 20th century onwards.

Student: I understand how art shows the presence of spirit in its links to knowledge, metaphysics, and ethics.

Teacher: Yes, those links are not far to seek.

Philosophy of History

Student: Can we see the action of spirit in history?

Teacher: Certainly, there are many ways in which spirit manifests itself in history. This is an important aspect of Hegel's philosophy. According to Hegel, spirit reveals itself in history, in a goal-directed action of spirit. For him, history is the theatre in which spirit comes to know itself, which is the purpose of spirit and the purpose of history. This manifestation of spirit in history occurs both in world history (primarily

European, in Hegel's approach) and in the history of ideas. Moreover, spirit manifests itself in its development in the different areas of human knowledge and activity. Hegel also believes firmly in progress and in a development towards a final achievement. He applies his famous dialectic logic to history, in which spirit comes to know itself through its opposite, namely nature. This progress is to be seen in history, in art, in religion, and in science, and the goal is absolute knowledge and the accomplishment of history.

Student: More specifically, what is the end goal of spirit in history?

Teacher: We find an affirmation of an end goal in history in Hegel's description of how subjective spirit meets absolute spirit. According to Hegel, knowledge is freedom, and truth is freedom, following the biblical principle stated by Jesus to the effect that the truth will set us free. Hegel viewed this principle in political terms as the fulfillment of the ideals of the French revolution.

Hegel thinks of absolute spirit as the culmination of subjective and objective spirit, and they are the same reality. Ultimately subjective and objective spirit, as forms of finite spirit, are merged within absolute spirit. There is a sense in which there is no transcendence because this would detract from human fulfillment. In this way some philosophers have identified this absolute spirit with objective spirit and removed the religious element altogether. In this sense absolute spirit embraces objective spirit, which is identified with social institutions and the communal aspect of human living.

Hegel also speaks of spirit in other ways as being present in history. Sometimes the spirit of a historical period is identified with a certain individual, usually a political ruler or monarch. Often a historical period is also associated with an artistic style. In addition, there is a connection between history and politics and the idea of justice. Spirit in time is also reflected in a particular ideology, and again these are political and economic aspects of spirit in history.

Student: There is also a religious sense of an end goal of history.

Teacher: In religious terms there is a sense of an end goal in connection with the end of the world, and of history, in the final judgment of humankind. Some held that this end was achievable in this world and in this life, a view which was attributed to Hegel and to some of the philosophers he inspired, for instance, Marx; but religious thought holds that it will be attained in the next life, at the end of time. Therefore, to think of a specific end goal of history, it is appropriate to establish a relation with religion and think of God's end goal for us and a final judgment at the end of history.

Student: We have chosen to maintain the distinction between finite and infinite spirit.

Teacher: Yes, we maintain the distinction between the different kinds of spirit. This means that there is a difference between finite subjective spirit and absolute spirit. These kinds of subjective spirit, finite and infinite, are both active and free by themselves, whereas objective spirit is rendered active through finite subjective spirit or by absolute spirit, or both.

Student: How will we consider the different kinds of spirit in relation to history?

Teacher: From the point of view of subjective spirit, we could consider the history of philosophy and ideas as the manifestation of finite subjective spirit. However, it can also be seen as the effect of absolute spirit. Absolute spirit is the source of finite subjective and objective spirit, as we have seen, and therefore history can be seen from the perspective of finite subjective spirit in a more limited way, or from the perspective of absolute spirit, because the latter is infinite spirit.

Student: If absolute spirit is the source of finite subjective spirit, as we have seen, and finite subjective spirit is the source of human action, does this not mean that everything is determined by absolute spirit? What is the point of speaking of finite subjective spirit in the first place?

Teacher: There are different kinds of subjective spirit. Absolute spirit contains subjective spirit but it is always infinite, as absolute and as subjective spirit. Finite subjective spirit is human spirit, as we have seen. The ultimate source of spirit lies in absolute spirit, which is its cause. However, free will is given to subjective finite spirit, leading to freedom of action, as we have seen, which means freedom of subjective spirit. Naturally finite subjective spirit cannot comprehend all aspects of history but it does act in history.

Student: Is there a more general sense in which finite subjective spirit appears in history?

Teacher: Yes, we could think of philosophy as encompassing all the kinds of manifestation of finite subjective spirit in history, if we think of philosophy broadly conceived as the history of ideas. These ideas are represented in all the branches of philosophy. Therefore, all aspects of reality find their expression in philosophy. However, to be more specific, in speaking of history, we can mention the spirit of the time or of the times, which is particularly apparent in political ideas, and also in art. Perhaps more than anything else, the spirit of an age is found in its various artistic expressions. Philosophical or political ideas appear regularly, and previous philosophical ideas can be revived at any time, but art is specific to a certain time, making it usually easy to identify the period when a work of art was made. Even when there is an attempt to revive or imitate a previous period, as was the case in the Renaissance in relation to Antiquity, art is still specific to a certain period. We can understand art here in a broad way to include fashion, which also reveals the spirit of a time. This spirit of the time, when expressed in artistic terms, has philosophical underpinnings and an ideal foundation.

Student: Does history determine the kind of spirit present at a certain moment in time? That is to say, does the spirit of a period in history determine all activity in that period?

Teacher: I do not think that we are completely determined and limited by history in that way, since it is possible to find in various periods of history different ways of doing things in the arts and in the sciences. Also, we are always exposed to the past and can easily return to it. What is curious is that when going back to the past and seeking to reproduce it, often a new period in history or art history actually comes into being. A good example of this is the Renaissance, as we have seen, in which a whole movement which sought to emulate classical Antiquity actually turned out to be quite original and novel. The tradition is thus never to be neglected when it comes to the arts and the sciences, because we can always learn from it, just as we can learn from past philosophers and should maintain a dialogue with them. A spirit of a time can be found, in particular instances, later in history.

Conclusion

Student: From our study of spirit in the history of philosophy and in the different philosophical disciplines, does our stress on the existence or presence of spirit indicate a classical rationalist or idealist position?

Teacher: We have seen how spirit is present, through philosophy and also religion, in the arts and in the sciences and in all fields of human knowledge and activity.

When it comes to our main position, namely that reality is essentially spiritual because perception and knowledge are ultimately spiritual, it seems that we are affirming an idealist position. However, there are different kinds of idealism. We do not deny the existence of matter, as Berkeley does, but we do say that it is subordinate to spirit, as stated in the Aristotelian tradition and by German idealists, in particular Hegel. We also do not affirm a kind of subjective idealism as Kant does, in which we cannot know reality in itself although it exists theoretically. We follow Hegel's objective or absolute idealism, which can be considered a kind of realism because there is nothing left after absolute knowledge is obtained and that knowledge is supremely spiritual. We do not claim to possess that absolute knowledge, but affirm that knowledge to be present for absolute spirit.

Student: Is there not a danger that idealism may in principle lead to relativism? In this sense idealism means that reality is as it appears to the knowing subject, and knowledge would be equivalent to perception, a theory denounced by Socrates, as held by Protagoras, in the dialogue *Theaetetus*.

Teacher: We have seen the meaning of objective idealism, which excludes any subjectivism or relativism. If one says that reality is as it appears to the individual finite subject, then there could be a danger of subjectivism, solipsism, or relativism, and the truth would not be an objective concept; but since all knowledge is contained in an infinite mind which is the source of anything related to spirit, in this way objectivity is ensured. This means that idealism and realism are at bottom not incompatible. Naturally, this is one of the perennial questions in philosophy, such as, for instance, the harmonization of free will and determinism. In this sense, the debate will remain open, but objective idealism is not incompatible with realism, and this kind of idealism is present in the philosophies of Plato, Berkeley, and Hegel.

Student: Is this position compatible with modern science?

Teacher: This position is not incompatible with realism in the sense that matter and the observable sense data are not denied. It is also not incompatible with the Aristotelian tradition and in particular with Thomism, for Aquinas also states that all reality is contained virtually in God. His philosophy and theology affirm the precedence of spirit over matter. Nothing is created that does not exist first as an idea in God or in God's intellect. In this way, ideas precede the coming into being of individual beings and the created universe. And naturally, God, who is intellect, precedes the world and creation, although time is created with the world. Matter is created by God. Aquinas' position, which follows in the vein of an Aristotelian realism, could thus be construed as idealism, more specifically as a kind of objective or absolute idealism—even though idealism is considered the opposite of Thomism, as it is interpreted by some Neo-Thomist philosophers, like Maritain.

Student: Could we not explain the reality of everything as starting from matter, or talk about an essentially material world that we know and translate into spirit? Some philosophers hold that even thought processes could be interpreted as material.

Teacher: Consciousness, which is spirit, is always ahead of particular theories, including materialistic theories. We can talk about prehistory, and things we have not seen or experienced, from a materialistic perspective, and mention the synapses of the brain as explaining all our thoughts and actions; but ultimately what we have is thoughts, perceptions, and intuitions. We cannot ignore these nor the fact that they accompany all the theories; hence we hold that spirit comes first and precedes matter, and that this position is more compelling than any materialistic theory. The other problem with a materialistic view or even a verificationist view, which requires that everything meaningful should have empirical confirmation, is that these are metaphysical positions that cannot be materially or empirically verified themselves. In this sense, there is no means of avoiding a metaphysical position, which is a spiritual position.

Student: One could avoid this objection by stating that knowledge is about theories and a theory is about reality, in such a way that the theory does not refer to itself.

Teacher: As we have seen, consciousness and the knowing subject always accompany its perceptions or thoughts and therefore materialism cannot be reasonably sustained.

Student: If philosophy ponders and reflects reality, can we then say that spirit is dominant both in philosophy and in reality?

Teacher: That is true, this is the conclusion we should reach. We have seen how spirit dominates in philosophy, because that has been the position of the majority of philosophers. Even if we do not wish to accept the weight of a majority, in the sense that the majority of philosophers made spirit dominant over matter in the history of philosophy—since a majority may not always choose the best option, as observed by Plato concerning the political domain—the argument for the dominance of spirit is quite strong, as found in Descartes for instance. He seems to follow a chronological order, in the sense that the subject discovers first spirit and only much later material objects, but we could think of this sequence as a metaphysical process and a discovery in which spirit metaphysically or ontologically precedes matter.

Student: What does this position of ours mean for science today, for instance?

Teacher: We realize that the dominant discourse about knowledge today comes from the sciences, and this is based on their contribution to technology and the ability to predict natural phenomena. The empirical and experimental element in science is crucial, as well as the consideration of the existence of matter. However, that is not to say that spirit does not exist in the sciences, as we have seen, or in the world. Our view integrates both material and spiritual elements.

Student: How can we sum up our findings?

Teacher: It is important to glean from the history of philosophy the concept of spirit, which is contrasted to that of matter. Obviously, it is impossible to exhaust the meaning of spirit, and volumes could be written about it, concerning what it means in the various languages, cultures, and religions. Spirit is more closely related to the humanities, philosophy, and theology than to the sciences; or at least it is more immediately and recognizably identified in the humanities and theology. However, we have seen the various connections between spirit and the sciences, and the presence of spirit in the various sciences through philosophy. We saw how it is related to existence and causality, which are central themes in philosophy and more specifically in theory of knowledge, and how it thus pervades all aspects of human existence and reality.

Student: Is there not a problem if we define spirit in a negative way, as opposed to matter? Even if we say that it is unlimited, infinite, unextended, we are using negative prefixes.

Teacher: Sometimes knowledge of the higher things is the most difficult, as we know from negative theology, which uses negative terms to describe God. Therefore it is not wrong to speak of spirit in this way. It is also important to bear in mind that what we experience most vividly is material objects with the senses, hence the difficulty in understanding and speaking of spirit.

If we start from general perception, and in spite of any skeptical position, we find spirit and matter. However, spirit prevails, especially if we think of spirit in a general way as consciousness. All the process of cognition implies some form of perception, over and above a general form of awareness. For instance, when we dream in the sleeping state we may consider this experience a certain kind of awareness, in the sense that the brain is certainly working and memory is active, although we may not consider it consciousness. We may learn nothing new in the process of sleeping, although scientists hold that this is an important activity in consolidating memory and even in solving problems. This kind of experience does not seem to constitute apprehension of new knowledge, and perhaps it cannot be called consciousness. However, consciousness, which is definitely a part of spirit, involves sensory and more abstract perception and knowledge, and therefore spirit is present in the form of consciousness. In this way, even sensory perception evinces the activity of spirit.

To recapitulate, we have seen the presence of spirit in the history of philosophy, both explicitly and implicitly. The ancients do not seem to speak of spirit explicitly in this way, even in the case of Plato and Aristotle, but much of what they say is classified as spirit by later philosophers who do use the term explicitly, namely Berkeley and Hegel. The ancients speak of ideas, forms, and universals, and these feature in logic, in metaphysics, and in theory of knowledge. They discuss the various forms of intellect, human and divine. They assign contemplative activity to humans and gods. These spiritual aspects dominate in the various fields of human activity and in the other philosophical disciplines.

The medieval period sees the appearance of "spirit" as an explicit term; however, it is more a theological category, applied especially in reference to God and particularly to the person of the Holy Trinity whose proper name is Holy Spirit. The connection between spirit and God is explicitly made: God is seen as spirit, and each person of the Trinity is also spirit.

Student: There are many developments in the theology of spirit during the Middle Ages.

Teacher: There is a rich theology on the spirit in the various churches, with respect to the special missions of the Son and the Holy Spirit, and the gifts and the fruits of the Holy Spirit.

An important domain of theology concerns the relation between the various divine persons, and particularly between the Son and the Holy Spirit. We have seen that there are disagreements regarding the procession of the Son, as proceeding just from the Father for the Orthodox and from the Father and the Son for the Western church-es. Therefore spirit is conceived explicitly in a theological and religious sense in the Middle Ages, especially for Christian philosophers and theologians. This identifica-tion of spirit with God is less explicit in the Jewish and the Islamic philosophical traditions, but all three traditions maintain the implicit spiritual categories that were present in Aristotelian philosophy and in Neoplatonism.

The modern period sees a focus on the human intellect and the question of cognition, as we have seen. The intellect is precisely a category of spirit. The term appears explicitly in a philosophical sense in Berkeley and in Hegel, and it is often opposed to matter and to nature, respectively. This allows us to look back the philo-sophical tradition in a new way and identify the presence of spirit in it, even if the terms used to refer to spirit are different. Berkeley clearly terms ideas instances or examples of spirit, in his opposition to the materialists. Finally, in Hegel, we see spir-it appear explicitly as the main description of reality. He still speaks of the different forms of knowledge and the human spirit, but spirit is a broad and encompassing category in Hegel as it was already in Berkeley, only it is more detailed in Hegel. For Hegel, spirit is reality; it is also knowledge and it pervades nature. Spirit is con-sciousness but also understanding and reason, and it is absolute knowing. We find it in nature, in the arts, in ethics, in history, and in the various fields of human activity. Most importantly it is identified with God, as infinite spirit. For Hegel, religion and philosophy are both ways of connecting with the absolute spirit. With Hegel we are allowed to use the three main different categories of spirit: subjective spirit, which can be human or divine (finite in the first case, infinite in the latter case), and also objective spirit, which is the object and the creation of subjective spirit, whether hu-man or divine, although Hegel stresses human objective spirit. We also speak of ab-solute spirit as identified primarily with God; but for Hegel it is also attainable by human beings, given his confidence in human reason.

We find spirit in the various disciplines, according to the philosophers, and we come to understand it also by expanding on the meaning of spirit based on philoso-phy. Spirit is real, hence it is a metaphysical category. In addition it is the most real object of knowledge and perception, as already stated by Berkeley and Hegel. Spirit is present in knowledge and in the human knowing subject. Spirit is in the ideas which exist in the various kinds of intellect. Spirit is present in the various categories and rules of logic. It is also present in the philosophy of nature and science, in aesthetics or the philosophy of art, and most importantly, in ethics. Even a materialist who would wish to deny the existence of spirit or subordinate it to matter would have to admit that there is no ethics without spirit and without the idea of a goal or the idea of right and wrong, which are not material and cannot be obtained from sense experience. Therefore ethics is a pivotal discipline in proving the presence of spirit, particularly in human knowledge and action. In this sense, human interaction would be impossible without ethics. We might do without ethics if we lived individually and in isolation, like Rousseau's noble savage, but that is not the experience of the vast majority of human beings. Finally, last but not least, spirit is present in theology and religion and it is identified with God.

Student: I understand the significance and preeminence of spirit.

Teacher: It is impossible to exhaust the meaning of spirit. We have sought to analyze it from a historical philosophical perspective and from a conceptual perspective by looking at the different philosophical disciplines as we find them today. We could mention other disciplines, because philosophy is always expanding and embracing new forms of knowledge and the arts. Speaking about spirit is an endless task, and much more could be said.

Student: We see that spirit is present everywhere in philosophy and consequently in the various branches of knowledge and human activity. What is its significance today?

Teacher: It is important to be aware of the significance of spirit, since it appears to have been partly neglected by philosophers after Hegel. In religion, it has always been present and holds pride of place, but in philosophy its significance has often been overlooked; hence our attempt to explain and highlight it again. By neglecting spirit, and its role in philosophy, which should defend spirit, philosophy itself becomes poorer and less significant to the other sciences and branches of knowledge and in its relation to the arts. For philosophy can be identified with knowledge and reason and intellect, and therefore it represents spirit itself. Philosophy can be made to serve other sciences, but initially it was considered the most important science and a broad and far-reaching kind of knowledge because it was not specialized and it embraced all kinds of knowledge and all the disciplines.

Student: I understand that an emphasis on spirit allows us to highlight also the significance of philosophy.

WiSa